高等学校教材

供临床医学及相关专业用

外科手术学基础
（汉英双语）

Fundamentals of Surgical Operation

第2版｜SECOND EDITION

主　审　郁解非

主　编　吴凯南　孔令泉

副主编　黄伟光　厉红元　曾晓华

编　者　（以姓氏笔画为序）

王忠良（重庆医科大学附属儿童医院）　　李　浩（重庆医科大学附属第一医院）

王学虎（重庆医科大学附属第一医院）　　李凤贺（重庆医科大学附属第一医院）

王瑞珏（重庆医科大学附属儿童医院）　　李英存（重庆医科大学附属儿童医院）

孔令泉（重庆医科大学附属第一医院）　　吴凯南（重庆医科大学附属第一医院）

厉红元（重庆医科大学附属第一医院）　　邹宝山（重庆医科大学附属第一医院）

冉　亮（重庆医科大学附属第一医院）　　徐　周（重庆医科大学附属第一医院）

朱　冰（重庆医科大学附属第二医院）　　黄伟光（重庆医科大学附属第二医院）

刘家硕（重庆医科大学附属第一医院）　　曾晓华（重庆大学附属肿瘤医院）

李　明（重庆医科大学附属第一医院）　　魏余贤（重庆医科大学附属第一医院）

人民卫生出版社

图书在版编目（CIP）数据

外科手术学基础：汉英对照 / 吴凯南，孔令泉主编 . —2 版 . —北京：人民卫生出版社，2018

ISBN 978-7-117-26180-7

Ⅰ.①外⋯ Ⅱ.①吴⋯ ②孔⋯ Ⅲ.①外科手术 - 医学院校 - 教材 - 汉、英 Ⅳ.①R61

中国版本图书馆 CIP 数据核字（2018）第 040418 号

人卫智网	www.ipmph.com	医学教育、学术、考试、健康，购书智慧智能综合服务平台
人卫官网	www.pmph.com	人卫官方资讯发布平台

外科手术学基础（汉英双语）
第 2 版

主　　编：吴凯南　孔令泉
出版发行：人民卫生出版社（中继线 010-59780011）
地　　址：北京市朝阳区潘家园南里 19 号
邮　　编：100021
E - mail：pmph @ pmph.com
购书热线：010-59787592　010-59787584　010-65264830
印　　刷：三河市潮河印业有限公司
经　　销：新华书店
开　　本：850×1168　1/16　印张：10
字　　数：289 千字
版　　次：2009 年 1 月第 1 版　　2018 年 4 月第 2 版
　　　　　2022 年 1 月第 2 版第 4 次印刷（总第 6 次印刷）
标准书号：ISBN 978-7-117-26180-7/R·26181
定　　价：30.00 元
打击盗版举报电话：010-59787491　E-mail：WQ @ pmph.com
（凡属印装质量问题请与本社市场营销中心联系退换）

前 言

本课程通过动物实验使学生了解外科手术的基本原则及操作技术。本书第 1 版于 2003 年出版发行,受到肯定。现根据教学师生的建议进行了部分修订,组织编写了第 2 版,以适应教学需要。

本教材主要内容包括无菌技术(如外科洗手法、穿手术衣、戴手套、无菌器械或用品的取用与传递等)和外科手术基本操作(如组织的切开、手术野的显露、止血、结扎、缝合等),前者要求学生能严格掌握,后者要求达到熟练程度。还要求学生对待实验动物要像对待病人一样认真、细致,严格执行无菌操作和有关规则,避免不必要的活组织损伤,为培养日后精湛的医疗技术和良好的医疗作风打下坚实基础。

本教材由长期从事医学教学和临床外科工作,汉英双语基础知识较好的教师担任主要编写工作,也有部分优秀青年教师参与编写。由国内已故知名资深专家、外科学老前辈郁解非教授对全书进行润笔和审校。可供七年制、五年制及医学留学生外科手术学基础教学使用,还可作为临床医学英语参考用书。

由于编著者水平有限,错漏之处在所难免。我们殷切期待广大读者对本书提出宝贵意见(联系邮箱:*huihuikp@163.com*),以便进一步修正和完善。本书在编写过程中得到了重庆医科大学、重庆医科大学附属第一医院的支持和帮助,在此致以衷心的感谢!

吴凯南　孔令泉
2018.3

目 录

手术室的一般要求和外科无菌技术

第一节　手术室基本规则

手术室是保证手术安全和手术顺利进行的场所。无菌技术是手术最基本的措施之一,所以手术室必须执行严格的无菌原则。

患有急性感染和上呼吸道炎症人员不应参加手术。进入手术室的非手术人员要严格控制以减少手术室环境的污染。经批准进入的人员(包括不参加手术的实习学生和参观手术者),要按照对手术人员的要求穿戴手术室专用的鞋、帽、衣裤和口罩,并要尊重工作人员的督促指导,严格遵守无菌原则。进入一个手术间的非手术人员不能过多,一般不超过 2~3 人。同一手术间一日连做数台手术者,应先做无菌或较清洁部位的手术,后做可能有明显污染部位的或有菌的手术。有明显感染的病人应在专供感染病人手术的手术间进行。每日工作结束后都应彻底清除污液、敷料、杂物及洗刷地面。手术室每周应彻底清洁、消毒一次。

手术室内应定期进行空气消毒。通常用乳酸或紫外线消毒。乳酸消毒时,紧闭门窗,按每 100 立方米空间用 80% 乳酸 12ml,原液或加入等量水后倒入蒸发碟内,点燃酒精灯使之蒸发完毕,熄火后 30 分钟打开门窗通风。采用紫外线消毒时,以每 10~15m² 地面面积使用功率为 30W 紫外线灯,照射 1 小时,照射源距地面 1.5m。每灯管可有效使用 1000 小时,故每次照射应记录使用时间。

铜绿假单胞菌感染手术后,先用乳酸进行空气消毒,1~2 小时后用 0.1% 苯扎溴铵(新洁尔灭)溶液擦洗室内物品,然后开窗通风 1 小时。

为破伤风、气性坏疽者进行手术后,可按每立方米空间用 40% 甲醛溶液 2ml 倒入高锰酸钾 1.0g 所产生的蒸气消毒封闭的房间,12 小时后打开通风。

为 HBsAg 阳性者进行手术后,地面和手术台等可洒 0.1% 次氯酸溶液,30 分钟后清扫。

第二节　手术人员的术前准备

一、一般准备

参加手术人员进入手术室后,首先在更衣室更换手术室专用的清洁衣裤、鞋、帽和口罩(图 1),以免将外部不洁物带入手术室内从而减少污染机会。帽子要盖住全部头发,口罩要求遮住口和鼻部。上衣袖口平上臂的上三分之一,下襟塞在裤内。认真修剪指甲并除去甲缘积垢。手、臂有化脓性感染,患呼吸道感染以及手、臂有创口者不能参加手术。

二、手、臂的消毒

皮肤皱纹及其深层毛囊、皮脂腺内都藏有细菌。据测，$1cm^2$ 手、臂皮肤上约有 4 万个细菌，1g 甲垢可有 38 亿个细菌。手、臂消毒可清除皮肤表面细菌，但不能完全消灭其深层细菌，手术过程中，这些细菌可随皮脂腺和汗腺分泌逐渐移到皮肤表面。因而，在手、臂消毒后，还要戴上无菌乳胶手套和穿灭菌手术衣，以防这些细菌污染手术野。

手术前手、臂的消毒方法很多。最常用的传统手、臂消毒法是肥皂液刷手后消毒液浸泡法。此法缺点是操作时间长，对手、臂皮肤刺激性较大。随着各类新型灭菌剂问世，新的手、臂消毒方法应运而生，不仅增加了消毒的可靠性，还简化了过程。

现将目前常用的几种手臂消毒方法介绍如下：

（一）肥皂液刷手消毒液浸泡法

该法分两个步骤。第一步是先用肥皂一般清洗手和前臂，初步除去油垢、皮脂，继用无菌毛刷蘸上肥皂液循序刷洗。从指尖开始，逐渐向上直至肘上 10cm 处。刷洗可分三段进行，每段之间应有重叠，手及腕为一段，腕到前臂上 1/3 为二段，前臂中份至肘上为三段。刷洗时可刷完一侧，再刷另一侧；也可在刷完两侧第一段后，再刷第二段，然后第三段。从指尖起，每个手指、手掌、手背等处皮肤的所有部位均要刷到，特别注意甲沟、甲缘、指间、皮肤皱纹等较隐蔽处，并适当用力，因为刷的次数和力量大小比刷的时间长短对刷洗效果更为重要。肥皂水用量以刷出泡沫为度。两侧刷一次用 3 分钟，之后以流水冲净。冲洗从手指开始，并始终保持肘低位，以免水反流至手部。如此反复刷洗三遍，总时间约 10 分钟。然后用灭菌巾依次由手部向上臂擦干。擦干过程不能逆行（图 2）。

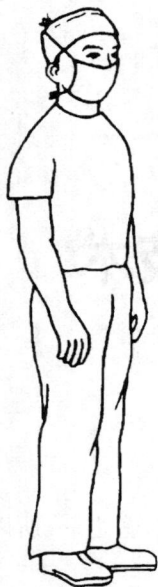

图 1　穿戴手术衣、帽和口罩

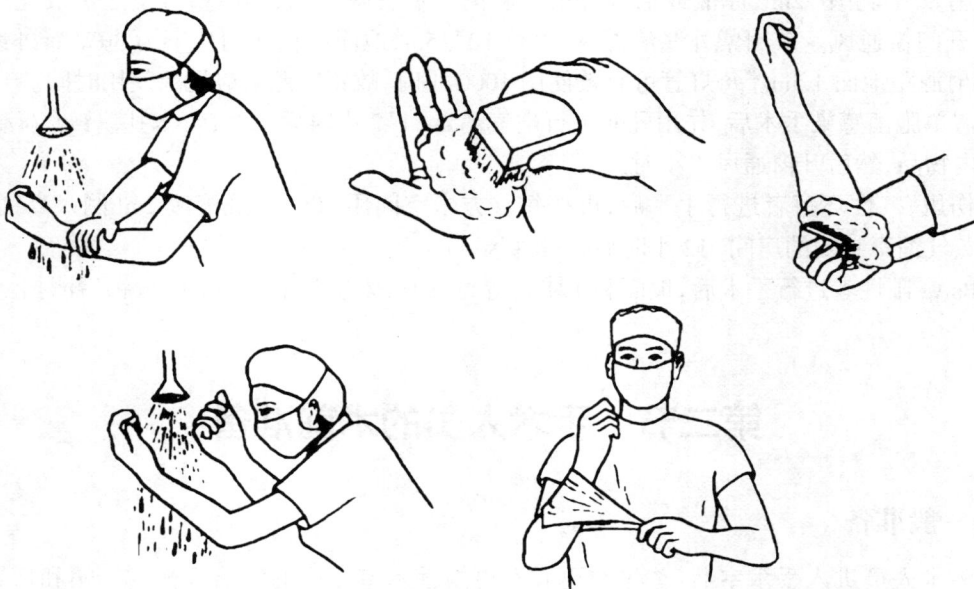

图 2　刷手和擦干

第二步用消毒液浸泡已刷洗的手、臂 5 分钟。常用的消毒液有 75% 乙醇，0.1% 新洁尔灭或 0.1% 洗必泰。手、臂伸入盛液的桶内，液面达肘上 6cm。浸泡时可同时用桶内小毛巾轻擦手、臂，使药液充分发挥作用。浸泡后手、前臂要保持拱手姿态,即手要远离胸部 30cm 以外,上限不高于下颌下缘,下限不低于剑突。刷洗后不能再触碰非消毒物品,否则需要重新刷手。

（二）洗必泰制剂手臂消毒法

4% 洗必泰（双氯苯双胍己烷）是国内一种新型的有效刷手液配方。按上法洗刷手、臂 3 分钟,流水将其冲洗干净,用无菌巾擦干,然后取纱布浸此液或泡沫由手部向上涂擦至肘上 6cm。

（三）络合碘手、臂消毒法

络合碘是碘和表面活性剂通过络合的方式而形成的不定型络合物。PVP- 碘（聚乙烯吡咯酮碘）,又称聚维酮碘或碘伏,是一种常用的络合碘,具有碘的强烈杀菌作用,但无碘酊对皮肤的强烈刺激。本法在西方国家应用较普遍,还可用于病人手术区的皮肤消毒。络合碘杀菌是其所含游离碘起作用。高浓度络合碘并不一定意味着高杀菌力,因 PVP- 碘浓度越高,碘与 PVP- 的结合越紧密,游离碘的含量与抗菌活性反而下降。故使用前必须了解其浓度。文献报道络合碘有效浓度为 0.1%~0.5%。采用本法可先用肥皂水刷手 3 分钟。流水冲洗干净,用无菌巾擦干后,取浸透 0.5% PVP- 碘的纱布,涂擦手、臂,此后即可穿手术衣,戴手套,进行手术。

洗必泰制剂和络合碘手、臂消毒比肥皂水刷洗消毒液浸泡法方便快捷。只要方法得当,效果可靠。一般洗必泰是阳离子表面活性剂,与碱类、肥皂、碘酊、乙醇等许多物质接触后可能失效,如应用不当,会影响消毒效果。

（四）免冲洗消毒剂消毒法

1. 摘除手部饰物,按要求修剪指甲,指甲长度不应超过指尖。

2. 洗手　在清洁双手时,应注意清洁指甲下的污垢和手部皮肤的皱褶处。用流动水彻底冲净,再用无菌巾擦干。整个过程应保持双手位于胸前并高于肘部,使水流向肘部。取适量洗手液,按照以下步骤进行洗手（图 3）:

（1）掌心相对,手指并拢,相互揉搓。

（2）掌心对手背沿指缝相互揉搓,交换进行。

（3）掌心相对,双手交叉,相互揉搓。

（4）弯曲手指,使关节在另一手掌心旋转揉搓,交换进行。

（5）一手握住另一手大拇指旋转揉搓,交换进行。

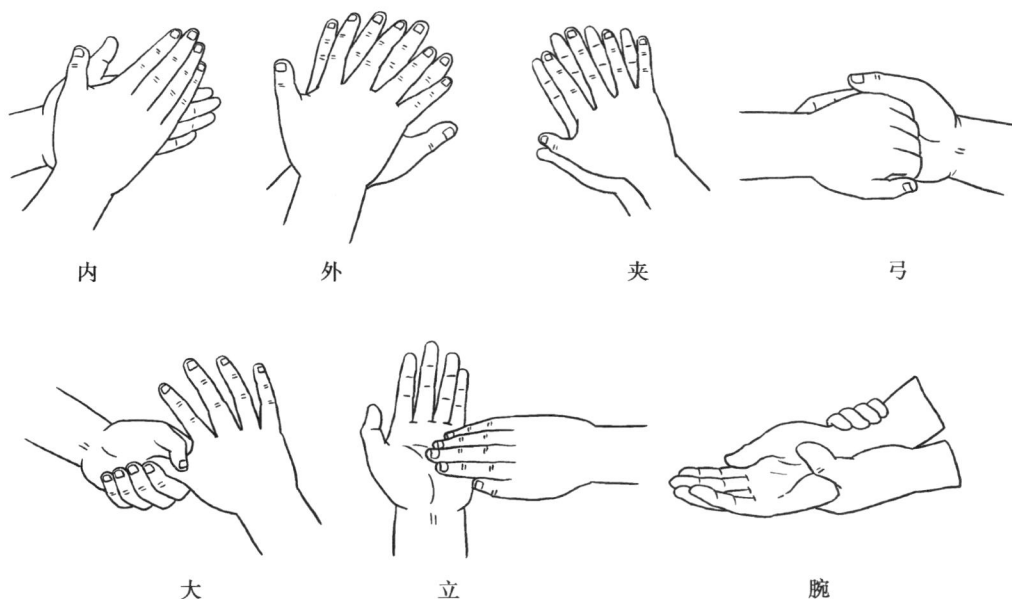

图 3　洗手步骤

（6）五个手指并拢在另一掌心旋转揉搓，交换进行。

（7）环形揉搓前壁至上臂下 1/3，交换进行。

（8）流动水冲净双手、前壁和上臂下 1/3，再用无菌巾擦干双手及手臂。

3. 手消毒　取适量免冲洗手消毒剂涂抹至双手的每一个部位、前壁及上臂下 1/3，并认真揉搓直至消毒剂干燥，手消毒剂的取液量、揉搓时间及使用方法应遵循产品的使用方法。整个过程应保持双手位于胸前并高于肘部。取适量消毒剂按照以下步骤重复两遍：

（1）掌心相对，手指并拢，相互揉搓。

（2）掌心对手背沿指缝相互揉搓，交换进行。

（3）掌心相对，双手交叉，相互揉搓。

（4）弯曲手指，使关节在另一手掌心旋转揉搓，交换进行。

（5）一手握住另一手大拇指旋转揉搓，交换进行。

（6）五个手指并拢在另一掌心旋转揉搓，交换进行。

（7）环形揉搓前壁至上臂下 1/3，交换进行。

4. 手消毒完毕，保持拱手姿势（双手远离胸部，手臂不能下垂），穿无菌手术衣、戴无菌手套。

（五）抢救紧急重危病人时术者手、臂的处理

在病人情况危急，来不及按常规进行手、臂消毒的情况下，可按以下方法进行手、臂处理：

1. 不进行手臂消毒而先戴一副无菌手套，接着穿无菌手术衣，然后再戴一副无菌手套，即可进行手术。

2. 直接涂擦络合碘 2~3 次后，即穿手术衣，戴手套，做手术。

3. 用 3%~5% 碘酊涂擦手、臂，干后，用 70%~75% 乙醇纱布涂擦脱碘，即可穿手术衣，戴手套，做手术。

三、穿手术衣及戴手套法

手术衣和手套都是用高压蒸汽进行灭菌处理的，而手术人员的手、臂仅是机械性和化学性消毒，前者显然更为可靠，所以，在刷手之后仍应严格按规程，以无菌手术衣和手套作进一步保护，以提高手术的安全性。通常是先穿手术衣后戴手套，偶有先戴手套后穿手术衣的情况。

（一）穿无菌手术衣法

穿衣时，先拿起反叠手术衣的衣领，在较宽敞处将手术衣轻轻抖开，此时切勿触及自身及周围人员和物品。提起衣领两角，看清袖筒入口所在，将衣稍向上掷，顺势脱手并将两手插入袖筒内、两臂前伸，由巡回护士在身后帮助向后牵拉，使衣就位。最后交叉两臂提起腰带（注意未戴手套的手不能碰及手术衣外面），并由巡回护士在身后将衣带系紧（图 4）。衣袖如过长，不能将其卷起，只能向上收拢。穿衣后，置双手于身体前方，勿举手超过双肩水平或下坠至腰部以下。

（二）戴无菌手套法

穿好无菌手术衣后，取一双尺码合适的无菌乳胶手套（手套尺码为中指尖至腕前横纹的吋数）。用左手提起手套口翻折部，看清左右，握紧手套口将右手插入右手套内戴好，再用已戴手套的右手插入左手套翻折部夹层内，让左手插入左手套内。最后分别将手套翻折部翻回，盖住手术衣袖口（图 5）。

通过以上操作，手术人员的手、臂、身躯及下肢（除脚部）均已完全被灭菌物品覆盖。整个操作过程的关键是裸露的手和手臂不可触及到手术衣和手套的表面。

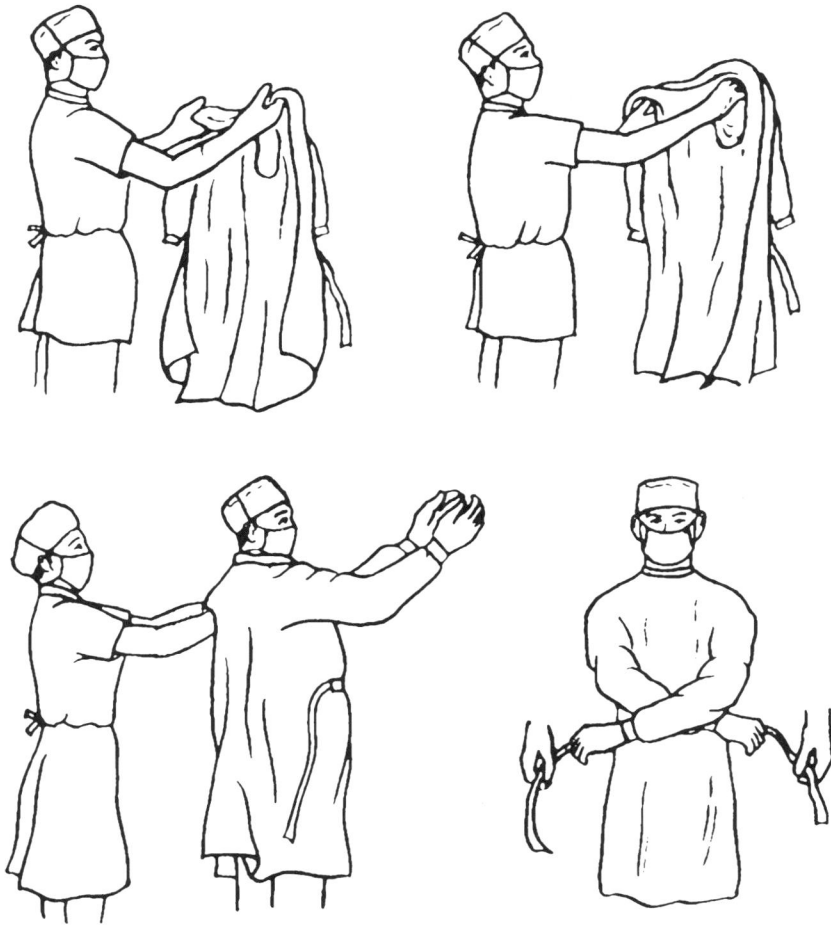

图 4　穿手术衣

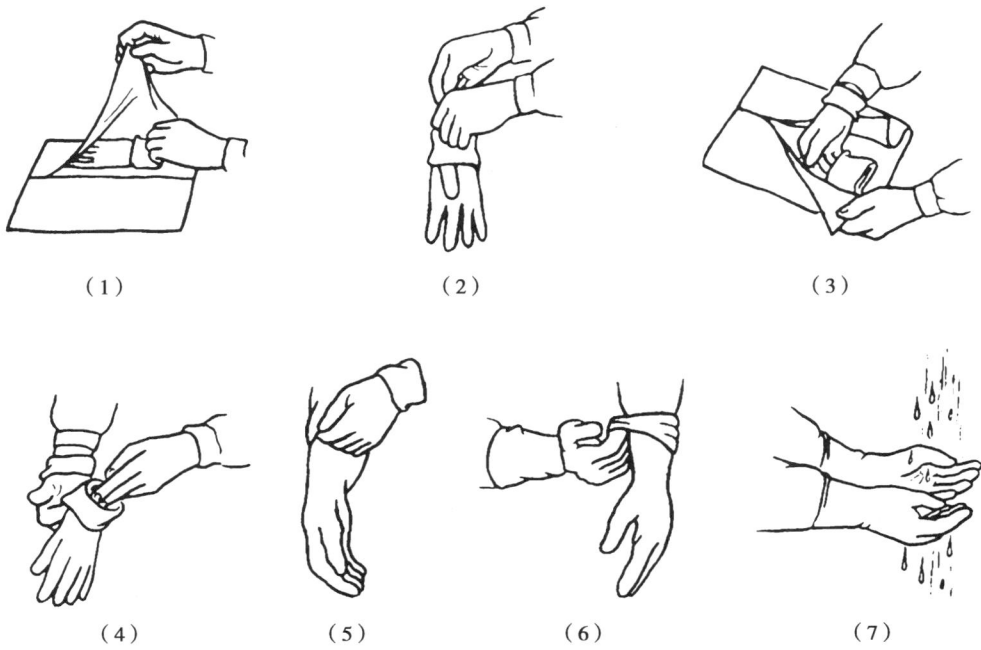

（1）　　　　　　　　（2）　　　　　　　　（3）

（4）　　　（5）　　　（6）　　　（7）

图 5　戴手套

第三节   手术台上病人的准备

一、体位

病人在手术台上应采取适应手术需要而且比较稳定的体位，以便到达并能充分显露手术区方便操作；同时应考虑麻醉的顺利进行，保证呼吸和循环畅通，避免压迫及过度牵拉大血管和神经干，还应照顾病人的舒适，避免牵强体位。为防止手术中病人体位的自主移动，可作适当填垫和约束以维持稳定。

绝大多数手术采用卧位进行，最常用的卧位有仰卧位、俯卧位和侧卧位。仰卧位（图6）适用于体前侧手术，最常用于经腹手术。根据需要，此体位可作一些细节调整。例如颈前部手术可在双肩下垫枕，使头后仰而突显颈前区（图7），面、颈侧部手术可将头转向健侧而更充分显露患侧（图8），会阴、肛部和某些泌尿生殖系手术可采用同时屈曲、外展双髋并架起膝部的截石位（图9）。俯卧位（图10）适用于体后侧手术，如背、臀、大腿后方等，此位如图11所示调整，更便于骶尾和肛直肠部手术的操作。侧卧位（图12）多用于胸部、肾区及采用胸腹联合进路的手术，侧转角度可视实际需要而定。

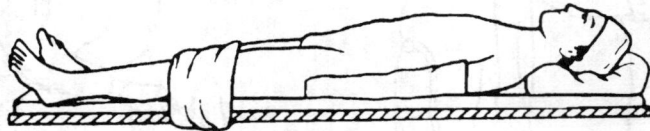

图6   仰卧位

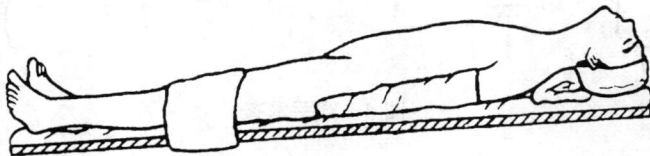

图7   适用于颈前部手术的仰卧位

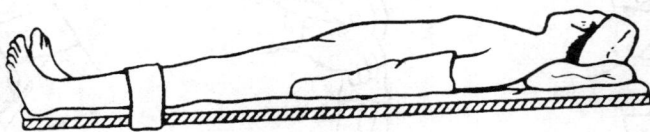

图8   侧头仰卧位

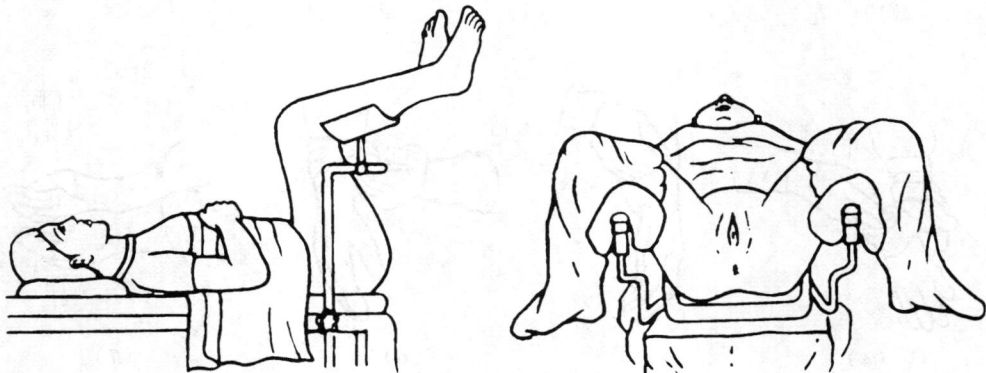

图9   截石位

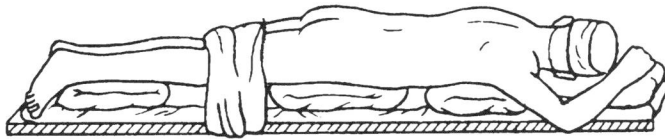

图 10　俯卧

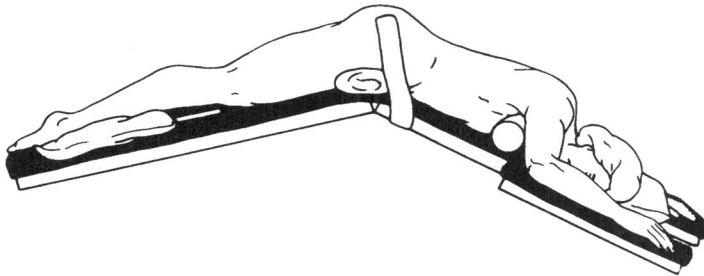

图 11　适用于肛直肠手术的俯卧位

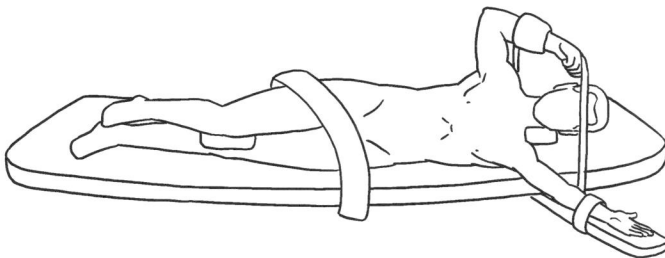

图 12　侧卧位

二、手术区准备

（一）术前手术区皮肤准备

手术区毛发应剃除，因毛发易藏污垢。一般腹部手术均应剃除阴毛，胸部手术应剃除同侧腋毛，头颅手术应剃除部分或全部毛发。剃除毛发时间一般在手术前一天（急症例外）。剃毛时勿剃伤皮肤。剃毛后用肥皂水将皮肤洗净，再用 3% 碘酊及 75% 乙醇涂擦，最后用无菌巾包裹。骨科手术要求更严格，有时需连续清洁三天。本课程动物手术时，先用剪刀剪去手术区长毛，后用脱毛剂涂擦脱毛（或在涂擦肥皂后用刀剃毛）。因脱毛剂对皮肤有强烈腐蚀作用，脱毛后需用大量清水冲洗，冲净后擦干。

（二）术时手术区皮肤消毒

通常由第一助手在已洗手并泡乙醇而未戴手套穿手术衣时，对手术区进行消毒。先用 2.5%~4% 碘酊涂擦皮肤一次，涂擦范围要够大，并从手术区中心部开始，逐步擦向外围。待碘酊干后，用 75% 乙醇脱碘两次（乙醇杀菌能力在 70% 浓度时最强，因其在室温中易蒸发，为保持其有效浓度，通常使用 75% 浓度）。碘酊对面部、口腔、肛门、外生殖器及婴儿皮肤等部位刺激太强，一般不用此液消毒。此时常用的消毒液为 1 ： 1000 新洁尔灭，红汞醑或 75% 乙醇涂擦两遍，植皮供皮区消毒则只用乙醇。

手术台上病人手术区皮肤消毒的任务，通常由手术组中已刷手而尚未穿手术衣、戴手套的第一助手施行，并由已穿手术衣、戴手套的器械护士协助。消毒区包括拟作切口的部位及其周围 15~20cm 范围内的皮肤。一般情况下，以海绵钳夹持蘸有消毒剂的小纱布块或棉球进行涂擦。

成人皮肤消毒多用 3.5% 碘酊涂擦 1 遍，干后用 75% 乙醇（含硫代硫酸钠更佳）脱碘 2~3 遍，或用碘伏原液涂擦 2 遍。黏膜、儿童皮肤和颜面、会阴、外生殖器皮肤可用稀碘伏液或新洁尔灭溶液涂擦 2 遍。

（三）注意事项

1. 涂擦应由消毒区中央开始，逐步向外周部分循序进行。各次涂擦的方向应一致，不可来回涂擦或涂擦四周后又返回中央。每两次涂擦应有 1/3~1/4 区域重叠，避免留有空白区。腹部皮肤消毒应先挤一些消毒液于脐窝内，消毒其他区后，再用纱布块擦拭并吸干脐窝。

2. 凡用碘酊、乙醇消毒者，应等碘酊干后，才另换海绵钳夹持乙醇纱布块脱碘，以便最大限度地发挥碘的灭菌作用。

3. 如手术区为感染伤口或在沾染较多的肛门、会阴等部位，消毒应从外周部开始逐步涂向中心区的伤口、肛门或会阴部。

三、铺手术巾

手术区皮肤消毒后，接着应在拟定的切口周围铺盖手术巾，以进一步完善无菌措施。小手术只用洞巾或 3~4 块小手术巾铺盖。中等以上的各部位手术，特别是涉及深部组织的手术，均需另加仅暴露手术部位的大布单，使切口外周体表至少有两层布单覆盖，并铺覆病人全部体表，铺巾一般是由第一助手和器械护士担任。为防止切口区皮肤深层细菌移至表浅层，近年有采用无菌黏性薄膜贴于手术区者。此时，宜先贴膜，后铺巾。以腹部手术为例，铺巾步骤如下（图 13）：

1. 用治疗巾四块或无菌小洞巾一块覆盖手术区，仅暴露切口部位。覆巾次序为手术区下方、上方、对侧、靠身侧。若穿好手术衣再铺巾，则依次为靠身侧、下方、上方和对侧。

2. 铺治疗巾之前必须看准部位，已铺下者不得随意移动，特别是不能向中心区移动；若必须向切口中心方向移动时，应另换一块重铺。

3. 所用治疗巾，宜将一边折起，折起之边靠手术区中心侧。铺好后用毛巾钳四把夹住每两块治疗巾之交角以利固定，一般不必夹住皮肤。

4. 较大手术在铺完治疗巾或孔巾后，需另铺一大的带孔布单（如腹单、剖胸单等）。它们通常由已戴好手套并穿手术衣之手术者铺覆。此单通常将器械台一并盖住。

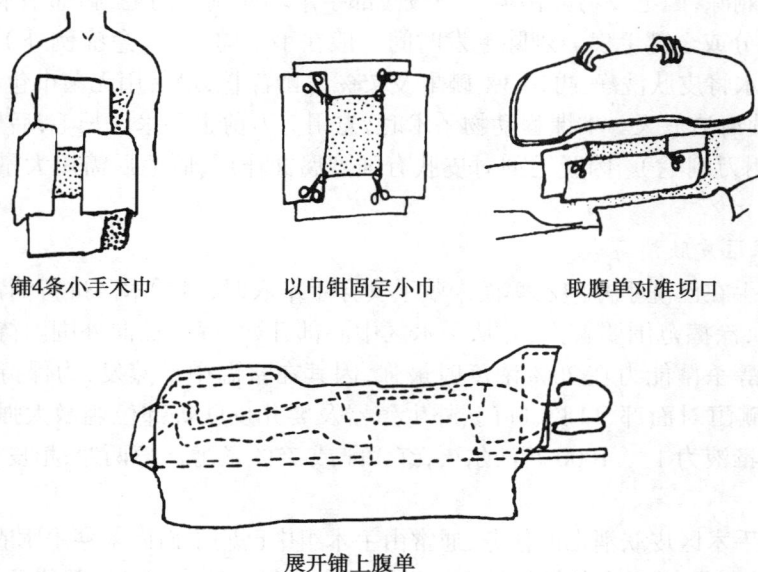

铺4条小手术巾　　　以巾钳固定小巾　　　取腹单对准切口

展开铺上腹单

图 13　腹部手术铺巾

第四节　手术进行中的无菌原则

参加手术人员在手术过程中,必须严格注意无菌操作,否则已建立的无菌环境、已经灭菌的物品及手术区域仍有受到污染、引起伤口或手术区感染的可能,从而导致手术失败。为此,在整个手术进行过程中,必须严格遵守以下规则,不得违反。手术组全体人员相互间应对任何破坏无菌条件的情况立即指出,以便及时进行补救。

1. 手术进行中,全体人员必须保持严肃认真,注意力集中,避免发生任何失误。

2. 手术人员穿灭菌手术衣和戴灭菌手套后,手和前臂不能触碰任何有菌物品,包括手术台以外的物品,手术台以下布单,自己的背部、腰以下、肩以上和其他手术人员的背部等都应该视为有菌地带,不得接触。

3. 手术开始前要清点器械、敷料,并准确记录。对胸、腹部等深部手术,术中严禁小纱布进入手术台。手术结束时,根据术前记录,应由两人认真核对器械、敷料数量(尤其是纱布块)。清点无误后方能关闭切口,以免异物遗留,产生严重后果。

4. 手术中,戴灭菌手套的手,不要直接触摸手术野中病人裸露的皮肤,必需时应垫有灭菌纱布,用完丢掉。皮肤切开后,需用两块纱布垫或小手巾覆盖其两侧,并用巾钳固定之。如已用无菌黏性薄膜敷贴,可免铺纱布或手术巾。切皮肤用的刀、镊,不可再用于深部操作。

5. 术中不可在手术人员背后传递器械及手术用品,坠落到手术台平面以下器械物品未经重新消毒,不能再用。

6. 术中手术组人员需互换位置时,应背靠背进行交换。

7. 额头出汗较多时,应将头偏向一侧,由他人代为擦去,以免汗液滴落于手术区内。

8. 术中如果灭菌单湿透,失去隔离作用,应另加无菌单遮盖。发现灭菌手套破损或被污染应立即更换。衣袖被污染时需更换手术衣或加戴无菌袖套。

9. 术中应尽量减少说话。必要的谈话或偶有咳嗽、喷嚏,不能面向手术区,以防飞沫污染。

10. 切开空腔器官之前,要用纱布垫保护好周围组织,以防止或减少污染。消化道管腔闭合后,要用无菌水冲洗手术者手套,相应吻合器械不再用于处理其他组织。

11. 参观手术的人员不可靠近手术人员或站得过高,并尽量减少在室内走动和说话。

12. 第一台无菌手术完毕,若要连续施行另一手术且手套未破者,不必重新刷手,仅需浸泡术前使用的消毒剂 5 分钟;如采用洗必泰或 PVP- 碘手、臂消毒法,可用术前使用的洗必泰或 PVP- 碘再涂擦一遍;然后穿灭菌手术衣戴灭菌手套。更衣时要先将手术衣自背部向前反折脱去,手套的腕部随之翻转于手上,用戴手套的右手指扯下左手手套至手掌部,再以左手指脱去右手手套、最后用右手指在左手掌部推下左手手套。脱手套时,手套的外面不能接触皮肤,否则需重新刷手。若前一手术为非无菌手术或术中手套曾有破口,需连续施行另一手术前应重新刷手和消毒。

(李　浩　孔令泉　吴凯南)

第二章

外科常用手术器材

了解各种手术器械的结构特点和基本性能是正确掌握及熟练运用这些器械的重要保证。

一、手术刀

（一）分型

手术刀（scalpel，surgical knife）由刀片和刀柄两部分组成。根据需要，各有多种型号，故刀片和刀柄都带有不同号码，以示区别（图14）。手术刀主要用以切割和分离组织。大圆刀片通常用于皮肤和一般组织的切开，小圆刀片用于较细微的切开，尖刀片则多用于挑开组织或脓肿。

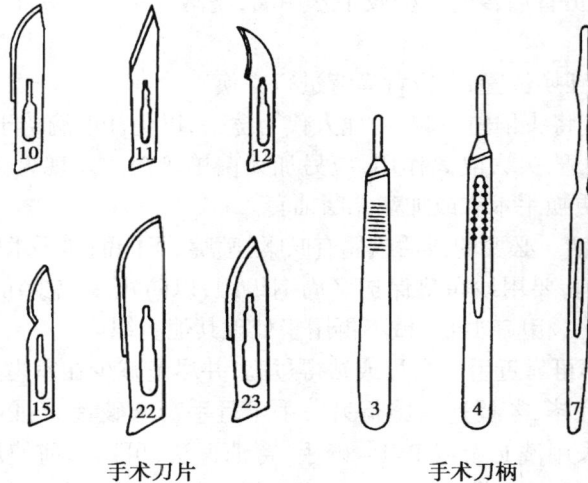

手术刀片　　　　　　手术刀柄

图14　手术刀的组成部分

（二）刀片装卸

刀片可自由装卸于刀柄。使用时，用持针器夹持刀片前端背部，将刀片的缺口对准刀柄前部的刀楞上，稍用力向后推即可装上。使用后，用持针器夹持刀片尾端背部，稍用力提起并向前推即可卸下（图15）。

（三）手术刀的使用

根据手术部位和组织性质的不同，可选用不同形状、大小的刀片，并选择不同的执刀方式。常用的执刀方式如下（图16）。

1. **执弓式**　为最常用的执刀方式。此法使用灵活，动作范围广，借示指加压作用可切割较坚韧的皮肤或组织，如各种胸腹部手术的皮肤切口。

2. **执笔式**　适用于短小切口如浅表的小脓肿，切开腹膜小口等；用力轻柔，操作灵巧准确，便于控制刀的动度和力度，如将刀片稍倾斜，可用作锐性分离和解剖组织，如解剖血管、神经等。

10

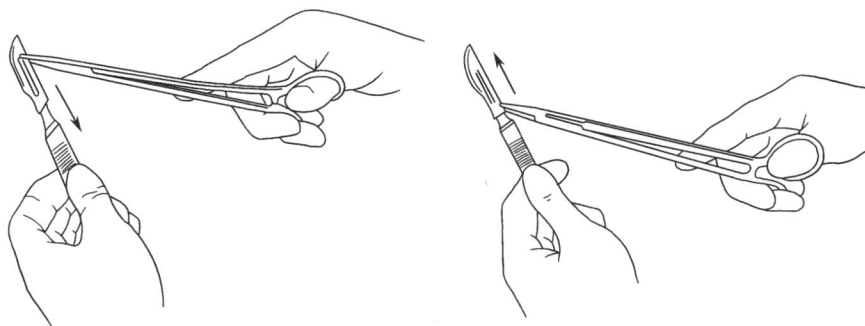

图 15　刀片装卸方法

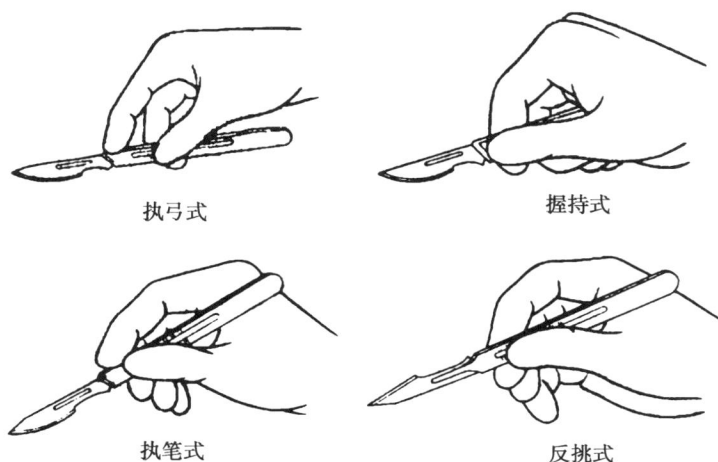

执弓式　　　　　　　　　　握持式

执笔式　　　　　　　　　　反挑式

图 16　执刀方式

3. 握持式　适用于切割范围较大、组织坚厚、用力较大的切开,如截肢切断肌肉、切开较长的皮肤切口等。

4. 反挑式　是执笔式的一种转换形式,刀刃向上挑开,可避免深部组织的损伤。适用于脓肿切开、挑破血管或胆总管等空腔脏器。

手术刀传递应防止误伤。传递时,传递者(常为器械护士)应握住刀柄与刀片衔接处的背部,将刀柄尾端送至手术者(图 17)。切不可将刀刃传递给手术者。

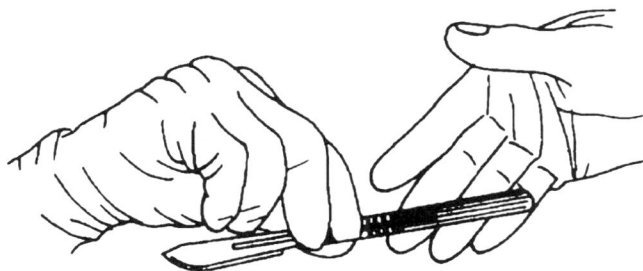

图 17　手术刀的传递

二、手术剪

手术剪(scissors)分为解剖剪和线剪两类。前者头钝,用以分离、解剖、剪开组织,其前端较圆薄,有弯直、长短之分;后者用以剪线和敷料,其前端尖而直(图 18)。

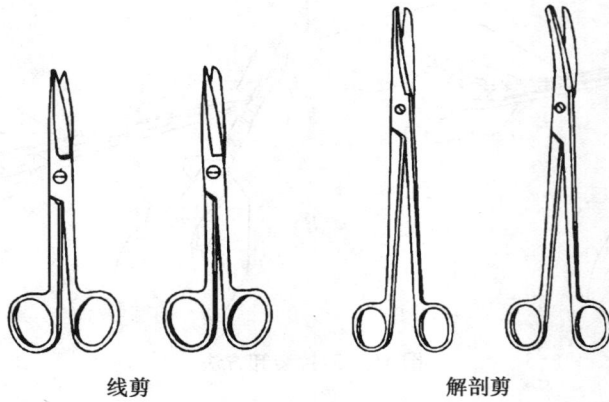

线剪　　　　　解剖剪

图 18　手术剪

正确的执剪方法是以拇指和无名指扣剪环,示指指腹抵其轴(图 19)。此持法可使剪刀在运用时维持稳定。使用各种带环手术器械时,均可采用这种方式握持。

图 19　持剪方式

三、手术镊

手术镊(forceps)主要用于夹持或提握组织,便于剥离、剪开和缝合。
手术镊根据其用途有长短、粗细及有齿和无齿之别(图 20)。

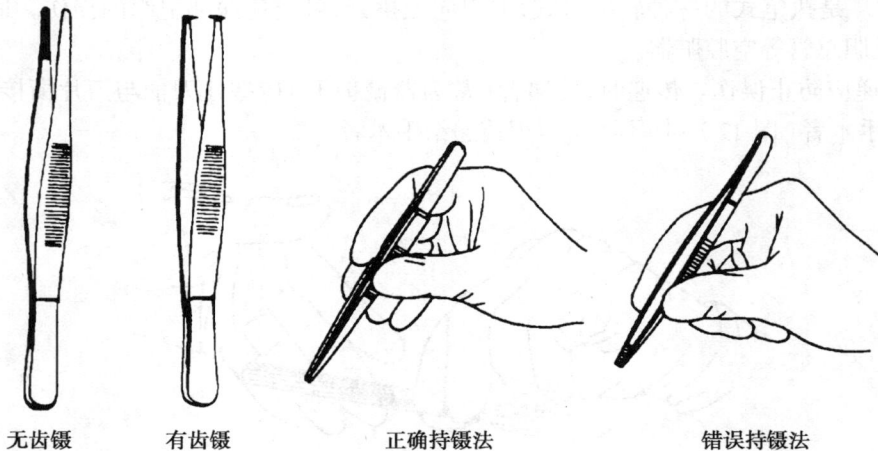

无齿镊　　　有齿镊　　　正确持镊法　　　错误持镊法

图 20　手术镊及其持握方法

有齿镊(组织镊,teeth forceps)　其前端有钩齿,无横行细槽,用于夹持较坚韧的皮肤、筋膜、肌膜、瘢痕等组织,对组织有一定的损伤,但夹持较稳固。

无齿镊(平镊,smooth forceps)　其尖端平,无钩齿,有横行细槽,用于夹持较脆弱的胃肠壁、腹膜、黏膜等组织和脏器。平镊对组织的损伤较轻微。

夹持血管、神经等精细组织时宜用尖头平镊。浅部操作用短镊,深部操作用长镊。正确的持镊姿势是拇指相对于示指、中指,把持于镊的中部。

四、血管钳

（一）分型

血管钳(止血钳,hemostat)有长、短、直(straight clamp)、弯(Kelly clamp)、有钩(Kocher clamp)、无钩之别。各型血管钳叶内侧全部或前半部有横槽,使钳夹的组织不易滑脱(图 21)。一般应用的血管钳长 14cm,主要用于止血,还可用以分离、解剖或夹持组织,但不应夹持布巾,也不宜夹持皮肤、脏器及较脆弱的组织。直钳用于浅部操作,弯钳用于较深部操作,长柄钳用于深部操作。主刀进行组织缝合时,通常由第一助手持直血管钳协助拔针。

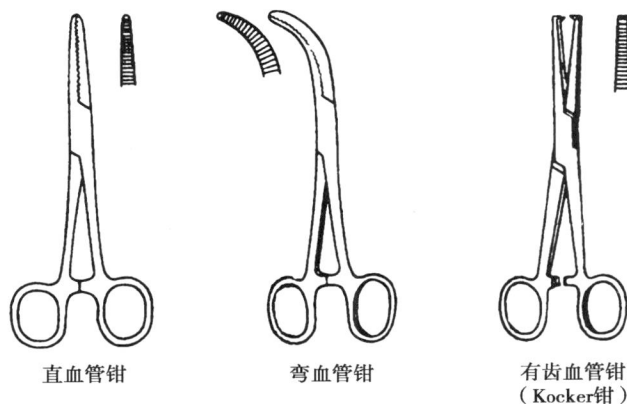

直血管钳　　弯血管钳　　有齿血管钳（Kocker钳）

图 21　各型血管钳

较细小、长度为 12.5cm 的血管钳称蚊式血管钳(mosquito clamp)。也有弯和直两种。通常用于较精细手术中的止血和分离,不宜做大块组织夹持。

有齿血管钳(Kocher clamp):在钳的前端有钩齿,用于夹持较厚、易滑脱的组织,也可用于需切除组织的夹持牵引等。该钳对组织的损伤较大,故不可用于一般止血。

（二）血管钳的运用

手术中最常用血管钳钳夹血管或出血点,以便止血。使用时,以拇指和无名指分别插入钳环内,用钳尖夹住出血点后闭锁血管钳齿扣(图 22)。

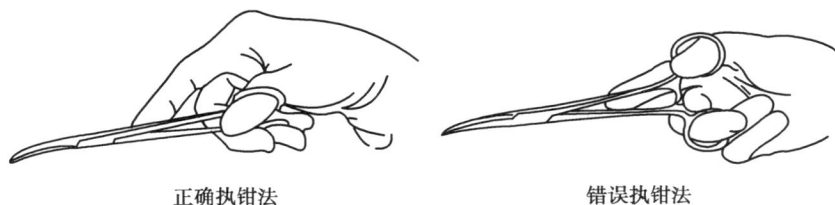

正确执钳法　　错误执钳法

图 22　血管钳执握法

结扎或缝扎出血点时需放开扣锁的血管钳。可用拇指与示指捏住血管钳的一个环口,同时以中指和无名指稍用力顶压另一环口,钳口即可张开。右手还可采用与钳夹同样的执钳法松开血管钳(图 23)。

五、组织钳

组织钳(鼠齿钳,Allis clamp)前端稍宽,带齿似小耙,闭合时互相嵌合,弹性好,可以牢固地夹持软组织而损伤较小,不易滑脱(图 24)。也常用于夹持组织或皮瓣,作为牵引。

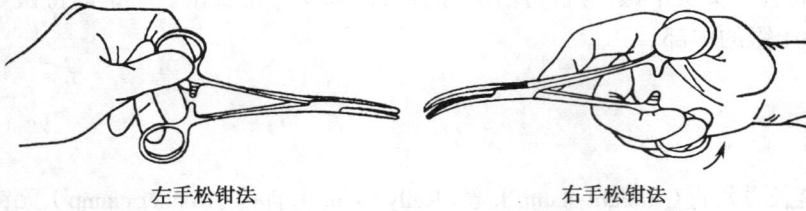

左手松钳法　　　　　　　　　右手松钳法

图 23　两种已扣锁血管钳的松开法

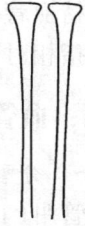

图 24　组织钳（Allis 钳）

六、巾钳

巾钳（towel clip）前端弯而尖，能交叉咬合（图 25）。主要用以固定布巾，以免移动或松开。在咬合固定时，注意勿损伤皮肤。

七、海绵钳

海绵钳（sponge forceps），又称卵圆钳（oval forceps）。它的前部呈环状，分为有齿和无齿两种（图 26）。前者用以夹持敷料作消毒用，或放在盛消毒液的大口量杯或大口瓶内，便于供手术台下向台上传递物品之用。后者用于夹提肠管等组织。手术台下用其取物时应注意钳的头端应始终朝下以免消毒药液倒流到柄端的有菌区域。

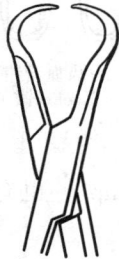

图 25　巾钳

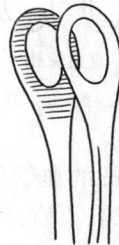

图 26　海绵钳

八、持针器

持针器（needle holder）也称针持。用以夹持缝针（通常用于夹弯针，直针不用）。持针器外形与血管钳相似，但要粗壮得多，臂长而支点与夹针端间距很短以利夹针稳固。缝合时用持针器的尖端夹住缝针中 1/3 与针眼侧 1/3 交界处，缝针与针持轴线呈直角关系，针上穿的线应适当重叠（一般间断缝合时重叠缝线全长的 1/4），并将缝线嵌在针旁持针器两叶尖端之间，以免缝合时脱落。

执持针器的姿势可与执血管钳相同，但如将其环口部用手掌整把握住，操作更为方便（图 27）。

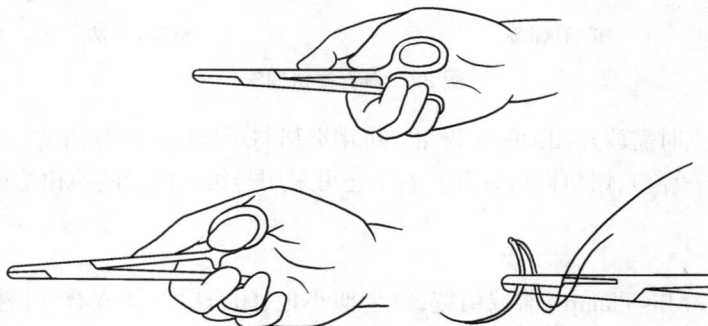

图 27　持针器及其握持法

九、牵开器

牵开器（拉钩，retractors）用以牵开妨碍操作和视线的组织，充分显露操作部位，以便于手术进行。拉钩有手持与自动两类，又可因使用场合不同而有各种形状和适合不同深度的拉钩，命名各异。常用的有甲状腺拉钩（thyroid retractor）、阑尾拉钩（appendix retractor）、腹腔拉钩（abdominal retractor）、深弯拉钩（Dever's retractor）、直角拉钩（rectangular retractor）等（图28）。

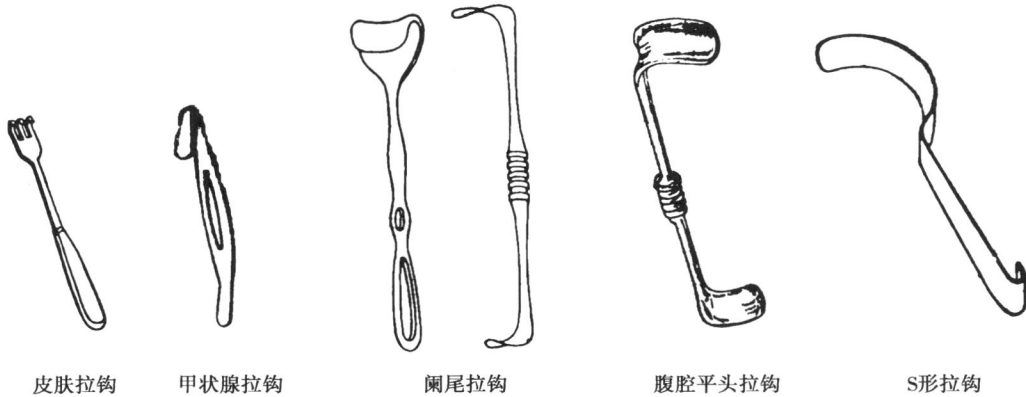

| 皮肤拉钩 | 甲状腺拉钩 | 阑尾拉钩 | 腹腔平头拉钩 | S形拉钩 |

图28　常用拉钩

使用拉钩不能用力过猛，以免损伤组织。牵拉柔软的组织，如肝脏、肠管等内脏时应在拉钩下方衬以纱布垫。

十、探针

普通探针是一支实心的可弯曲金属条，用来探查窦道、瘘管、伤口和管腔。其头圆钝，以避免损伤组织或在探查时产生假道。

有槽探针用于窦道瘘管切开或脓肿引流时引导工具（图29）。

十一、吸引器头

外接吸引器用以吸去手术区内的积液。它是一支金属或一次性硬塑料的双套管。外套管有多个孔眼；内管尾端与负压吸引器的管道相连。外套管管壁有很多小孔，可防止吸引时内管前口被周围的固体物堵塞，以保持吸引通畅（图30）。

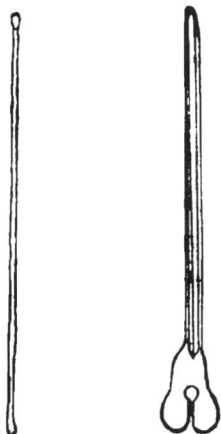

图29　普通探针与有槽探针

图30　吸引器头

十二、缝针与缝线

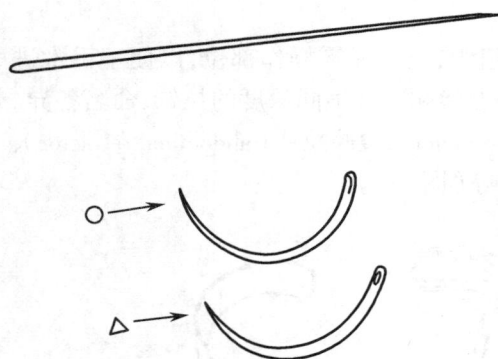

图 31   各种缝针

缝针（needle）   根据针断面形状缝针有直、弯、圆、三棱之分（图 31）；针有不同长度,弯针还有不同弯度。三棱针（或三角针）有锐利的刃,能穿透较坚硬的组织,故适用于缝合皮肤、软骨及乳腺腺体等组织,但损伤较大。其他组织的缝合通常都用圆针。弯针与直针相比更便于深部操作。

另有无损伤缝针,集针线为一体,针尾嵌有与针粗细相似的线,用以缝合血管、神经等。

缝线有不可吸收和可吸收两大类；其原料有天然纤维和人工合成纤维两类。

（一）不吸收缝线

丝线是最常用的不吸收手术缝线,与肠线相比它的优点是组织反应较小,价廉而操作方便。在相同直径的基础上,丝线的抗张强度高于肠线,因此可选用较细的线和针,减少缝合导致的组织损伤,容易打结而且线结牢靠。它的缺点是不被吸收,长期留下异物,遗留于泌尿道黏膜面、胆道黏膜面的线结可能成为复发结石的核心。此外,丝线为多股搓合,用于非无菌性手术时,细菌可能侵入其纤维之间而潜伏,一旦感染,不易清除,常导致慢性脓窦形成。

常用的不吸收合成缝线由高分子合成材料制成,如尼龙线、涤纶线等。尼龙线多用于腹部或其他部位的减张缝合。高分子合成线抗张强度高,组织反应小,但打结后容易松开,故必须连续打结 5~6 次,剪线时线尾宜长,以防松脱。

（二）可吸收缝线

有天然及合成两大类。通常所用天然可吸收缝合材料为肠线,它在体内能够逐渐被蛋白酶消化。常用的合成可吸收性缝合材料为聚羟基乙酸。它在体内可被水解而不是被蛋白酶消化。

肠线有普通和铬制两种。普通肠线在组织内 5~10 天之间被吸收；在铬酸盐溶液内浸泡过的铬制肠线吸收时间可延后到 1 至数周,实际吸收时间取决于铬酸盐的浸泡时间。由于肠线吸收过程有一定的组织反应,加之使用不方便等缺点,目前临床已很少使用。

聚羟基乙酸（polyglycolic acid, Dexon）为常用的可吸收合成缝合材料。这种缝线组织反应小,一般在 60~90 天之间完全被吸收。因其强度比肠线大,故使用时可取比肠线相对较细的线达到相同效果,但因线质较硬,打结后较易松开。这一缺点可借采用多纤维制品克服。虽然此类缝线也适用于深部组织缝合,但主要用于缝合皮肤及皮下组织。新一代可吸收合成缝线"POS"抗张强度高,组织反应小,而且质地柔软,不需采用多纤维制品。

缝线根据抗张强度及粗细分为各种号码。正数号码越大表示缝线越粗,抗张强度越高,"0"数越多则越细。

十三、引流物和导管

油纱布（条）即纱布浸有凡士林或石蜡油,主要用于保护无表皮的创面,以保持其滑润无损,有时用于填塞脓腔以保持其引流口畅通。

橡皮片引流条用乳胶手套胶皮剪制成条状,主要置于术后易有渗血积聚的甲状腺、阴囊及乳房等手术区的皮下层作为引流,防止积血。

卷烟式引流条用薄胶管或旧手套胶皮制成管状,裹以纱布条,成为形似烟卷的引流物。常置于腹腔内以防止或引流积液。

引流管多以乳胶管或塑胶管制成,用于深部术野的引流,防止积血、积液和积脓。

T形管以乳胶或硅胶制成,通常用于胆总管的引流。

导尿管有粗细之分,可用于一次性导尿或留置导尿,也可用于膀胱造口、胃造口或液气胸的引流等场合。蕈状导尿管与气囊导尿管因其前端膨大,置入膀胱或其他腔隙内充气或充液后,可防止脱出。前列腺切除后置气囊导尿管,气囊有压迫创面减少渗血的作用。

套管式引流管由内外两管组成。外管前端有数个小孔,后端还有一小孔。内管后段较长于外管,可接负压引流器或注液冲洗。外管后端应捆紧在内管上,便于维持负压。此种引流管主要用于盆腔和膈下等深部腔隙的引流,可防止负压吸引时内管被堵塞(图32)。

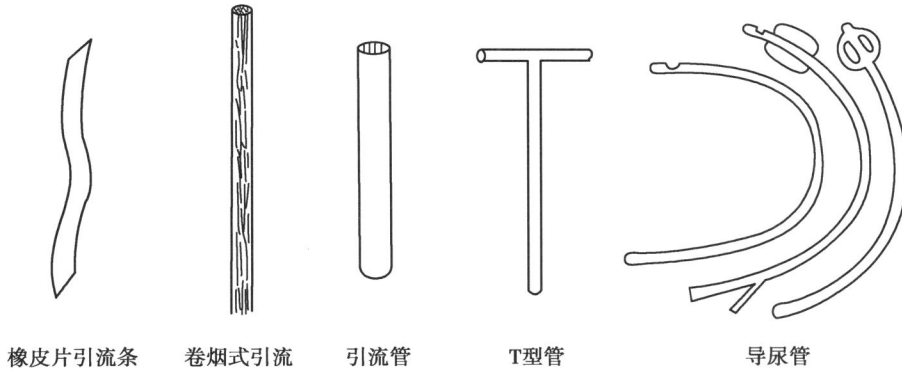

橡皮片引流条　卷烟式引流　引流管　　T型管　　　　导尿管

图32　几种常用引流物和导管

（徐　周　李凤贺）

第三章

外科手术的基本操作

第一节 组织的切开

一、切开的基本原则

1. 充分显露手术野,便于手术操作。

2. 力求减少对组织的损害,如切口部位应尽量靠近病变部位,不要作超过实际需要的切开,用锋利的刀剪作切开以减少损伤等。

3. 力求减少功能的损害,如皮肤的切开要与皮肤张力线平行,不要在负重部位如足跟部切开,在关节部位应避免纵行切开,避免损伤重要的血管、神经、腺体导管等。

二、皮肤切开

在做较长切口时,由术者与助手各以其手掌将预定的切口两侧皮肤压按固定,然后在其间切开（图 33 ）。做短小切口时,由术者以左手拇指及示指将切口皮肤向两侧按压,在两指间切开。

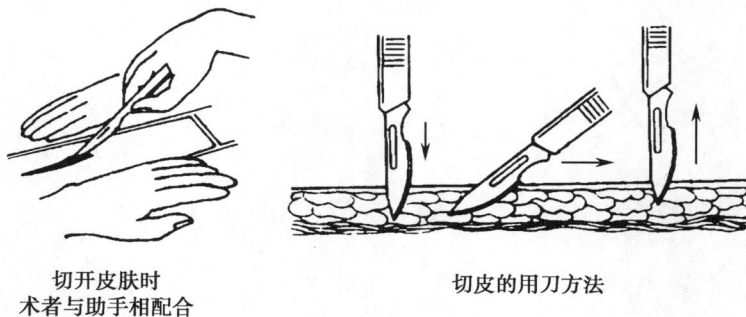

切开皮肤时
术者与助手相配合

切皮的用刀方法

图 33 皮肤切开

切开皮肤时,刀片必须与皮肤平面垂直,避免倾斜。先将刀柄向上抬起,用刀刃尖部切开皮肤全层,逐渐将手术刀放平至与皮肤间成 30°~45° 角,以刀刃圆凸部切开皮肤,直至切口末端,将刀柄抬高,以刀刃尖部结束切开（图 33 ）。切开时要做到方向准确,用力稳定,力求一次切开皮肤全层,深浅均匀一致。

三、筋膜和腱鞘切开

一般可先作一小切口,再用组织剪伸入其深面,张开剪刀,使之与深部组织钝性分离并剪开。如果切开处筋膜下间隙较窄,切小口后可伸入弯钳分离,然后用刀或剪扩大切口。

四、肌层切开

手术径路通过肌层时,如能顺其肌束或纤维的方向钝性分离,可减少出血,也有利于愈合。然而,许多手术必须切断肌肉,方能达到深部。此时,将肌层予以横断。出血点可借结扎或缝扎止血。电刀切割可以减少出血。有时用两把有齿血管钳夹住肌束,在两钳之间切断,然后结扎或缝扎肌肉断端。

第二节　组织的分离

组织的分离是指各种正常及病理组织的游离借以充分显露病变的组织或器官,而便于进行处理。

一、锐性分离

用手术刀或组织剪进行分离,有分离面准确、整齐而损伤较少的优点。这种分离必须解剖关系清楚,并在直视下进行,要避免盲目操作而致血管、神经和器官的损伤。此法较多用于离断解剖关系清楚的组织及坚韧的纤维组织。

二、钝性分离

多用于疏松组织的解剖,可用血管钳或组织剪不断插入、张开,用刀柄或剥离子(用弯血管钳夹持的极小纱布球)逐步推开,甚至用术者的手指直接剥开等法进行分离。钝性分离用力要适当,否则可撕裂血管、神经或脏器。

用剪同时进行锐性及钝性分离比较方便。先以闭合的剪刀由浅层插入要分离组织深面的间隙中,微微张开进行分离,辨清组织结构后剪断已分离的部分,继而反复向前插入、分离并剪开,以扩大分离范围,直至达到预期目的。

第三节　止　　血

一、压迫止血法

这是手术中最常用的止血方法之一。压迫出血点可使血流减慢或停止,有利于血栓形成而止血,适用于微小血管出血,特别是静脉性出血。通常的做法是用手握纱布压迫创面片刻。有较汹涌出血而情况紧急时可用手指捏住出血部位或出血血管的近心段以便寻觅血管破口。温盐水纱布有加速血凝的作用,常用于压迫创面渗血。对于某些难以控制的出血或渗血,有时可用纱布条填塞达到止血目的。填塞物在手术后 5~7 天逐渐取出。

二、结扎止血法

有钳夹结扎和缝合结扎两种方法。

(一)钳夹结扎

用血管钳直接钳夹出血点(图 34)。钳夹时血管钳应与出血组织创面垂直,以钳尖准确夹住出血点(钳夹的组织应尽量少)。然后由一人将血管钳尖端向下,轻轻提起,用结扎线绕钳尖套住出血点,保持线的紧张度并打一单结,在收紧线结的同时将血管钳轻轻松开移去,第一个单结收紧后,再打第二个结,为保证可靠结扎,有时需连续打三个单结。打结时两手用力要均匀,在拉紧结扎线时,两手中的结扎线受力处与结扎处三点应在一条直线上,避免偏位,防止组织撕脱或线结脱落。

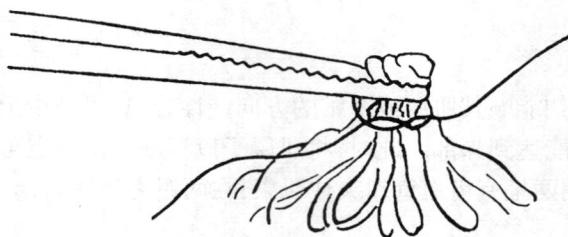

图 34 钳夹结扎止血法

对需切断的较大血管,可先用血管钳游离其一小段,用两把血管钳钳夹,在两钳之间将血管切断,然后分别用线结扎两断端止血。

（二）缝扎止血

缝扎又称贯穿缝合或 8 字形缝扎（图 35），常用于闭合大血管的断端,可防止结扎线脱落。在缝扎大血管时,应先游离一段血管,上三把血管钳。在近心侧两把与远心侧一把之间切断血管,然后在一、三两钳处结扎,再在中位血管钳处作 8 字形缝合。切断的组织可能会有较大血管而需行 8 字形缝扎,此时应注意避免缝针刺伤所含血管,否则可导致出血或血肿形成。有时可先作一道结扎,然后在结扎线结的远侧作贯穿缝扎。

三、电凝止血法

高频电流可以凝固组织（过强电流可使组织液化）。将电凝头接触夹住出血点的血管钳,通电后使组织凝固而达到止血目的（图 36）。有时可用电凝头直接烧灼小的出血点。电凝止血的优点是操作简捷,伤口内不留异物（线结）。它还可通过内镜进行远距离止血操作。电凝止血不宜用于较大血管的止血,因凝固的血管壁可坏死脱落而导致术后大出血。

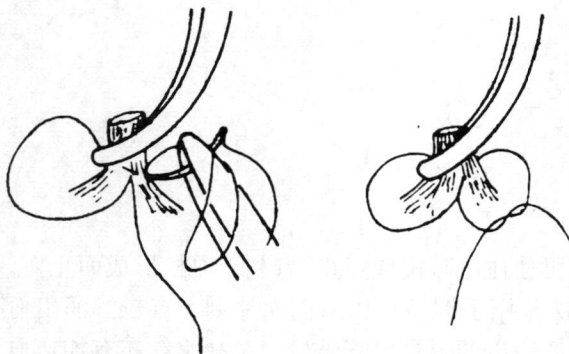

图 35 缝扎止血

图 36 电凝止血

四、止血物品止血法

用以上方法难以止血的创面,如肝或骨断面等处的出血,可用明胶海绵、纤维蛋白泡沫体、氧化纤维素、胶原丝等促凝物品或骨蜡填敷（骨）于创面达到止血作用。

五、金属夹止血法

金属夹止血多用于经不住缝线结扎的脆弱组织（如脑）的止血和不便显露的深部组织的止血。此法除有止血作用外,还可在术后 X 线检查中作为定位标志。经内镜（如腹腔镜、胸腔镜）检查或手术可用此法替代无法操作的结扎法。常用的金属夹用钛或银制成,上夹时需用特制的夹钳。

第四节　结　　扎

手术中止血需用缝线进行大量结扎,组织缝合后也需结扎,故结扎是外科最基本而且十分重要的操作之一。结扎的要求是安全可靠、操作便捷;因此,要选用合适的缝线和进行规范的操作。

一、各种线结

（一）方结

也称平结,是外科手术中最常用的一种。它由两个方向相反的单结组成,多用于结扎较小的血管和各种缝合时的结扎。如打结操作正确,此结牢固而不易脱落（图 37 ）。

单结　　方结　　三重结　　外科结　　假结　　滑结

图 37　各种线结

（二）外科结

打第一单结时线连绕两圈,可增加线与线之间的接触面,再打第二个单结时不易滑脱或松动,故外科结比方结更为牢固可靠,但操作比较费时。通常用于结扎较大血管或缝合处张力较大的结扎（图 37 ）。

（三）三重结

是在方结的基础上多打一单结,且第三个单结与第二个单结的方向相反。此结不易松脱,故也适用于结扎较大的血管和张力较大的组织缝合。尼龙线、肠线打结后易松开,故常用三重结。缺点是组织内残留的结扎线头较大（图 37 ）。

（四）假结

又名十字结,由两个方向相同的单结组成,此结容易滑脱,手术中忌用（图 37 ）。

（五）滑结

滑结与方结的基本结构相同,即由二个方向相反的单结组成,但因打结时操作方法不当,形成一个一侧线段围绕另一线段两圈的结,此线结容易滑脱,故名滑结。在打方结时如两手拉线用力不均匀,只拉紧一根线,虽然打结时两手交叉仍是用一侧线段围绕另一被拉紧的线段打结,但是形成的是滑结,而不是方结（图 38 ）。滑结极不可靠,应避免。

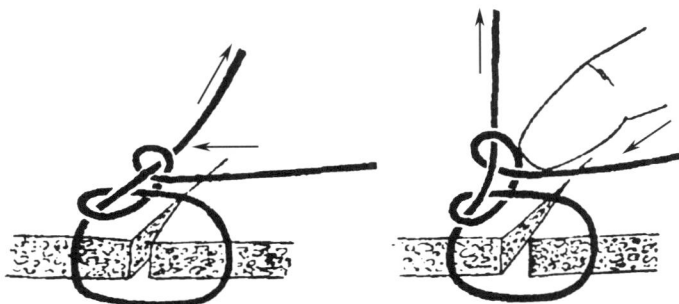

图 38　滑结的形成

二、各种打结方法

（一）单手打结法

单手打结法是一种简便迅速的打结方法，左、右手均可操作，但应防止操作不当导致滑结（图39）。

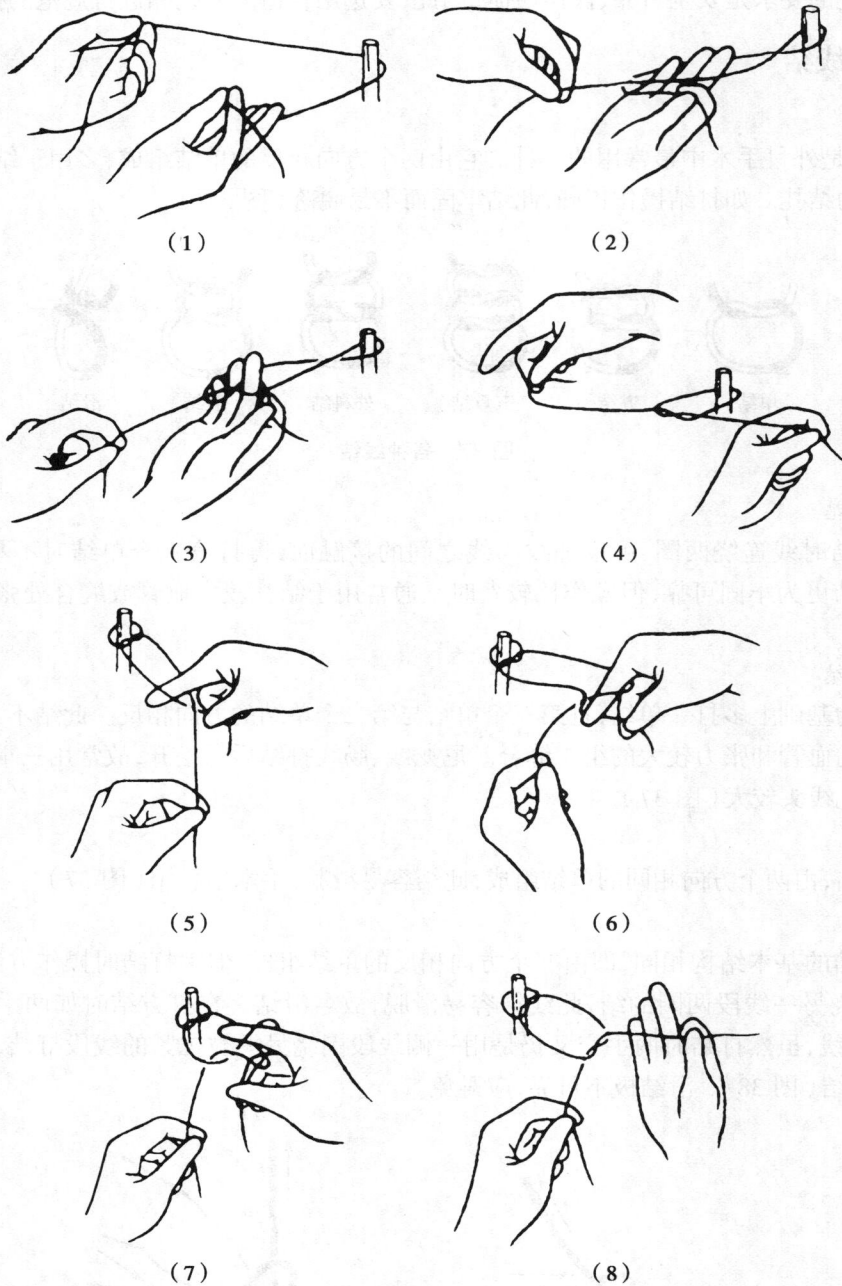

（1）

（2）

（3）

（4）

（5）

（6）

（7）

（8）

图39　单手打结法

（二）双手打结法

除用于一般结扎外，对深部或组织张力较大的缝合结扎较为可靠、方便（图40）。另外，双手打结时，也便于做外科结。

（1）

（4）

（7）

（2）

（5）

（8）

（3）

（6）

（9）

（10）

（11）

（12）

（13）

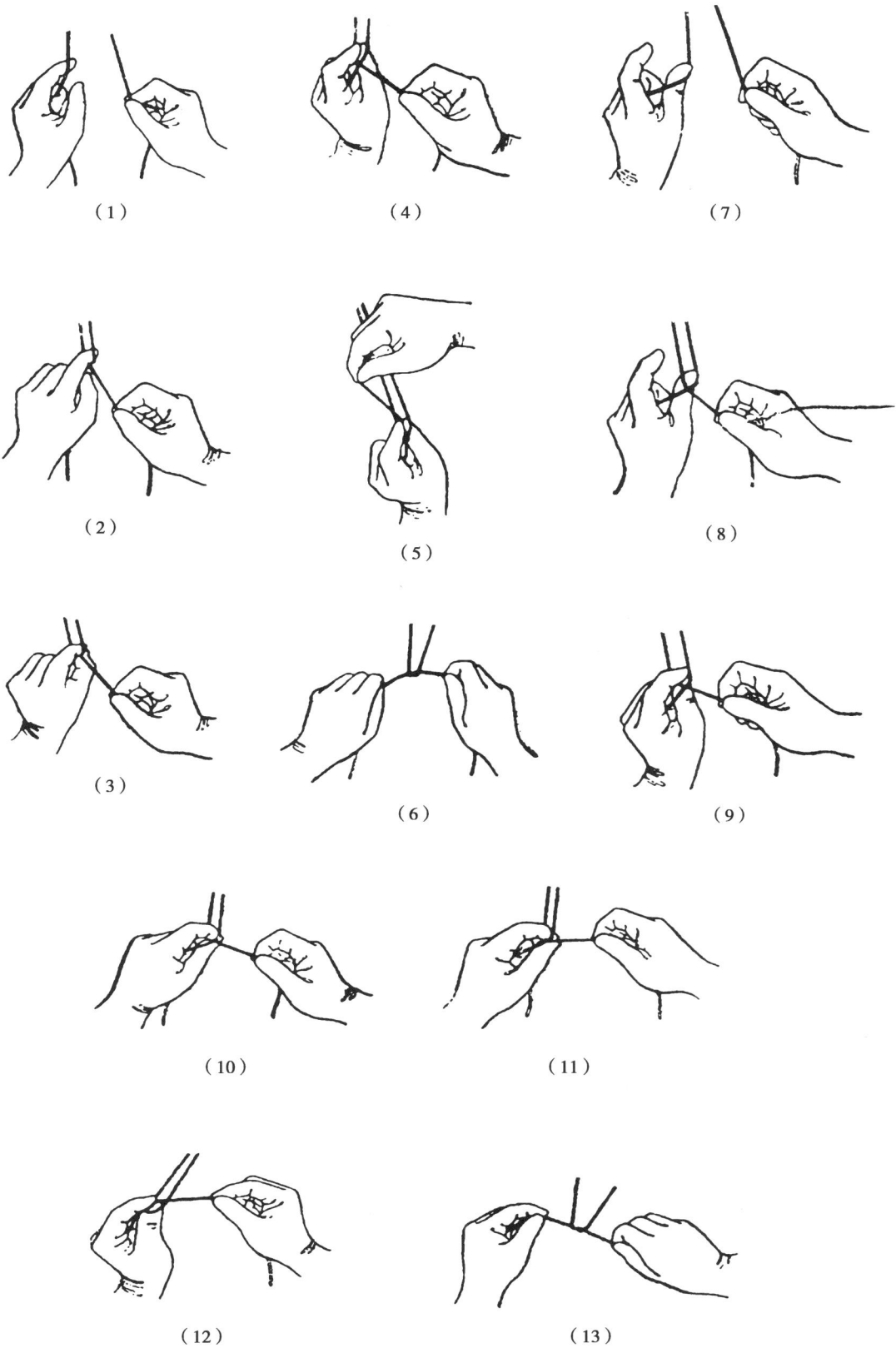

图 40 双手打结法

（三）器械打结法

用持针器或血管钳打结适于线头短而用手打结有困难时；器械打结结扎较浅组织时可少花穿线时间并节省缝线，尤其是采用肠线作为缝合材料时。打结方法见图41。

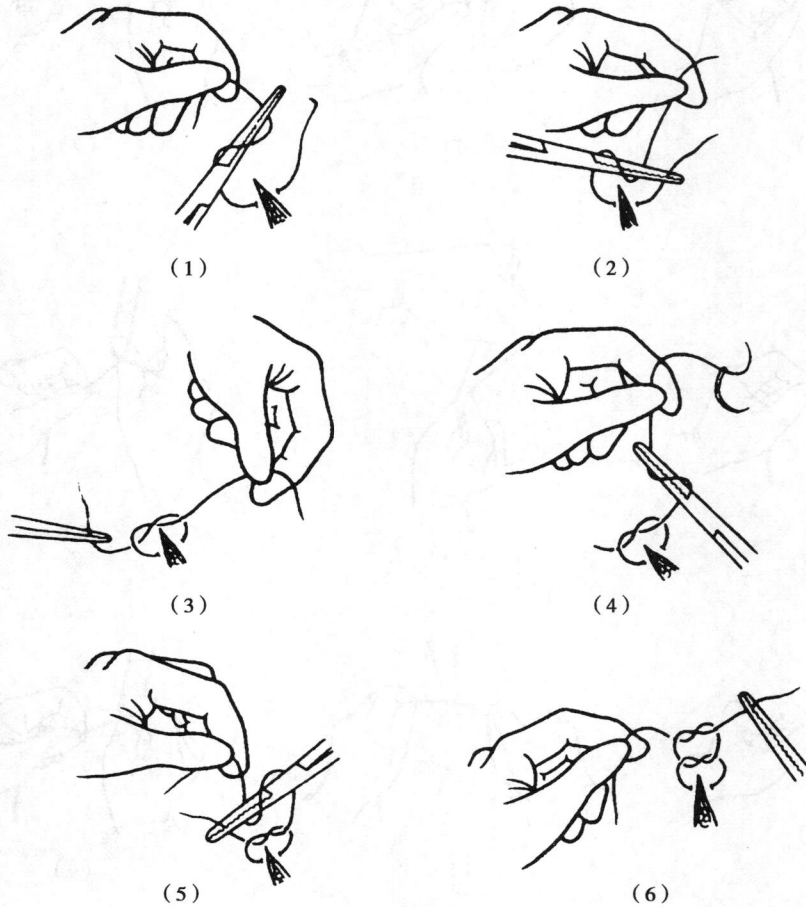

（1）   （2）

（3）   （4）

（5）   （6）

图 41   器械打结法

（四）深部打结法

用于较深位置或重要血管的结扎。宜用一段较粗而长的线，用血管钳尖端夹住线的一端，深入术野深部套住钳夹出血点的钳尖，然后按双手打结的方法进行操作。拉紧线结时，用一只手的示指将线结慢慢顶向结扎点，用力的方向与另一只手相反（图42）。

三、打结时注意事项

1. 打结收紧时，要求三点（两手用力点和结扎点）成一直线，成角或把结扎点向上提容易使结扎点撕脱或线结脱落。

2. 要打成方结，二个单结的方向必须相反。

3. 二个单结收紧线时，必有一次两手需交叉，否则即成滑结。

4. 操作中两手用力要均匀，不然也容易成为滑结。

5. 打结时用力要轻柔均匀，徐徐拉紧，否则易断线或未扎紧而滑脱，导致再出血，甚至发生大出血。

6. 打结时，要选择质量好而粗细合适的线。结扎前用盐水浸湿，能增加线之间的摩擦力和线的强度。干线易断裂。

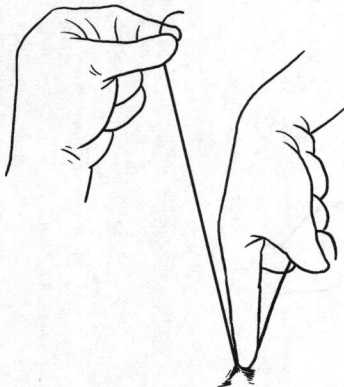

图 42   深部打结法

第五节　缝　　合

一、缝合的基本原则

1. 分清层次,对合相同组织。如交错对合,将影响愈合并加重愈合后的功能障碍。

2. 创口边缘要彼此靠拢,对合整齐。创缘两侧缝合的宽度和深度适宜、对等、针距恰当。过宽或过深的缝合,在打结后将造成缝合组织两创缘内陷,宽度深度不等时,打结后两创缘则不在同一平面,影响组织的愈合。组织缝合的宽度、深度及针距,应根据所缝组织的厚薄、强度、缝合的具体方法以确定。

3. 缝合的组织应能承受缝线的牵拉,如皮肤、黏膜肌层、筋膜、胸膜、腹膜、肌膜、神经鞘等。而脂肪、肌肉等脆弱的组织通常不予缝合。

4. 缝合时打结不可过紧,以免缝线压榨组织,影响局部血液循环,使愈合延迟,甚至导致组织坏死。

5. 要避免缝合时形成无效腔,因其不仅妨碍创缘的对合,而且腔内可积液,易并发感染,这些都将推迟组织的愈合。创口深者不应全层缝合而需逐层缝合。这是避免无效腔形成的主要方法。

6. 手术者应根据术中情况选择缝线。清洁切口或沾染很轻的伤口,经清创后,可选用不吸收线;污染较重者则应选用可吸收线。血管的缝合或结扎,应选用不吸收线,因可吸收线一旦吸收过早,可导致出血。穿过胆道或泌尿道黏膜的缝合应尽量采用可吸收线,以避免残留缝线继发结石形成。胃肠道的吻合和缝合,多用内外两层缝合,穿过黏膜的内层缝合终将脱落,故使用可吸收线或不吸收线均可。

二、缝合方法

主要有间断和连续之分。以下是几种常用缝合方法。

（一）单纯间断缝合法

最为常用,多用于皮肤、皮下、腱膜等组织的缝合。缝针于创缘一侧进入组织,从对侧相应部位穿出（图43）。缝合稍厚的组织时,要注意尽量接近垂直方向进针与出针,否则将引起创缘向内或向外翻转。

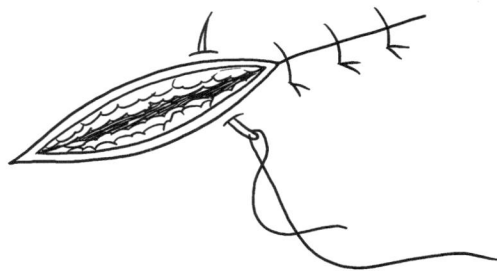

（二）双重间断缝合（“8”字缝合）

结扎较牢固,可用于腱膜、肌腱、韧带等强力组织的缝合。不同的进行程序可使8字的交叉在创口的深面或浅面（图44）。

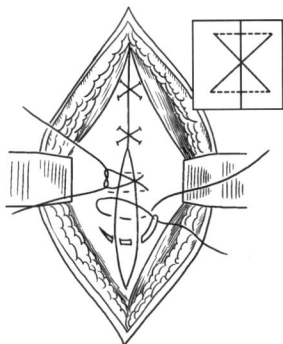

图43　单纯间断缝合

“8”字交叉在浅面　　　　　　“8”字交叉在深面

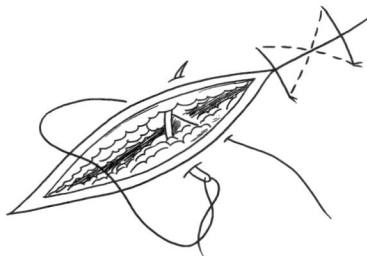

图44　8字缝合

（三）单纯连续缝合

常用于腹膜的缝合，先作一单纯间断缝合，打结后用其长头连续缝完创口全长，结束时将缝针所带双股缝线与该线连续的单股缝线结扎（图45）。此种缝合法具有缝合速度快、创缘对合严密、有一定止血效果等优点。但是遗留在组织内的缝线较多，一旦术后早期缝线断裂，则整个缝合可能裂开。

（四）扣锁缝合

开始与结束的方法与单纯连续缝合法相同，只是每一针从前一针的线袢内穿出（图46）。此法有防止创缘翻转及更好的止血作用。此法更多用于胃肠吻合时后壁内层缝合。

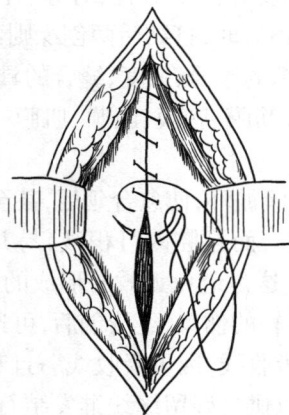

图45　单纯连续缝合　　　　　　　　　图46　扣锁缝合

（五）减张缝合

主要用于腹壁切口的减张。特别是切口处张力大或全身情况较差时，为防止切口裂开，在常规切口缝合之外加用此缝合，缝合线将除腹膜以外的腹壁予以全层缝合（图47）。结扎前缝线穿过一段橡皮管或纱布作为衬托，以防高张时皮肤被缝线割裂。结扎时线不能抽得过紧，以免影响血运。

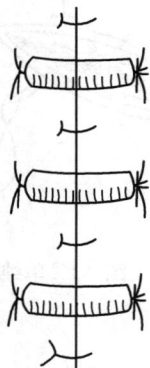

肌肉
腹膜

图47　减张缝合

（六）内翻缝合

胃肠道和膀胱的壁由多层组织组成，其内层黏膜面对合后不能彼此愈合，故缝合时均采用内翻法以保证外层组织良好接触和愈合，否则可致黏膜外翻而引起胃肠液或尿液的外漏，形成胃瘘、肠瘘或膀胱瘘。内翻缝合形式众多，详见第十二章胃肠道手术基本原则。

（七）外翻缝合

此法可使缝合组织的边缘向外翻出，常用于血管缝合，目的是使血管内膜面在缝合后能保持平滑，避免粗糙面形成血栓（图48）。此外，缝合松弛的皮肤时（如阴囊皮肤缝合），为避免创缘内卷，也可用外翻法（图49）。

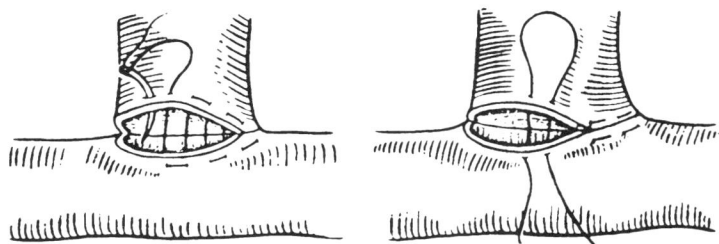

图 48　吻合血管的外翻缝合

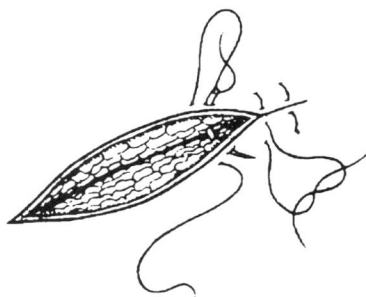

图 49　阴囊皮肤的外翻缝合
可避免创缘内卷

三、缝合注意事项

1. 各种手术缝线,(包括可吸收者),对机体均为异物,故应力求减少其在组织内的存留。缝线的选用以能承受组织张力为度,并非越粗越好。残留在组织内的线头越少越好。如无特殊需要,应多采用间断缝合。

2. 被缝线结扎的组织都会发生缺血,加上缝线的刺激,局部会有一定的炎症反应,故缝合线骑跨的组织不宜过多。

3. 应按解剖层次缝合,不得遗留无效腔。无效腔可能导致积血、积液,会延迟愈合,甚至继发感染。

4. 结扎缝线不可过紧或过松,以创缘紧密相接为准。过紧会加重组织缺血而妨碍愈合,甚至发生坏死。过松则组织对合不全而影响愈合。缝合皮肤时,应保持皮肤平整、对合良好。

5. 同一层次和性质的组织缝合时,不可夹有其他组织,否则可能妨碍愈合。

第六节　剪线和拆线

一、剪线法

结扎后应在离线结不远处剪去多余的线。留在体内的线头,在保证线结稳固的前提下,应尽量剪短以减轻异物反应。所留线头的长短,应根据线的性质、粗细及组织的性质而定。通常丝线留1~2mm,可吸收线留3~4mm。结扎重要血管、较多组织或缝合处张力较大时,所留线头应稍长,例如丝线头应留2~3mm。

打结者结扎完毕后将双线尾并列提起,保持一定的张力。剪线者持剪微张刃口,以前端顺线尾向前滑至线结外,继而稍向上倾斜约45°,直视下将线剪断(图50)。如此所留线头一般为1~2mm左右。增大倾斜角或者提高剪刀头,留线可增长。皮肤缝合线以后需拆除,故所留线尾应较长,以便利拆线的操作。所留线尾一般长1cm左右。

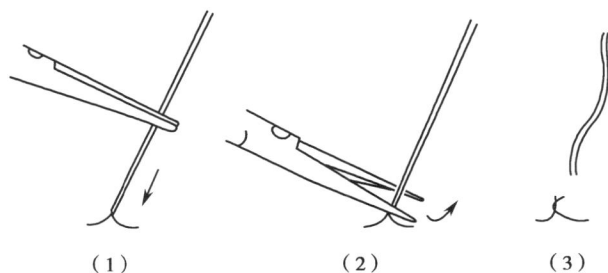

（1）　　　　　　　（2）　　　　　　　（3）

图 50　剪线

二、拆线法

皮肤切口的缝线在伤口初步愈合后需拆除。如保留过久,可能发生针孔感染。根据病人全身情况、组织愈合能力、缝合张力、缝线种类等因素决定拆线日期。一般切口用丝线缝合者,在头、面、颈部术后 4~5 天拆线;胸腹壁的缝线术后第 7 天、上肢和下肢切口 9~12 天、减张缝线 10~14 天拆线。对年老、体弱、营养不良或手术部位的血液循环不佳(如有周围血管病)的切口,以及关节附近活动度大的切口,均应推迟到术后 10~14 天拆线;或先作间断拆线,2~3 天后再酌情全部拆除。切口如有炎症或感染出现,应适当提前拆线。已化脓者应张开切口,予以引流。

拆线时应注意勿使暴露在皮肤外面的一段缝线通过皮下组织抽出,以防止后者被污染。

除去敷料后,用皮肤消毒液作局部(包括缝线)消毒。镊子提起线尾,用线剪在紧贴皮肤针孔之上线结之下剪断线袢,随即可将整个线袢抽出(图 51)。局部再次消毒,覆盖无菌纱布。

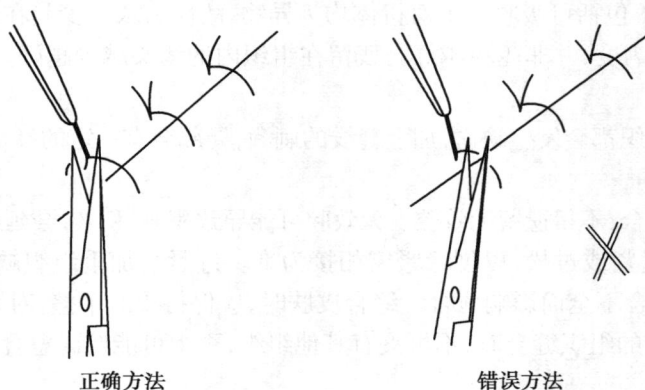

正确方法   错误方法

图 51   皮肤缝线的拆除

第七节   换   药

一、概述

换药又名更换敷料,是对经过初期处理的创口作进一步处理的总称。包括检查伤口,清洁伤口及更换敷料。是预防和控制创面感染,消除妨碍伤口愈合因素,促进伤口愈合的一项重要外科操作。

二、换药目的

1. 观察伤口   观察伤口是否需要进一步特殊处理。
2. 改善伤口环境   去除影响伤口愈合的异物、坏死组织、脓液及分泌物,保持伤口引流通畅。
3. 缩短疗程   促进新生上皮和肉芽组织生长及伤口愈合,减少瘢痕形成。
4. 保护伤口   包扎固定,防止继发性损伤及污染。

三、换药适应证

1. 缝合伤口到期需要拆线者。
2. 伤口放置引流物,需要松动或拔除者。
3. 伤口有渗出或出血征象者。
4. 引流液、渗出液、血液湿透敷料者。

5. 需要观察和检查局部情况者。

四、换药间隔时间

1. 无菌外科切口,一期缝合的伤口一般术后 2~3 天更换敷料 1 次。

2. 分泌物多,感染较重伤口,应增加换药次数,每日 1~2 次,必要时随时更换。

五、换药操作

1. 佩戴口罩、帽子,洗手,准备换药物品。

2. 去除敷料

(1)轻柔慢慢揭开敷料两侧胶布,连同外层敷料一并移除。

(2)伤口内层敷料及引流物,用无菌镊取下,揭起时应沿伤口长轴方向进行(图 52)。若内层敷料与创面干结成痂,可用无菌生理盐水浸湿,待敷料与创面分离后再轻轻顺创口长轴揭去,如还有少许与伤口粘连,则可用另一把镊子夹生理盐水棉球按压粘连处的伤口创面,另一把镊子再轻轻揭去敷料。

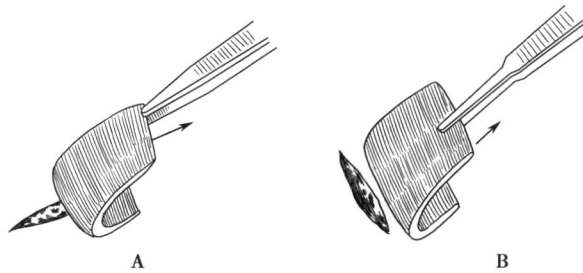

图 52　揭除敷料方式
A 正确;B 错误

3. 创周皮肤处理

去除敷料后,用消毒液(75% 乙醇或 5% 聚维酮碘)在伤口周围由内向外消毒 2 次(图 53),勿使消毒液流入创口内。要用双手持镊操作法,注意无菌操作,右手镊子可直接接触伤口,左手镊子专用从换药碗中夹取无菌物品,递给右手(两镊不可相碰),镊尖保持朝下。消毒范围应超过无菌敷料覆盖范围。若创周皮肤太多脓液,可先用干棉球由内向外擦拭,然后再作皮肤消毒。

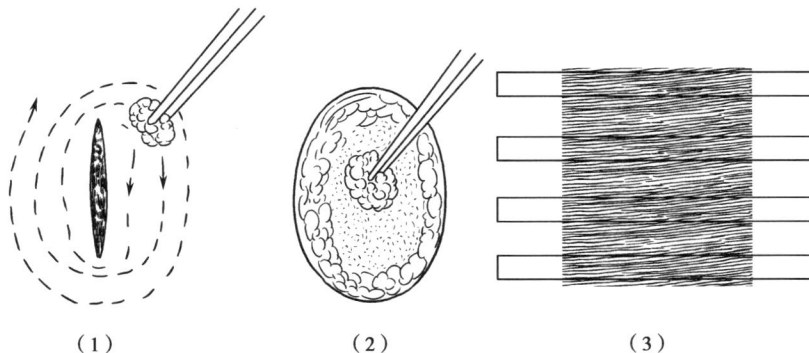

图 53　创口处理顺序
(1)创周皮肤处理;(2)创面处理;(3)创面覆盖和包扎固定

4. 创面处理:

(1)创周皮肤处理完毕后,用生理盐水轻柔拭去创面分泌物(图 53)。注意:在拭去分泌物时切忌反复用力擦拭,以免损伤创面肉芽或上皮组织;擦拭创面棉球不宜太湿,否则不但不能清除分泌物,反而使脓液外流污染伤口周围皮肤;擦洗创面周围皮肤棉球不得再洗创口内面。

（2）脓腔深大者,棉球擦洗时应防止脱落在创口内。

（3）脓腔可用3%过氧化氢水溶液（双氧水）、0.1%新洁尔灭、生理盐水顺序冲洗。

（4）创面清洗后,应彻底清除伤口内线头、坏死组织等异物。

（5）最后用消毒液消毒创周皮肤。根据伤口情况选择凡士林纱布、药物纱布或盐水纱布覆盖,或放入引流条等（图53）。

5. 包扎固定

创口处理完毕后,覆盖无菌干纱布,胶布粘贴固定,必要时绷带包扎（图53）。胶布粘贴方向应与身体长轴垂直,长度一般相当于敷料宽度2倍~2.5倍。

（李英存）

第四章

动物外科实习要求

动物外科这一课程的目的是通过动物实验体验外科手术的基本概念,并初步熟悉外科手术的各项实际操作。通常采用家犬作为实验动物,在专设的实验室中进行一些模拟的人体手术。

第一节　实验室规则

动物手术实验室设有更衣室、洗手间、手术间、器械用品室等,基本上与临床医院的手术室设施相同。进入实验室进行实习,同样要遵守以下规则:

1. 进入实验室应首先更衣(包括戴口罩、帽子)。参加手术者,必须洗手消毒,穿戴手术衣和手套,并自觉遵循无菌原则。手术中受到沾染,必须及时重新消毒处理。

2. 经常保持室内清洁卫生,注意随时清除动物的排泄物。每次实习后应清理环境。

3. 保持室内安静,不可嬉笑喧闹。

4. 爱惜物品,正确使用各种手术器械、布巾等。每次实验前清点器械,实验后负责洗净归还。若有丢失或损坏,要追究责任。节省乙醇、纱布等易耗用品。

5. 爱护实验动物,不得戏弄实验动物。注意安全,避免被动物咬伤。

6. 每一手术组由主刀,第一、二助手,器械护士等手术人员和麻醉师,巡回护士等5~7人组成,各人员要求有明确分工,又要充分合作,密切配合,共同完成手术。

7. 每次实验前由主刀,麻醉师和第一助手完成动物的麻醉和皮肤准备(手术区去毛和清洁),术后由主刀和麻醉师将动物送回动物房,器械护士和第一助手(若有第二助手也参加)清洗器械,擦干后交回并清点。巡回护士负责手术台周围的清洁。

8. 手术中各人员的分工如下:

主刀:通常站在动物右侧主持手术,负责施行切开、分离解剖、止血、打结、缝合等。术后写手术记录交老师修改。

第一助手:站在主刀相对位置。手术开始前检查手术用器械,负责消毒手术野,铺无菌巾;术中协助主刀,为主刀提供操作便利的条件,如擦血、止血、打结、牵引与固定拉钩,以充分显露手术野等。

第二助手:一般站在主刀左侧,主要协助显露手术野,固定拉钩和剪线,清理手术野及其周围,需要时也可协助擦血。

器械护士:站在动物脚端右侧,主要负责术前清点、术中供应和术后核对器械和敷料(包括针线)并随时保持手术台整洁。

麻醉师:在动物头端,监控麻醉,使手术在无痛安静情况下进行,并监测动物的生命体征,计划术中补液。

巡回护士：在手术台以外负责术前器械、敷料清点登记，随时补充手术台上所需物品等辅助工作，和手术人员对外联系等有关事宜。

第二节   手术前实验犬的处理

在实施动物实验之前有以下各项工作需予完成。

一、接触实验犬

在即将进行动物手术实习之时，每一手术组将获得由动物饲养中心提供的实验用犬一条。在实验室技师的协助下，将犬从动物房带至实验室。狂躁不安的犬可用钢制夹钳（图 54）或专用套索（图 55）套住其颈。在强制制动情况下，用网罩套住其嘴（图 56）或用索带将其嘴捆住（图 57）。之后，可分别将其前、后肢捆绑。此时即可开始进行麻醉。

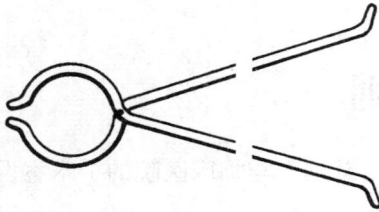

图 54   捕犬钳

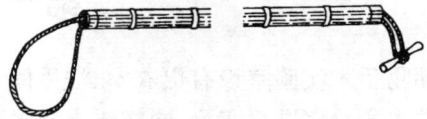

图 55   捕犬套杆

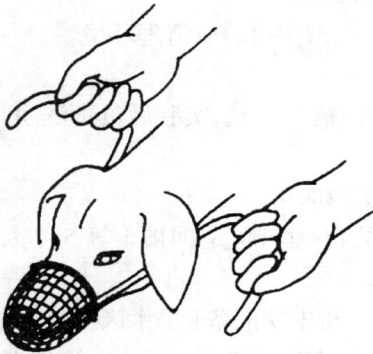

图 56   犬嘴用网罩套住

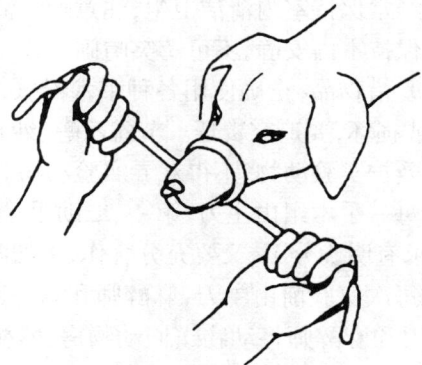

图 57   犬嘴用布带捆绑

二、麻醉

受约束的实验犬被带至实验室后，首先在磅秤上测其体重。如因其躁动而影响顺利测重，可人犬同测。读数减去人重后，即可获得犬的体重数。根据测得的体重，推算所需麻醉剂的用量，并通过适当途径给药。

犬的手术以采用全身麻醉为妥。本实验室通常用2.5%巴比妥钠进行腹腔内注射,静脉内注射或肌内注射。用药剂量为每公斤体重25~30mg。腹腔内注射此药后,麻醉作用将在10~15分钟内出现,并可持续3~4小时。另一选择是通过相同渠道给以2.5%硫喷妥钠,剂量为每公斤体重25mg。此药更多用于静脉注射。注射后麻醉作用可迅速出现,但一次剂量仅能维持麻醉作用45分钟左右。此药更多在采用巴比妥钠麻醉、手术未结束而麻醉作用已消失时作为追加麻醉之用。

采用经静脉麻醉剂注射时,通常可利用犬前肢前侧的头静脉(图58)或后肢小腿段外侧的隐静脉(图59)。注射时先注入药液的2/5~1/2,然后放慢速度缓缓注入。一旦出现麻醉迹象,即终止注射。

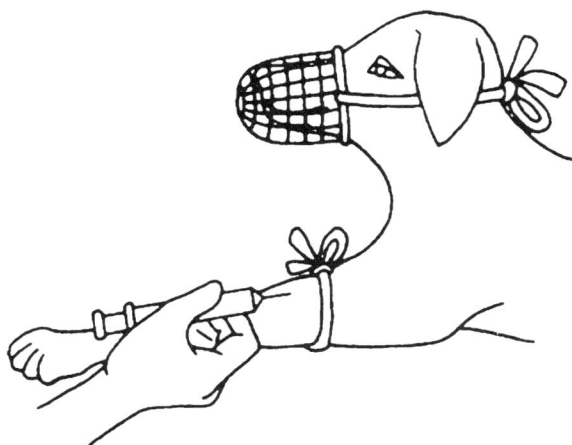

图 58　犬前肢头静脉穿刺

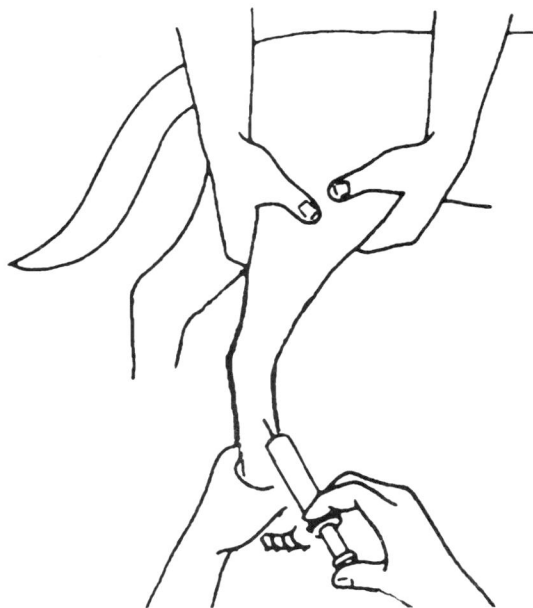

图 59　犬后肢隐静脉穿刺

麻醉后,置动物于手术台上,拉出其舌头,以维持其呼吸道畅通。此时,麻醉师即开始专注监视动物的生理状态。

如需追加麻醉药,可通过动物舌部静脉给予。

三、实验动物手术前备皮

实验动物皮肤长有密毛,术前应进行手术区去毛处理,去毛一般在麻醉后进行,方法有人工剃毛和脱毛剂脱毛两种。

（一）人工剃毛

本法虽然比较古老,如操作得当,效果仍佳。关键是要把毛剃净而又不损伤皮肤。动物麻醉后固定体位,充分显露手术区,先用剪刀将手术区毛剪短。剪毛应在动物身体自然状态下进行,切不可用手将毛提起,因为动物皮下组织疏松,提毛下剪易将皮肤同时剪破。毛剪短后,用肥皂水浸透剪毛处余毛,以左手将皮拉紧,右手持剃刀,顺毛的方向,尽量水平用力,按术野要求将毛剃光。

（二）脱毛剂除毛

优点是操作简单,除毛彻底;但药液有强烈臭味,如果操作不当还可引起皮肤损伤。

常用的脱毛剂有硫化钠、硫化钡、硫化砷等,其中硫化钠因水溶性好使用较多。临用前将硫化钠用50℃左右的热水配制成15%溶液;用钳夹纱布块蘸该溶液涂于手术区皮肤,使毛浸透1~2分钟后,可使毛呈黏糊状并与皮面脱离,用布将糊状物揩掉。最后用大量水冲洗皮肤并擦干。

除上述各项术前处理外,还有一些术后处理需予注意。在动物手术结束之时,应仔细缝合皮肤。手术后创口并不覆盖敷料,也不予包扎,因动物在麻醉作用消失而恢复意识后,将拒绝并抵制任何敷料的存在。手术后将动物送回动物房,并在术后头几天内尽量抽时间随访其术后恢复过程。认清施术的动物,便于以后继续用该动物进行手术实习。

（李 浩 孔令泉）

第五章

静脉切开术

一、适应证

1. 急需输液而静脉穿刺有困难者,如休克、严重脱水、大出血时静脉塌陷,穿刺不易成功。
2. 需要在较长时间内保证输液道高度通畅者,如进行大手术时。
3. 需要长时期反复或持续静脉内滴注者,如血液透析、静脉高营养滴注等。
4. 通过静脉进行某些诊治手段,如心导管检查,中心静脉压测定等。

二、静脉的选择

人体四肢浅表静脉均可用作静脉切开,最常用的是大隐静脉,因其解剖位置比较恒定。其他如头静脉、贵要静脉等均可切开。

静脉切开输液持续时间较长或输入高渗葡萄糖液等对静脉内膜有刺激的液体,都可能引起静脉炎,甚至静脉血栓形成,造成该段静脉闭塞。因此,静脉切开部位应优先选择在静脉的远心段,以便必要时还可利用其近心侧部分进行切开。

三、手术步骤(以大隐静脉切开为例)

1. 在小腿内踝前上方找到大隐静脉后,用碘酒及酒精消毒手术野皮肤,铺无菌巾。
2. 作一与大隐静脉平行或交叉、长约 1.5~2cm 之切口。
3. 切开皮肤后,用弯蚊式血管钳或小弯血管钳沿血管走行方向在皮下组织中边分离边寻找大隐静脉,找到后游离一段约 1.5cm(图 60)。
4. 用弯血管钳挑起已游离的静脉,在其深面引过中号丝线二段。用一段丝线结扎切口内已显露静脉之远端,结扎后暂不剪线以便作牵引之用。另一段丝线置于静脉之近端暂不结扎(图 61)。

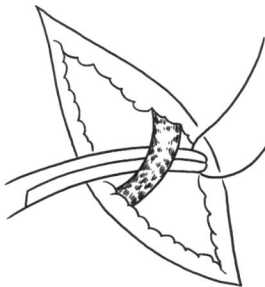

图 60　分离大隐静脉

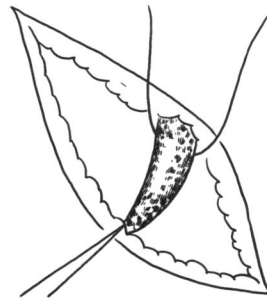

图 61　先结扎静脉远端

5. 牵引远端已结扎的丝线,用锐利的小尖剪剪开静脉壁的前半(或用针头横穿过静脉腔,切开静脉壁的前半,即针头浅表侧血管壁)。将塑料管口修剪成斜面,另一端连接于盛有生理盐水的注射器,排出空气后,管口斜面向下插入静脉切口。插入后见到管内有回血时,推注射器内液体,如无阻力,也无渗漏,表示塑料管已成功插入(图62,图63)。

6. 将近端未结扎之丝线围绕插有塑料管的静脉进行结扎(图64)。

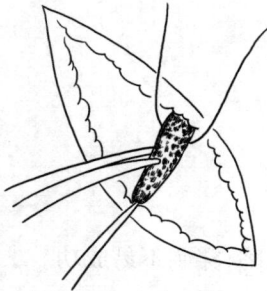

图 62　剪(切)开静脉壁　　　　图 63　向静脉内插入导管　　　　图 64　结扎静脉切开的
近端并缝合皮肤切口

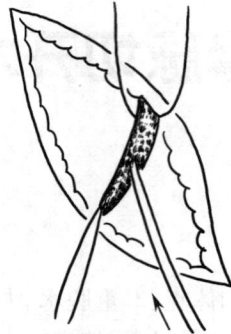

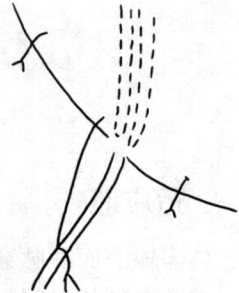

7. 取走注射器,将塑料管尾部连接在输液器之橡皮管上。注意这一操作中勿使空气进入输液管道。

8. 用三角针细线缝合皮肤数针。其中一针结扎后再绕塑料管结扎之,以免塑料管滑出。

9. 调整液体流速。

四、注意事项

(一)插管后如液体不流或流通不畅应考虑以下情况

1. 围绕塑料管的结扎过紧,压迫或闭塞了管腔。需剪去结扎线后再行结扎。

2. 塑料管插入静脉壁夹层。此时用注射器推注液体有阻力或渗漏,需重插。

3. 静脉受刺激而痉挛。局部热敷或输入 0.25% 普鲁卡因 1~2ml 可获得缓解并证明血管痉挛。

(二)输液时出现漏液,应考虑以下情况

1. 静脉近端结扎太松。需重新结扎。

2. 塑料管已刺破静脉。此时需在破口以上重作静脉切开。

五、术后处理

1. 塑料输液管可因患者躁动而脱出,术后应注意输液管的固定。

2. 输液结束时,剪断固定塑料管的缝线,拔除塑料管,压迫 1~2 分钟。

【实习】

使狗侧卧于手术台上,按以上方法及切开与缝合的原则在狗的下肢作静脉切开。狗的大隐静脉位于小腿外侧。

(黄伟光)

深静脉穿刺置管术

一、适应证

1. 外周静脉穿刺输液困难,需长期输液治疗。
2. 需行肠道外静脉营养者,高渗、高刺激性溶液(如脂肪乳,高渗葡萄糖、氨基酸、化疗药物)。
3. 抢救治疗,危重病人需快速扩容、血管活性药物及采血困难病人急症处理。
4. 中心静脉压(CVP)测定,一般选取颈内和锁骨下静脉,股静脉测不出数值。
5. 血液透析、血浆置换等。
6. 血管介入手术的操作通道。
7. 禁忌证 穿刺点近心端或远心端血栓形成,穿刺部位的感染等。

二、穿刺静脉的选择

1. 颈内静脉,优先选择右侧,因右侧颈内静脉走行较平直。
2. 锁骨下静脉,优先选择右侧,因左侧有胸导管。
3. 股静脉,优先选择右侧,因右侧股静脉走向较平直。

三、穿刺步骤(以人股静脉穿刺为例)

1. 了解、熟悉病人病情与病人或家属谈话,做好解释工作,争取病人的配合。必要的术前检查:如凝血功能、血小板计数等。
2. 会阴部备皮。
3. 准备器械等相关用品:中心静脉穿刺套装,消毒深静脉穿刺包,无菌手套、口罩、帽子、消毒液(络合碘或碘酊、乙醇)、2% 利多卡因、肝素钠生理盐水、注射器、肝素帽、缝针、无菌敷料。
4. 选择穿刺点,可在进行操作前标记(图 65)。
(1)体位:穿刺侧大腿外展、外旋 30°~45°。
(2)穿刺点:腹股沟韧带下方 2~3cm,腹股沟皱褶上方 1cm,股动脉内侧 0.5~1cm。
(3)穿刺针与皮肤夹角:30°~45°(图 66)。
(4)穿刺方向:针尖稍指向脐。
(5)深度:因病人的肥胖程度,差异较大。
5. 使用络合碘消毒 2 遍,或使用碘酒及乙醇进行术野消毒,铺无菌巾。
6. 局麻及定位 2% 利多卡因 2~5ml 进行局部浸润麻醉,麻醉及试穿过程:进针—回抽(无血)—注射麻药—进针—回抽,若回抽有暗红色血液提示进入静脉,可按此部位、方向、深度进行穿刺。

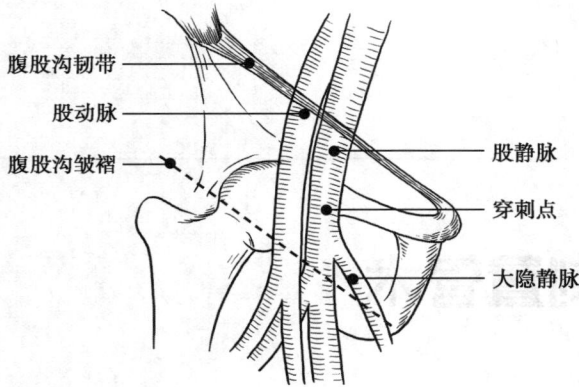

图 65 股静脉解剖示意图

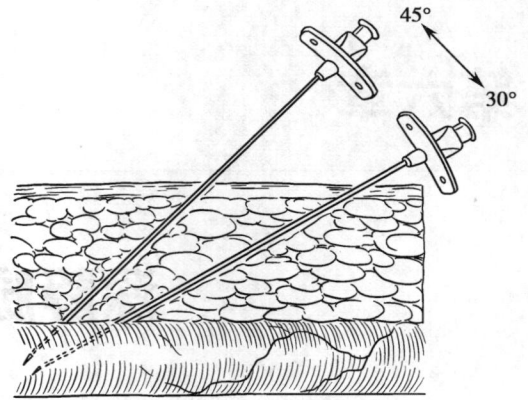

图 66 股静脉穿刺角度的选择

7. 穿刺 局部采用尖刀刺破皮肤,约 2mm 大小,按照原先确定的穿刺部位、角度、方向、深度进行穿刺,穿刺过程中保持负压,进入静脉后,可有突破感,回血通畅,呈暗红色。深静脉专用的穿刺针尾部有单向阀门,可进行测压,若为普通穿刺针,则去除注射器,若为喷射状鲜红色回血,则证明为穿刺动脉,若为滴出暗红色血液,则为静脉血。

8. 置管 沿穿刺针置入金属 J 形导丝,用力适当,无阻力,深浅合适,不能用力外拔。固定导丝,退出穿刺针,沿导丝置入静脉导管,在静脉导管进入皮肤前,确保导丝已从导管尾端穿出,捻转导管前进。若前进困难,可用皮肤扩张器扩张皮肤及穿刺隧道。股静脉导管置入深度可在 20cm 以上。

9. 退出导丝,注射器回抽血顺畅,确认导管位于静脉内。以肝素盐水封管。缝合固定导管,敷贴或无菌纱布包扎固定。

四、注意事项

1. 必须严格无菌操作,以防感染。
2. 如抽出鲜红色血液表示误入动脉,应立即拔出,压迫穿刺点至少 5 分钟以上。
3. 尽量避免反复穿刺,一般穿刺 3 次不成功应停止,可在超声引导下进行穿刺。
4. 术后可进行 X 线透视,确定导管位置。

(王学虎)

清 创 术

一、一般概念

外伤创口不可避免地要受到细菌污染,其程度因致伤条件和环境不同而异。清创术是对新鲜外伤创口进行清理、最大限度地减轻污染,使其接近无菌,从而预防创口感染的一种手术。为此,手术中要求尽量去除可能导致感染的污染组织、异物及挫伤严重或失活的组织。清理后的创口在一定条件下可予缝合,以争取一期愈合。已感染的创口不是施行清创术的对象。

二、清创术基本原则

1. 术前处理　全面仔细检查伤员,了解是否有其他需要优先处理的严重复合伤。
2. 积极防治休克、失血、脱水和其他并发症。
3. 争取时间,尽早清创　污染创口内细菌随时间的推移而迅速增加并不断侵入创口周围甚至远处组织。因此,愈早处理创口,效果愈好。超过一定时限,清创术不仅不能预防感染,反有引起扩散的可能。通常在伤后 6~8 小时以内的新鲜创口,经彻底清创缝合后,绝大多数不致于感染,可一期愈合。因为此时细菌增殖数不多,基本限于创面而未大量侵入周围组织。以后,感染的可能就愈来愈大,原则上不应进行清创术,除非是头、面部伤(血液循环良好)、刀刃切割伤(失活组织较少)、致伤环境较清洁而污染少、伤后即开始应用有效抗菌药物者。清创术原则上应在伤后 6~8 小时内施行,条件好者(上述头面部伤等情况)在伤后 8~12 小时内仍可进行。对于创口污染严重或估计入侵细菌毒力大者,伤后 4~6 小时即可能转为感染,通常只能作一般清洗,不宜按污染创口进行清创术。

清创后的创口缝合与否,应根据创口情况而定。对于受伤时间不长,污染程度不重、污染清除满意的创口,可在清创后予以缝合;对于受伤时间较长、污染较严重、清创不满意者,清创后不应予以缝合;对于处于二者之间者,可只缝深层组织后延期缝合皮肤和皮下组织或缝合后留置引流物。

战伤创口一般按感染创口处理,尤其是深在的创伤。因为战伤创口污染严重,易发生厌氧感染,组织损伤广泛而全身情况又多较差。

三、清创步骤

1. 术者戴手套,以无菌纱布覆盖伤口,剃去创口周围毛发。左手固定纱布,右手持无菌毛刷蘸肥皂水刷洗伤口周围皮肤,并以大量生理盐水冲洗。冲洗时避免冲洗液进入创口。如此刷、冲两遍。
2. 去除覆盖伤口的纱布,以生理盐水或 1:1000 新洁尔灭冲洗创口,清除异物。擦干伤口周边皮肤。此时如见创内有活动性出血,可用血管钳暂予钳夹。
3. 换手套,无菌纱布覆盖伤口。以碘酊、乙醇棉球消毒皮肤(注意:碘酊和乙醇勿接触创面)。在伤口周围铺手术巾。
4. 检查伤口,了解其范围及受损组织。进一步清除异物、血块或组织碎片。再以生理盐水冲洗创口。

5. 切去创口边缘约 0.2~0.5cm 宽及被压碎、挫伤的皮肤,切去污染、失活的皮下和深部组织。操作时宜始终以刀片的一侧面向污染的组织,另一侧面向健康组织。在处理深部创面时,可适当扩大创口,并切开深筋膜以加强显露。失活组织通常呈暗红色或灰白色,切割时不出血,失活肌肉在给予刺激时不收缩。如创口有深在的创道,应尽量切开,清除其中血块与坏死组织,勿使遗漏而成为感染的隐患。

6. 清创中对污染的肌腱和神经原则上不应予以切除,只能将其周围疏松膜样组织予以清除。如有断裂,原则上应予吻合,如污染严重或缺损过多,则不应勉强吻合,可用有色缝线带住断端便于以后二期缝合时作为寻找断端的引导。

非主要的小血管破裂,可予结扎;影响器官或肢体血运的血管损伤时,应予修补或吻合;需要血管移植时,必须是污染较轻而彻底清创者。

骨损伤时,完全游离的小骨片可去除,但取走后缺损较大难以填补的较大游离骨片及有软组织相连的骨片均应保留,以避免骨的延迟愈合、畸形愈合或不愈合。

关节囊破裂者,应去除血块、异物、修整囊壁组织,用大量生理盐水冲洗关节腔,然后用肠线予以缝合。关节内不置放引流物,可注入 20 万 ~40 万单位青霉素和 0.5~1g 链霉素以预防感染。如因缺损过大而无法缝合,可用附近筋膜或肌肉覆盖,不可使关节软骨外露,以免软骨坏死而致感染。

7. 经上述处理后认为清创已彻底时,用生理盐水再冲洗创口一次,对符合缝合条件的创口,可全层(创口浅者)或分层(创口深者)缝合。如清创不够彻底或止血不够满意,可留置橡皮引流条 24~48 小时。如创口不够缝合条件,可用凡士林纱布或干纱布松松填塞创腔,以利引流。

皮肤缺损较多,影响创口缝合时,可作松弛切口或进行植皮术(清创彻底者)以达一期愈合目的。

缝合中应注意肌肉和皮肤的张力不能太紧,否则可因血供受阻(尤其是肌肉血供)而导致危险的厌氧感染。

四、术后处理

1. 用夹板等固定肢体于功能位以避免或减少功能损害,将肢体远端略抬高以利静脉回流并减轻局部组织肿胀。

2. 严密观察,及时了解局部和全身的变化。伤情严重者,应加强全身治疗。

3. 积极防治感染。对破伤风及气性坏疽等严重并发症,必须提高警惕。术后常规肌注 TAT 1500 国际单位以预防破伤风。对污染严重的创口,全身应用抗生素。

总之,清创的目的在于减少创口感染的机会,争取创口一期愈合。因此清创必须彻底,但同时应尽量减少组织的破坏和功能的损害。

【实习】
狗侧卧于手术台,由教师在臀部或大腿部作一处人为创伤,按以上原则和方法进行清创术。

(曾晓华)

第八章

脓肿切开引流术

脓肿形成的原因很多,如感染等,是外科常见疾病之一。脓肿切开引流术是一项基本的外科手术操作技术。

一、适应证

1. 脓肿形成后,浅表脓肿触诊包块波动感明显,且经穿刺证实有脓液,深部脓肿需经穿刺或超声检查证实脓液存在。

2. 特殊部位脓肿需积极手术切开以便引流减压,如蜂窝组织炎、手部感染及其他特殊部位的脓肿,应在脓液尚未聚集成明显脓肿前施行切开引流手术,以减轻或降低感染扩大风险。

二、手术步骤

1. 消毒铺巾　消毒区域:脓肿及超过脓肿边缘 10~15cm 以上的周围区域皮肤。消毒顺序:脓肿未破裂者,由里向外同心圆式消毒;脓肿破裂者,应由外向里同心圆式消毒,最后消毒脓肿破溃处。用碘酊、乙醇常规消毒,铺无菌巾。

2. 麻醉选择　用 0.2%~0.5% 利多卡因或者普鲁卡因,沿切口做局部浸润麻醉(图 67)。

3. 脓肿穿刺　脓肿局部穿刺抽得脓液后可留针,需明确感染性质的患者,常规将抽出的脓液送脓液培养和药敏试验。若为深部脓肿不易定位时,可将穿刺抽脓的空针留在原处,作为切开标志。

4. 切开引流　一般在波动感明显的部位进行切开。切口方向应平行于脓肿所在区域主要血管和神经的走向,尽量避开以免损伤。切开皮肤、皮下组织后,找到脓肿的部位,可将脓肿壁作一纵行小切口或用止血钳钝性分离脓壁进入脓腔排出脓液。再用示指伸入脓腔深部,分开腔内的纤维间隔,再扩大脓肿壁切口,使引流通畅(图 68~ 图 71)。

图 67　局部麻醉

图 68　切开皮肤

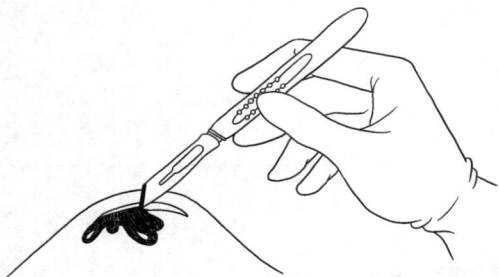

图 69 挑开脓肿切口

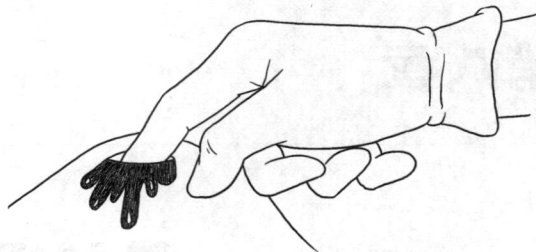

图 70 手指探查脓肿并分开间隔

5. 置引流条(油纱) 按脓肿大小与深度放置凡士林纱布条(油纱)引流或烟卷引流(图 72)。若脓腔较大,预计引流可能不畅者,也可在脓腔两侧处切开做对口引流。若有活动性出血可用止血钳钳夹后结扎,一般渗血用凡士林纱条按一定顺序紧紧地填塞整个脓腔以便压迫止血并稍微加压包扎预防出血。术后 2 天轻柔取出全部填塞敷料后,改换抗菌纱布,以后每次换药时,根据脓液减少和脓腔缩小情况逐步向外拔出引流条,并剪掉引流条的拔出部位,直至脓腔完全愈合。

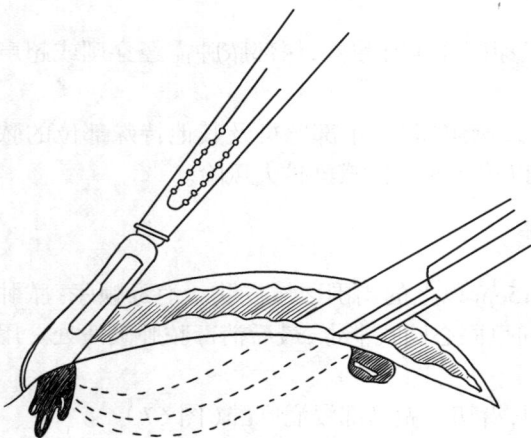

图 71 脓肿全长挑开

图 72 脓腔充填油纱

三、注意事项

1. 脓肿在波动感最明显处切开,手术刀切入脓腔的时候一定不要向下用力过猛,以免切穿脓腔后壁伤及脓腔周围正常血管神经等组织。

2. 深部脓肿切开前,需先穿刺抽出脓液,并确定部位和深度。

3. 脓肿切口应选在较低部位并有足够长度,满足低位引流畅通。

【实习】

实验兔俯卧固定于操作台,老师首先在实验兔子背部皮下注入 30% 脂肪乳 20~30ml 以作为实验的脓液。然后学生按照上述手术步骤进行操作。

(冉 亮)

第九章

拔 甲 术

一、适应证

1. 甲下积脓、嵌甲伴甲下感染、外伤致甲下积血或指（趾）甲与甲床分离者、顽固性甲癣。

2. 甲下血管瘤、甲周疣、甲下外生骨疣的辅助治疗。

二、禁忌证

1. 有出血倾向者。

2. 伴严重内脏疾患。

3. 瘢痕体质。

4. 精神障碍。

5. 炎症性皮肤病,如慢性放射性皮炎、化脓性皮肤病、复发性单纯疱疹、炎症明显的痤疮、着色性干皮病等。

6. 白癜风活动期。

三、麻醉

指根神经阻滞麻醉。在指根背侧作皮丘,垂直进针至指骨,注入 2% 利多卡因 0.5ml,然后向指骨内外侧各注入 2% 利多卡因 0.5~1ml,至局部软组织肿胀（图 73）。

四、手术步骤

1. 常规碘酒、酒精消毒患手 / 足至腕 / 踝关节以上,铺巾,按如上方法进行指 / 趾根神经麻醉。

2. 用橡皮条拉紧扎缚于指（趾）根部,以血管钳钳夹固定,防止出血过多,并能维持麻醉效果（图 74）。

伸肌腱　　　背侧神经
掌侧神经　　屈肌腱

（1）　　　　　　（2）

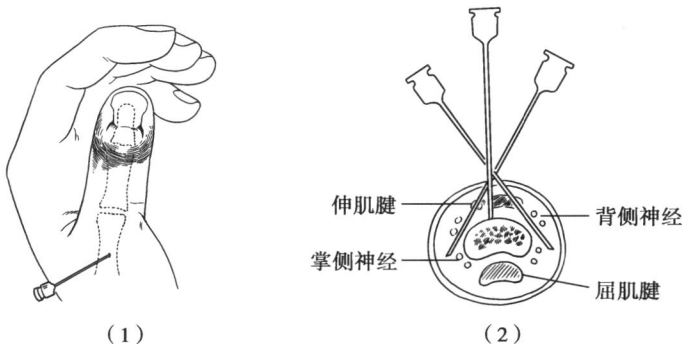

图 73　指 / 趾根神经阻滞麻醉
（1）进针部位;（2）进针方向

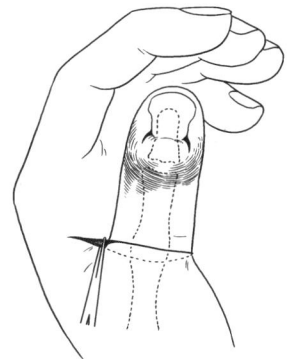

图 74　指根部橡皮条捆扎止血

3. 术者用左手拇指和示指捏紧病指末节两侧,固定患指/趾便于操作,同时可控制出血。在甲根以尖刀刺入甲与皮肤之间,顺甲根分离甲上皮肤,于两侧甲根处皮肤各作一纵行切口。

4. 再以尖刀自指甲尖端刺入甲下,顺甲床面将指甲与甲床分离。

5. 当指甲完全游离后,用止血钳夹持指甲的一侧向另一侧翻卷,使指甲脱离甲床。

6. 检查无甲角残留后,用凡士林纱布覆盖甲床,然后用消毒纱布包扎(图75)。

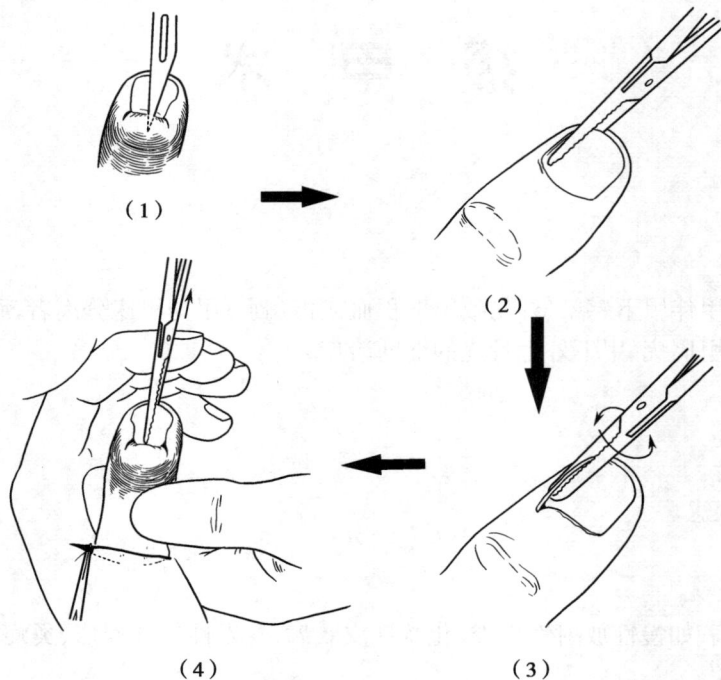

图 75　拔甲步骤
(1)固定手指,分离、切开甲根皮肤;(2)分离甲床;(3)翻卷拔甲;(4)拔出指甲,检查有无残留

五、术后处理

1. 换药　感染性创面每日换药直至创面愈合。无菌性创面5~7天更换敷料。

2. 可疑甲周细菌感染就医者术后使用抗生素5~7天。

六、注意事项

1. 指(趾)根麻醉时,麻醉药中不可加入肾上腺素,否则可能引起指动脉痉挛,导致手指/足趾坏死。

2. 指(趾)根部捆扎止血时,切勿将橡皮筋闭环套于指(趾)根部,以免术后因未及时取下而发生手指/足趾坏死。

3. 用尖刃刀分离甲上皮时,应注意不要使其损伤,以免日后从甲上皮生出的指甲畸形。分离甲床面时,应紧贴指甲,刀刃指向指甲背面,注意不要损坏甲床组织。拔除指甲后,如甲床不平整,宜用刀刃将其轻轻刮平,以免日后新生的指甲高低不平。

4. 为防止损伤甲床,也可在用尖刀分开指甲尖端的甲床后,用蚊式止血钳插入间隙,在分开止血钳时即可使指甲脱离甲床。

5. 甲癣拔甲时,因指甲较脆,难以翻转拔甲,可在甲下分离后直接拔出。

（王忠良）

第十章

诊断性腹腔穿刺术

诊断性腹腔穿刺是一项重要辅助诊断措施,某些腹部情况在诊断和治疗决策上有困难时,通过观察经套针从腹腔内吸出液体的性质(清亮的或浑浊的,漏出性的或渗出性的,血性的或化脓性的等)可帮助诊断,吸出的液体还可行实验室检验,如查胰腺炎的淀粉酶、微生物培养等。诊断性腹腔穿刺是安全、容易的操作,它的确诊率可达 90% 或更高。

一、适应证

1. 为确定病变性质或部位不明急腹症的诊断,尤其是有休克征象、腹膜刺激征和短时间内红细胞计数迅速下降者。

2. 为明确肠梗阻时肠管有无坏死。

3. 为确定病理性或外伤性空腔脏器穿孔所致化脓性腹膜炎是否存在。

4. 为确定腹部闭合性损伤时腹内有无脏器损伤,是实质性还是空腔脏器的损伤。

二、禁忌证

有某种腹内肿瘤(尤其是腹主动脉瘤),显著腹胀,弥漫性腹腔粘连存在时应禁止作腹腔穿刺。另外,不要对易激动的、不安静的或不合作的病人进行腹腔穿刺。

三、操作步骤

1. 准备无菌腹腔穿刺包。

2. 让病人处于仰卧位　消毒,铺巾,穿刺点通常选在右侧麦氏点或其左侧对称点,有时也可选在脐水平线与腋前线相交处(图 76)。

3. 麻醉　局部麻醉。

4. 切口　在穿刺点作一长约 1cm 的切口,将穿刺套针经过皮下组织、肌肉及腹膜缓缓刺向腹腔。在针尖刺穿腹膜时,推送针头的手可有落空感。

5. 引流管的置入　拔出锐利的针芯,把细塑料管经套针的外管送入腹腔抽吸腹腔液。如抽不到液体可变换针头方向、塑料管深度或改变体位再抽吸。结束后,将穿刺套针和塑料管拔出。

6. 缝合切口　通常只需缝合 1 针以关闭皮肤切口。

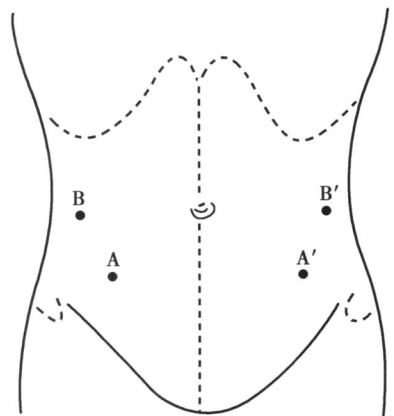

图 76　腹腔穿刺术的进针点

四、注意事项

1. 在穿刺时,病人应保持安静,不要移动身体,不要咳嗽,否则穿刺针可能损伤腹内脏器。
2. 为避免损伤,穿刺要轻柔缓慢,不可使用暴力。

【实习】

行腹腔内麻醉后,将狗固定于仰卧位。老师首先向腹内注入适量的亚甲蓝钠,然后按上述步骤作诊断性腹腔穿刺术。

（魏余贤）

剖 腹 术

一、常用腹部切口

（一）腹直肌切口

是最为常用的通过腹直肌的纵行切口［图 77（1）］。在腹直肌前鞘被切开后，沿肌纤维方向将腹直肌纤维向两侧分开，其间血管、神经则需切断、结扎。然后，同时切开腹直肌后鞘及腹膜进入腹腔。这种切口操作简便、迅速，便于向上向下延长，必要时可加横切口（"⊢"形）以扩大术野，或向上延长至胸部（胸腹联合切口）。其缺点是纵行切口对腹腔内压力的承受能力较差；切口过长时，切断神经较多，而易引起切口内侧腹壁的松弛。

（二）旁正中切口

也是一种纵行切口，皮肤切口位于正中线旁 1.5~2cm［图 77（2）］。手术方法大致与腹直肌切口相同，只是在切开腹直肌前鞘后并不分开腹直肌纤维，而是游离腹直肌的内侧部分，把它向外侧牵开，然后切开后鞘等组织。这种切口除有与腹直肌切口相似的优点外，最重要的优点是不引起神经损伤，但操作比腹直肌切口略为复杂。

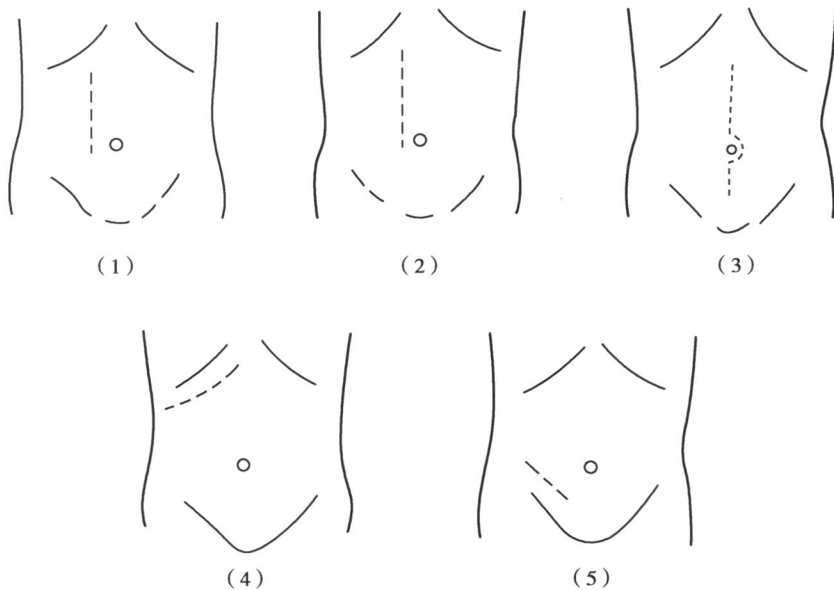

（1）   （2）   （3）

（4）   （5）

图 77　常用腹部切口

（1）右经腹直肌切口；（2）左旁正中切口；（3）正中切口；

（4）右肋缘下切口；（5）右髂窝斜（麦氏）切口

（三）正中切口

在正中线将前腹壁切开，也就是经过白线的切口［图 77（3）］。它的最大优点是简捷、省时，损伤和出血少。缺点方面除了具有一般纵行切口的缺点外，最主要的是白线血供少，缺乏肌肉保护，故愈合比其他腹部切口差，切口疝的机会比较多。

（四）肋缘下切口

是起于剑突下 2cm，与肋缘平行、向左或向右斜行切开达腋前线的斜行切口［图 77（4）］。腹壁各层肌肉和腹膜均按此方向分开或切开。由于切口方向与腹壁张力线大致平行，故缝合时张力较小而愈合牢固。此切口在右侧多用于胆道手术，左侧多用于脾脏手术，它显露手术野较佳，但因伸延困难而偏局限，且切开缝合所费时间较长。

（五）髂窝斜切口

在髂前上棘与脐连线的中 1/3 与外 1/3 交界处（右侧即 McBurney 点）作一与该线垂直的切口，长 6~8cm［图 77（5）］（右侧者也称 McBurney 切口）。在同一方向（即沿腹外斜肌纤维方向）切开腹外斜肌腱膜，然后顺腹内斜肌及腹横肌纤维方向将此二肌劈开，最后沿皮肤切口方向切开腹膜。此切口在右侧因便于显露盲肠与阑尾而常用于阑尾切除术，左侧者常用于乙状结肠造口术。此切口方向与皮肤张力线相符，分开的肌肉纤维方向又交错排列，故伤口愈合较好，很少发生伤口裂开或切口疝。它因切口小而局限于髂窝区，故对腹腔其余部分骚扰很少。但显露范围局限，切口伸延又有一定困难是它的缺点。

二、剖腹手术操作（以脾切除术为例）

脾切除术适用于很多脾脏病理情况，其主要适应证有腹部损伤引起的脾破裂，晚期血吸虫病、黑热病、疟疾引起的巨脾症（多伴有脾功能亢进），多种原发性脾功能亢进症及特发性血小板减少性紫癜和家族性溶血性贫血等血液病。

近年发现脾切除后，可因免疫缺陷而导致有致死可能的暴发性感染，特别容易发生于儿童；因此，当前对脾破裂，很多人主张避免脾切除而予以修补、部分切除、脾动脉结扎或切除后行碎脾移植。

人的脾切除术操作较复杂，其方法不属本课程范围。狗脾与人脾解剖不同，它有较长的系膜，且十分游离，脾切除术的操作远较人的脾脏切除容易。本实习在狗身上行脾切除术，主要目的在于锻炼基本操作，包括剖腹切口、大血管的切断结扎等。

（一）作左侧腹直肌切口

1. 自肋缘下 2cm 处在腹部正中线左侧 1.5cm 作一长 8~10cm 之纵切口。

2. 切开皮肤、皮下组织，用直血管钳钳夹止血和细丝线结扎后，以皮肤巾覆盖切口边缘以外皮肤以减少手术野污染机会。

3. 切开腹直肌前鞘，然后将腹直肌沿其纤维方向钝性分开，注意止血，腱划处必有血管经过，可先置两把弯血管钳，然后在两钳之间切开，中号或细丝线结扎之。

4. 手术者用镊，第一助手用弯血管钳同时提起切口中部之后鞘与腹膜（二者实际上紧密粘连在一起）予以切开。切开前必须肯定未夹住腹内组织。切开处两侧边缘分别用钳夹住，便于下一步操作。

5. 用剪刀或刀子将后鞘与腹膜之切开处向上下延长。切开的长度应与皮肤切口保持一致，特别要注意不能过分向上端延长，否则有切开胸腔导致动物死亡的可能。延长切开时须将腹膜提起，或手术者和第一助手用手指插入腹膜之开口处下面，进行保护和引导，在两手指浅面切（或剪）开腹膜，注意避免误切大网膜或其他内脏。

6. 进入腹腔后手术中所用纱布均须经盐水浸湿以减少对腹膜和内脏的刺激。

（二）切除脾脏

1. 首先找到胃，尽量将其牵向手术野之右侧，当可相继见到胃脾韧带和脾脏之一部分。用手指衬盐水纱布抓住已显露于手术野的部分脾脏,然后放下胃而将脾全部提至手术野中。送回被挤出切口外之其他器官或组织,用盐水纱布覆盖填塞于脾脏周围,仅使脾脏显露于手术野。

2. 分离并切断胃脾韧带,每次都同时切断其中的一支胃短血管。切断前先上三把血管钳,在血管的胃侧两把与脾侧一把之间切断。胃侧端用中号丝线分两次结扎,以免术后胃扩张(术后胃肠道麻痹)导致线结滑脱出血。

3. 手术至此,已进入小网膜囊而清楚显露脾系膜(人脾通常无系膜)在其中段找到脾动脉与脾静脉。首先游离处理脾动脉。同样用三把血管钳钳夹,在血管近心侧二把钳与远心侧一把钳之间切断之。近心侧断端予以两次结扎。先围绕最近端的一把血管钳用中号丝线三重结扎,然后围绕另一把血管钳用圆针中号丝线行"8"字缝扎。行"8"字缝扎时两次进针点力求在同一部位以免漏扎血管。此后再三重结扎远心侧脾动脉断端。注意脾动脉结扎后,可见脾脏体积缩小,包膜皱缩,这是因为脾血有出无进所致。随后同法处理脾静脉。

4. 自脾下极起分次切断脾系膜,每一切断先上血管钳两把,然后在钳之间切断,以免失血。系膜全部切断后,脾脏即被切下。系膜侧钳夹点用中线一一结扎。腹腔内的止血均宜采用三重结。

（三）缝合切口

1. 检查止血是否彻底并进行必要的止血,同时检查有无纱布或其他异物遗漏腹内,最后清除腹内残留血液,再次观察有无遗漏的出血点。肯定腹内止血,无异物残留、无积液后,即开始缝合切口。

2. 先用数把血管钳夹住腹直肌后鞘及腹膜层切开之边缘及上下角。置盐水纱布一块于腹膜与内脏之间以保护后者,并避免缝合时内脏向切口外鼓出。

3. 提起上角部血管钳,自上角开始用圆针中线作连续缝合以免内脏经间断缝合线之间的空隙突出。第一针在血管钳上方打结(结扎第一单结后,才放去血管钳,完成第二单结后剪去线尾),缝线之带针段在靠近结扎处由第二助手拉紧。

4. 逐针作连续缝合,针距约 0.5cm。缝合时注意使缝线保持拉紧以免缝合之切口松开。作最后几针时取出腹腔内纱布。

5. 最后一针在后鞘腹膜层切口下角血管钳之下方进针,缝前拉长线之重叠段使成双线,引出缝针后,一手提住双线之尾端,一手拉紧缝针将线抽紧,先是打一单结,绕至血管钳之上方,再打一方结以完成结扎。距该结 1~2mm 处,剪断多余之缝线,以免松开。

6. 腹膜缝合后应以洁净之消毒盐水冲洗伤口。

7. 吸干冲洗液,用圆针中线间断缝合腹直肌前鞘。针距仍保持 0.5cm 左右。

8. 取出覆盖皮肤之皮肤巾,相继用盐水和乙醇纱布擦拭切口周围皮肤。

9. 用圆针细线间断缝合皮下组织。针距 1~1.5cm。

10. 用三棱皮肤针细线间断缝合皮肤。针距约 1cm。

（曾晓华）

第十二章

胃肠道手术基本原则

1. 胃肠道内容物含细菌多,尤其是下消化道(如结肠)更多。故在进行胃肠道手术时,应特别注意无菌操作技术。例如:在准备切开其腔道至完全缝合时,应使用盐水纱布垫覆盖切开边缘以外所有的手术野,各手术者之手尽量不接触胃肠道黏膜面;接触过黏膜面的各种器材均已污染,应集中于一个盛器,勿随意乱放;胃肠道切开处缝合后,施术者须用盐水冲洗或另换无菌手套,已污染器材也不再使用。以上措施目的在于尽量减少手术野污染机会。

此外,对于结、直肠手术病人,因结、直肠内含细菌特别多,应在手术前进行必要的肠道准备,包括无渣饮食、清洁灌肠和口服抗菌药物。

2. 胃肠道创面的愈合有赖于其浆膜渗出的纤维蛋白。因此,胃肠道的缝合通常采用内翻式,以期浆膜面能平整对合而有利于愈合。如内翻不善(主要是缝合处黏膜外翻)势将引起胃肠缝合处或吻合口漏。这是一种极为严重的手术并发症。为了保证内翻妥善,胃肠道的缝合习惯上分内外两层进行。近年有主张只缝一层者,尤应注意操作,勿使黏膜外翻。

3. 胃肠道内翻缝合时,要注意内翻不可过多,否则有导致梗阻之可能。

4. 胃肠道所用缝合方法有全层缝合和浆肌层缝合两大类。前者缝针穿过胃肠壁全层,通常用于内层缝合;后者缝针只穿过浆肌层或黏膜下层,不进入黏膜面,通常用于外层缝合。这两类缝合法又各有连续和间断之分。连续缝法更多用于内层缝法,因它兼有对胃肠壁切口边缘的止血作用,常用的缝合法有连续扣锁缝法(图78)和连续水平褥式(Connell)缝法(图79)。间断缝法既用于内层也用于外层缝合。常用的外层间断缝法有单针浆肌层(Lembert)缝合(图80)、间断水平褥式(Cushing)缝法(图81)和间断垂直褥式(Halsted)缝法(图82)。此外胃肠壁的小破口,通常可用荷包口缝法(图83)将其内翻。

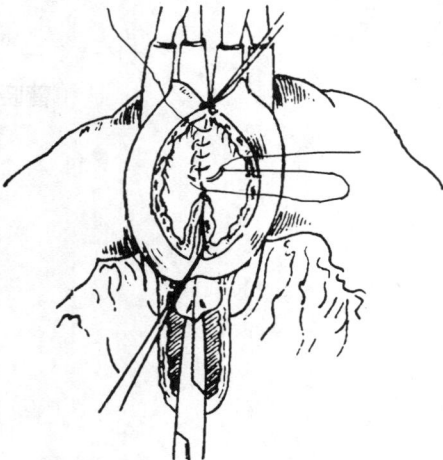

图78　全层扣锁缝合

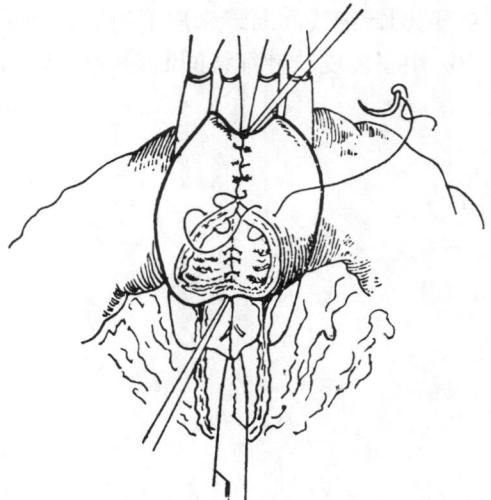

图79　连续褥式缝合(Connell缝法)

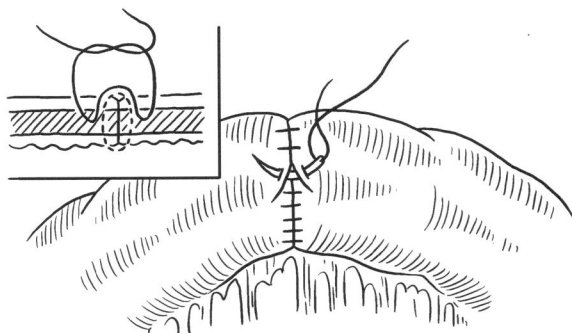

图 80　间断浆肌层缝合（Lembert 缝法）

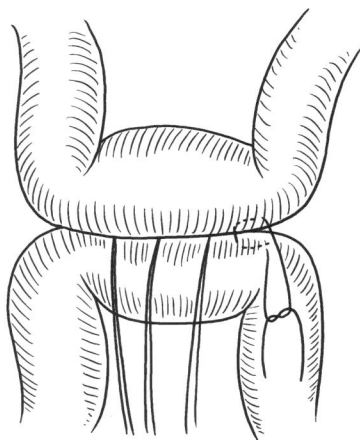

图 81　间断褥式缝合（Cushing 缝法）

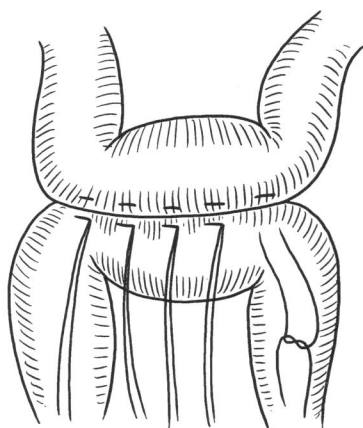

图 82　间断垂直褥式缝合（Halsted 缝法）

图 83　荷包缝合

胃肠道缝合所用缝线，在国内一般全部采用丝线，但内层缝合也有采用铬制肠线者。

5. 胃肠道各段血供情况不尽一致。胃的供血血管多，侧支丰富。小肠除十二指肠和首段空肠略差外，一般尚佳，结、直肠的供血血管较少，且侧支也不多。此外，肠道的血管均来自系膜，故多自系膜侧进入肠壁，末梢在对系膜侧。鉴于以上血供特点，在肠切除切断肠管时，断面应略为偏斜，使对系膜缘比系膜缘多切一些。这样不仅保证了对系膜侧肠壁的血供，还可减少吻合口狭窄的可能。此外，行肠侧面吻合时，宜将肠壁切口作在对系膜缘，以保证切开处两侧边缘的血供。这些手术原则在结肠手术时尤为重要。

6. 胃肠道吻合手术中应避免吻合口张力过大，以免影响血供导致愈合不良而发生吻合口漏。张力过大常来自于腔内积气、吻合口受牵拉等情况。

7. 胃肠道缝合处或吻合口附近，不应留置引流物，否则不利于愈合。需要引流者，引流物不应紧靠缝合处或吻合口。

8. 胃肠道手术时，操作应特别轻巧，胃肠不宜过分暴露，不需要显露的组织均应以盐水纱布覆盖。这些都是为了减少对胃肠道的刺激进而减少术后胀气和粘连形成。

9. 胃肠道吻合的方式通常有开放式与闭合式两种。开放式吻合时胃肠腔完全敞开，逐针缝合。故污染机会多，但操作方便，技术性并发症少。闭合式则在胃肠腔不敞开的情况下进行吻合。这种吻合操作较复杂而技术性并发症多。但最大的优点是大大减少了手术野污染的机会。当前因术前准备的进步和预防性抗菌药物的广泛应用，开放式吻合法已被普遍采用，但操作中仍必须注意前述预防和减少污染的措施。

（黄伟光）

胃穿孔修补术

胃穿孔是一种外科常见病。常系急性消化性胃溃疡的并发症或由胃的外伤引起。胃癌有时也可有此并发症。穿孔的胃有多种处理方法,穿孔修补术是最为简单易行的一种手术治疗方法。

【实习】

用狗模拟人的胃穿孔进行修补。手术步骤如下:

1. 作右侧腹直肌切口(切口步骤参考脾切除术)。

2. 找到胃,使其显露于手术野,由教师在适当部位作一戳孔。

3. 充分显露穿孔部位,周围用盐水纱布妥为保护,防止胃内容物流向腹腔扩散污染。

4. 先在穿孔处作与胃主轴方向垂直的胃壁全层缝合封闭破口(图84),再用浆肌层内翻缝合法加固一层(图85)。穿孔小者可根据具体情况直接用浆肌层内翻法修补。

5. 修补不满意时,还可将一片大网膜缝在修补处,使大网膜覆盖其上以防缝合口溢漏。

6. 修补破口后,术者用干净盐水冲洗手套。

7. 清理手术野,确定无出血,无异物,更应注意清除可能流向腹腔的胃内容物。

8. 缝合腹部切口,步骤同脾切除术。

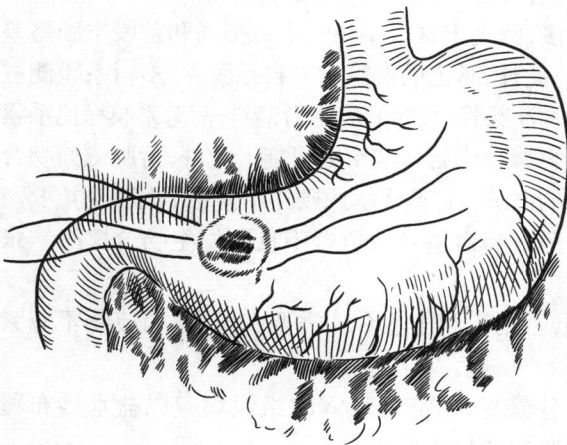

图84　全层缝法闭合穿孔

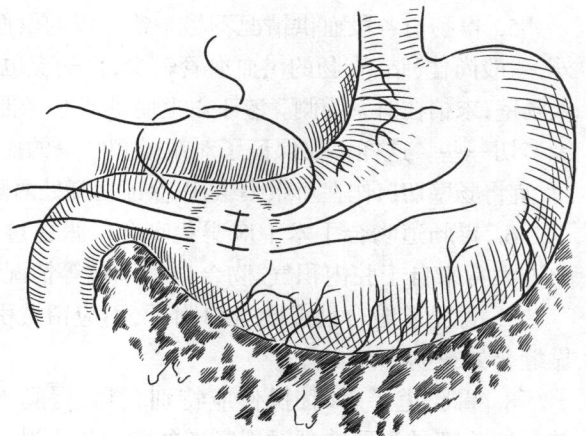

图85　浆肌层内翻缝法加固修补处

(魏余贤)

胃 造 瘘 术

胃造瘘分为临时性和永久性两种,主要适用于以下两种情况:

1. 各种原因引起的进食困难,如食管良性狭窄、食管肿瘤所致梗阻、颌面部严重外伤等。

2. 某些腹部大手术后,如需要长期放置胃肠减压,为避免需鼻胃管吸引所致不适,在某些腹部手术后作为胃肠减压之用;小儿经鼻腔插管不合作或因胃管太细达不到减压目的;肺功能障碍倾向的高龄或高危患者;门静脉高压患者,为避免经鼻腔插管引起大出血风险等。

【实习】

用狗模拟人行临时性胃造瘘术,采用荷包缝合法(Stamm 法)。手术步骤如下:

1. 常规消毒铺巾,作左侧腹直肌切口进入腹腔,用爪形肠钳(Babcock's clamp)钳夹胃前壁中部,测试胃壁是否容易与腹膜靠近(图 86)。

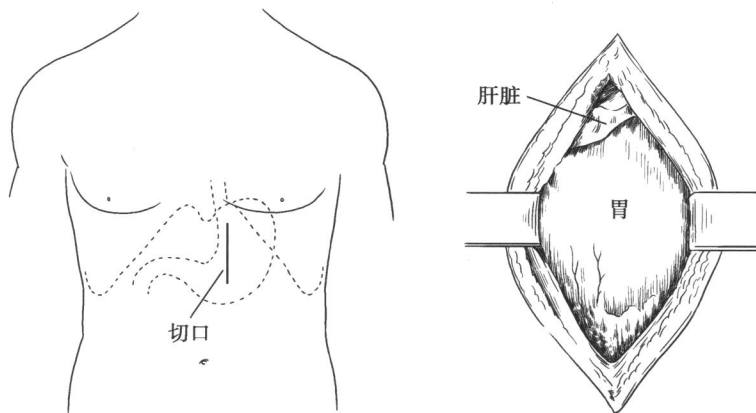

图86　左侧腹直肌切口进入腹腔

2. 在钳夹组织周围作一浆肌层荷包缝合,暂不结扎,并在周围垫好纱垫以免污染(图 87)。

3. 在荷包缝合中央垂直胃长轴方向切开胃壁,吸尽胃内容物,充分止血后将蕈形导管(或带侧孔的橡胶管或 Foley 导管)置入胃内 10~15cm,然后收紧、结扎荷包缝合线(图 88,图 89)。

4. 在距原荷包缝合线 1cm 处做第二层荷包缝合结扎,必要时可做第三层,同样相距 1cm(图 88,图 89)。

5. 将导管穿过大网膜,使大网膜覆盖于造瘘口处,从侧腹壁戳口将导管引出体外,检查充分引流后,将造瘘口附近的胃壁与腹膜以丝线缝合固定,并将引流管固定在皮肤上(图 88,图 89)。

6. 清理手术野,确定无出血、异物后,逐层关腹。

图 87 浆肌层荷包缝合

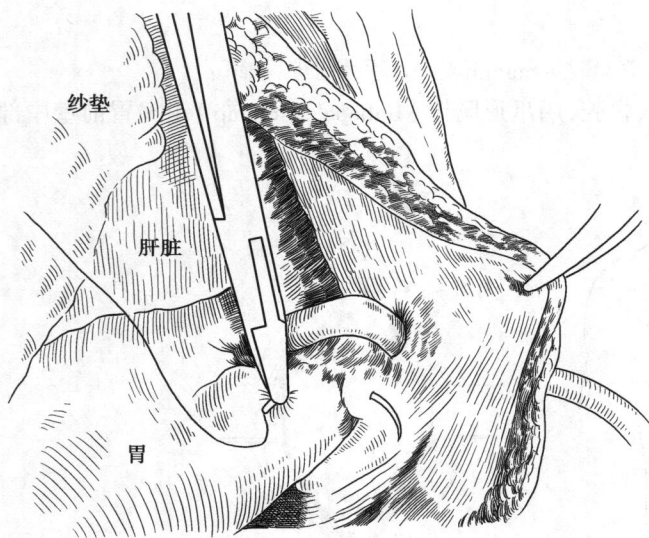

图 88 置管及固定

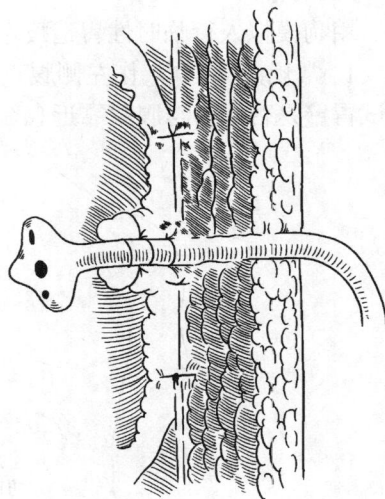

图 89 关腹

（王瑞珏 厉红元）

第十五章

阑尾切除术

急性阑尾炎是最常见的外科急腹症之一,最常采用的治疗方法是阑尾切除术。

【实习】

狗无阑尾,但其盲肠较长,很像人的阑尾而略粗大。故可用切除阑尾之方法切除狗的盲肠,以体会阑尾切除术之操作过程。

一、作麦氏(McBurney)切口

1. 在脐与髂前上棘连线中 1/3 和外 1/3 交界处作一长约 5cm 的斜切口,与连线大致垂直。切口 1/3 在连线上方,2/3 在连线下方。

2. 切开皮肤、皮下;顺切口方向切开腹外斜肌腱膜。

3. 显露腹内斜肌后,主刀与第一助手交替用血管钳插入肌纤维中分离肌纤维直至见到腹膜。然后将两把拉钩放入肌肉裂口内,顺切口方向反向牵拉,扩大肌肉裂口。至此,腹膜即可充分显露。

4. 提起腹膜,确认未夹住深部组织后,将其切开。用血管钳将腹膜裂口固定于四周的治疗巾上,以防切断盲肠时污染切口。

二、寻找盲肠

在右腹找到升结肠(小肠较细,肠腔多塌陷呈扁条状,表面光滑,结肠较粗,管状,表面有纵行肌纹)。然后逆向追踪,当可找到回盲部和盲肠。狗的末段回肠对系膜缘有一起自回盲部沿肠长轴方向走行的长 4~6cm 的血管是其特有的解剖标记。见到此血管即可确认为末段回肠无疑,借此当可辨认盲肠所在。

三、切除盲肠

1. 拉出盲肠,用盐水纱布保护周围手术野。仔细分离其内侧系膜样组织,妥善结扎。至此盲肠即被游离。

2. 用中号丝线在距盲肠根部约 0.5cm 处作一经浆肌层荷包缝合。缝妥后暂不收紧结扎。

3. 用血管钳压距荷包缝合远端约 0.5cm 处盲肠壁,在压榨处用中线作一结扎。

4. 在结扎线远端约 0.3cm 处夹一直血管钳,然后在二者之间紧贴血管钳切断盲肠。注意勿使残端污染手术野。为此,在切断盲肠之前应在周围用盐水纱布予以保护。用石炭酸烧灼盲肠残端借以破坏黏膜组织,再用乙醇棉签去除残余石炭酸,最后用盐水擦净,取去周围之盐水纱布。用蚊式钳夹住结扎线结,将残端送入荷包缝线圈内,同时收紧荷包缝线并结扎之,即可内翻盲肠残端。

使用石炭酸烧灼盲肠黏膜的目的是破坏其分泌功能,防止盲肠残端作荷包缝合后形成黏液囊肿。

5. 如残端内翻不完善,可再作一荷包缝合或"8"字内翻缝合;也可加盖邻近的脂肪组织。

四、关腹

按腹壁原有的解剖层次,分层缝合腹膜(圆针、中线)、腹内斜肌肌膜(细线)、腹外斜肌腱膜(细线)、皮下组织(细线)和皮肤(三棱针、细线)。

(邹宝山 孔令泉)

第十六章

小肠部分切除吻合术

一、肠部分切除的适应证

1. 疝、肠扭转、肠粘连、肠系膜血管栓塞及其他引起肠坏死的病变。
2. 肠瘘、肠管较大损伤等估计修补成功可能性不大者。
3. 小肠局限性炎症、结核肉芽肿等引起肠道狭窄者。
4. 肠道肿瘤或有肿瘤倾向的病变。

二、小肠部分切除吻合的操作步骤

1. 切口　一般应在病变部位附近选取；手术若为探查性质，多采取右侧腹直肌切口。
2. 探查并决定切除范围　根据需要进行腹内脏器的探查以进一步明确诊断，尤其是外伤性病人，要注意多处损伤的可能。在此基础上确定肠管切除范围。
3. 显露拟切除的肠祥　把病损肠祥提出切口外。如为坏死肠管，动作要轻巧，以免拉破而严重污染腹腔。将其他正常的肠管纳入腹腔，覆盖好盐水纱布垫。一般在离病变的近、远两端各 3~5cm 处切断。如为恶性肿瘤，分别离肿瘤二端不少于 5cm，并应将区域淋巴结一并予以广泛切除。切断部位的肠管必须正常以保证愈合。
4. 处理肠系膜血管　在与拟切除肠段相应的肠系膜中找到主要供应血管，在其两侧系膜组织中分别作一戳孔。通过三把全齿弯血管钳夹住血管，然后在近侧两把与远侧一把之间剪断血管。用中号丝线分别妥善结扎。近心端双重结扎（结扎一次及 "8" 字贯穿缝扎各一次）。然后，以结扎点为尖端扇形切开肠系膜（图 90）。如因系膜中脂肪较厚而不能辨认血管，可在灯光下透照血管走向后钳夹、切断并结扎。

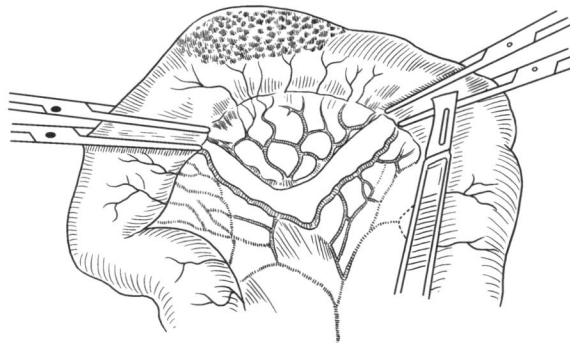

图 90　扇形切开系膜

5. 切除肠管   在肠管拟予切断处,分别将附于肠管的肠系膜各剥去 1cm(图 91)。确认拟保留肠管血运无碍后,各用直组织钳两把分别并列钳夹拟切除肠管的两端,钳的尖端在系膜侧,钳身略斜(偏斜角度不超过 30°),以切除较多对系膜侧肠壁面保证吻合口血运,并抵消吻合时内翻缝合可能引起的吻合口狭窄(图 92)。钳夹时应使剥去系膜的肠管留在健侧,以便于吻合时该处肠壁的内翻。钳夹后用手指从置钳处分别向上下端将肠内容物挤出,在离置钳处 5cm 处在上、下肠管上分别上一臂长而富有弹性的肠钳(或在该处用橡皮筋一条,穿过系膜围绕肠管)阻断粪流。最后用盐水纱布妥善保护手术野,在每一对直组织钳之间切断肠管,取去预定切除之病损肠袢。

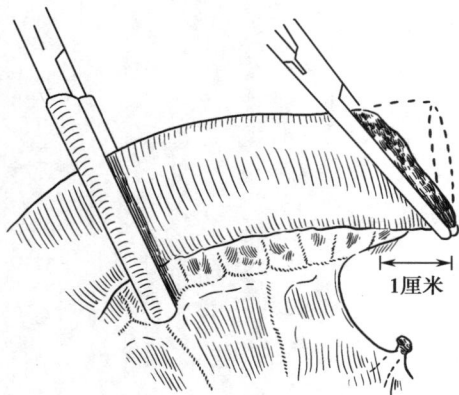

图 91   肠断端系膜侧的游离

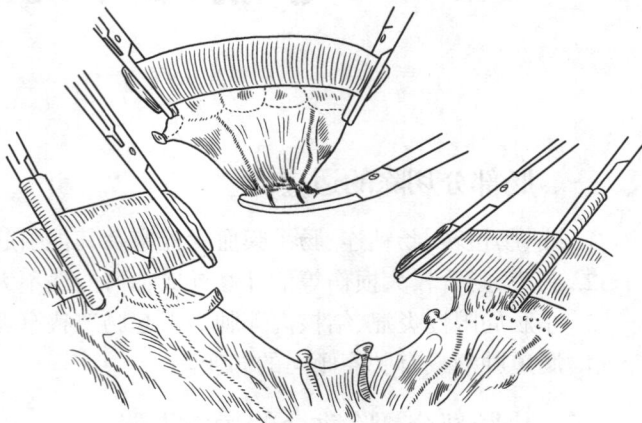

图 92   斜切肠管

6. 肠吻合(一般选用小圆针、细丝线)通常有闭合式或开放式两种操作方法。以端 – 端吻合为例,操作方法如下。

(1)闭合式吻合:健侧肠断端直组织钳不予开放。靠拢两端的组织钳,紧挨组织钳在肠断端间作间断浆肌层(Cushing 或 Halsted)缝合,但缝线暂不抽紧结扎。待整圈肠管全层缝妥后,才拉紧各线头,抽出钳子,分别结扎各缝线,对合两断端。最后绕吻合口再作一圈间断 Lembert 缝法。这种吻合方法最大限度地减少了肠内容污染腹腔的机会,因肠粘膜面未敞开于手术野。其缺点为肠切断面止血可能不完全;如缝针刺入一侧肠壁太深,可能穿到对侧肠壁,以致抽紧缝线后形成吻合口隔膜,把肠腔分为两个或更多小腔而引起梗阻。故进针时既不能太浅(要穿透浆肌层),又不能太深。为了避免吻合口被分隔引起梗阻,开始进行外层 Lembert 缝合时,应先用手指测试吻合口通畅度。如发现肠腔被分隔,应立即拆除有关缝线,重新缝合。

(2)开放式吻合:靠拢两组织钳,在两肠断面二端分别作一 Lembert 缝合作为牵引;同时,作一排 Lembert 缝合对合吻合口后壁(图 93)。取去直组织钳,敞开肠腔,吸去腔内残留内容物,并进行必要的止血。然后,在直视下进行间断全层缝合(图 94,图 95),再以 Lembert 缝合完成前壁外层缝合(图 96)。此法虽污染机会较多,但简便安全,在严格按胃肠道手术原则行事和预防性抗菌药物的辅助下,开放式吻合目前已成为肠吻合的主要方式。

7. 吻合完成后,检查吻合口内翻是否完善,特别注意其系膜侧,必要时可加强一、二针。

8. 检查吻合口大小及通畅度(图 97)。

9. 吻合后系膜扇形切开所形成的裂隙需用几针间断缝合予以消除,以防发生内疝(图 98)。

10. 清理手术野,确认无出血、无积液,亦无异物残留后分层缝合腹壁切口。

〔附〕肠切除后,在连接两断端再建它们之间的连续性方面,有对端(端 – 端)、侧 – 侧、端 – 侧(丁字形)等三种形式。本段所述吻合方法是对端吻合。其优点在于符合正常生理状态;缺点是有引起吻合口狭窄导致梗阻的可能,且在吻合直径不相称的两段肠道时有一些不便。侧 – 侧吻合要在切

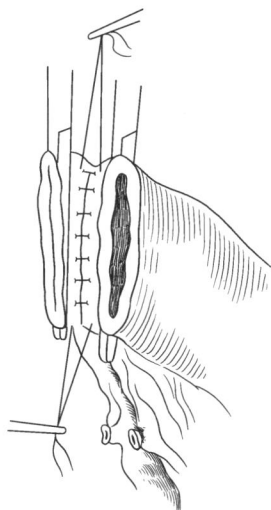

图 93　吻合口后壁外层间断浆肌层缝合

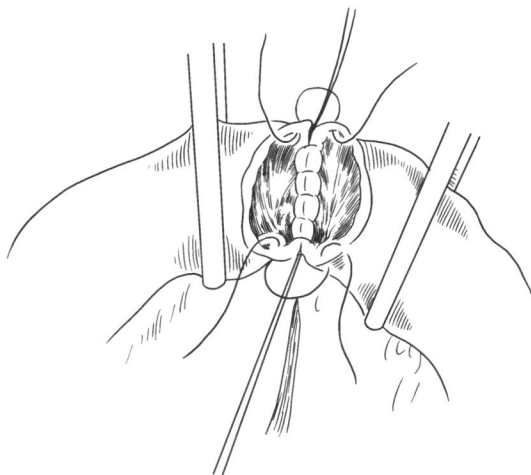

图 94　吻合口后壁内层间断全层内翻缝合

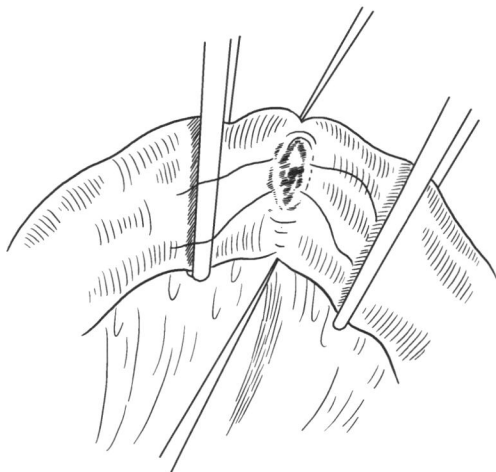

图 95　吻合口前壁内层间断全层内翻缝合

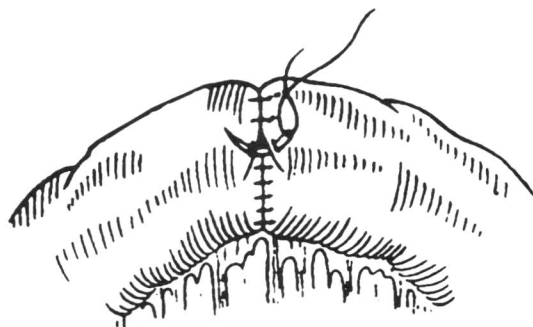

图 96　吻合口前壁外层间断浆肌层缝合

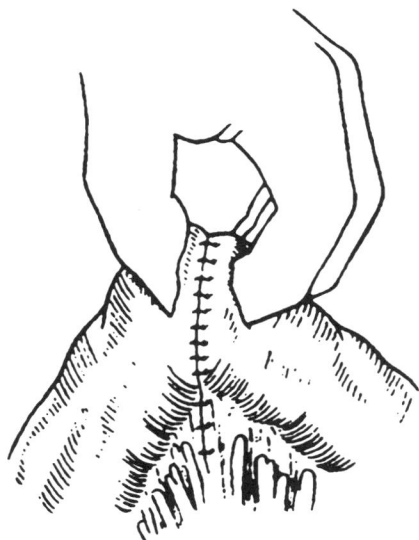

图 97　探明吻合口大小及通畅度

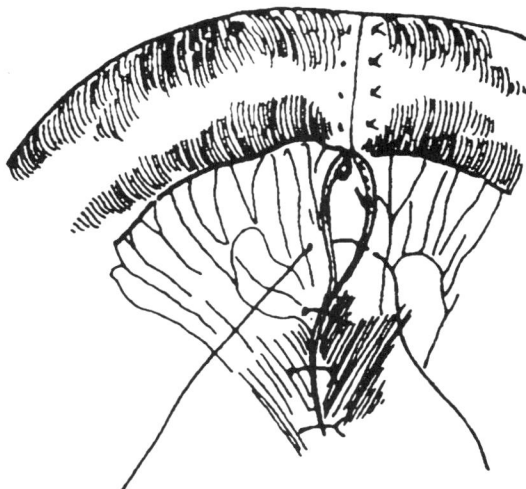

图 98　修复系膜裂口

除病损肠道后,先以内翻缝合法封闭断端,然后在其邻近肠壁对系膜各作一长短相应的切开,进行吻合。有时,病灶未能(如晚期肿瘤)或不需(如肠粘连)切除,可将病灶上下侧肠袢拉拢,分别纵行切开,进行吻合。此种吻合的口径不受吻合肠道直径不等的限制而便于吻合直径不相称的两肠袢,不致引起狭窄。但是,吻合口与封闭端之间往往有盲腔,可能造成某些不良后果。端 – 侧吻合是在切除病灶后闭合一个断端,在该段肠道的侧面作一切开,与未封闭的另一断端作吻合。这种吻合适用于回肠与结肠之间的吻合,因为它更接近回肠与盲肠之间的正常解剖情况。

【实习】

1. 全班分为若干小组,每组 2~3 人;分别用离体猪肠进行体外端 – 端、侧 – 侧及端 – 侧吻合。每次吻合完成后,将水灌入肠腔,测试吻合口是否通畅,吻合是否严密而不漏。

2. 以动物手术组为组合,用犬经腹直肌切口切除部分小肠并进行端 – 端吻合。

（刘家硕　孔令泉）

第十七章

胃空肠吻合术

一、适应证

1. 作为某些影响胃肠间连续性手术的组成部分。例如胃十二指肠消化性溃疡或胃癌施行胃大部切除后以胃空肠吻合术重建胃肠间连续性(通常称 Billroth Ⅱ式胃大部切除术);又如胰头癌病者施行胰十二指肠切除者等。

2. 幽门附近梗阻性病变不能用其他方法缓解者。例如胃十二指肠溃疡并发瘢痕性幽门梗阻而无施行其他手术的条件时。

3. 胃癌无法切除时作为缓解或预防幽门梗阻的姑息性处理。

4. 十二指肠病变切除困难,作为解除梗阻或旷置原发病灶的手段。例如十二指肠结核、十二指肠憩室等。

5. 其他 如为预防胃内容滞留而在行迷走神经切断术时加行胃空肠吻合等。

二、吻合口位置

胃空肠吻合可经结肠前或结肠后进行。前者是将空肠绕横结肠前方牵至胃前壁进行吻合,而后者则将空肠穿过横结肠系膜戳孔牵至胃后壁进行吻合。

三、手术步骤

(一)结肠前吻合

1. 体位、切口 仰卧位,作左上腹直肌切口。

2. 找到空肠并确定拟作吻合的部位 提起横结肠,在横结肠系膜根部,脊柱左缘找到十二指肠空肠曲(它的标志是屈氏韧带,韧带位于左膈脚和十二指肠空肠曲之间)。空肠吻合部位应选在距屈氏韧带15cm 以内,吻合口大小在 5cm 左右。用小圆针细丝线将计划的吻合口两端肠壁浆肌层各缝一针作为标记。

3. 缝合系膜间隙 拉起横结肠系膜和空肠系膜,由基部向肠管侧用小圆针细丝线将两层系膜间断缝闭数针,以防术后发生内疝。

4. 确定胃前壁吻合部位 一般选择胃前壁最低位大弯侧,尽量靠近胃角切迹垂线处作为吻合部位。如为恶性肿瘤病人的姑息治疗,则吻合部位应离肿瘤边缘至少 5cm,以免在短期内因癌扩展而阻塞吻合口。吻合部位选定后,将已有缝线标记的空肠袢绕结肠前提至胃大弯处(图 99),置空肠近端(输入端)于右侧,在拟定的吻合口两端将胃肠壁浆肌层缝合各一针,打结后暂不剪线,作为牵引,有利于吻合的操作。

5. 缝合吻合口后壁外层 在二牵引线间,用小圆针细丝线作一排胃肠壁间断浆肌层缝合,针距为 0.5cm。

6. 切开胃壁和空肠 在拟定吻合口的四周和后方放置盐水纱布,预防下一步骤操作中可能发生手术野污染。离胃肠壁浆肌层缝线 0.5cm 处先后切开胃壁和空肠浆肌层,用小圆针细丝线缝扎可见到的黏膜下血管(最好能带一点浆肌层组织,以免剪开黏膜后黏膜层过多地外翻),然后剪开胃和空肠黏膜,随时吸去胃肠内容物。在切开胃壁和空肠时,注意切口两端勿超越牵引线范围,一般离牵引线 0.5cm,两切口需等大,并应互相平行(图 100)。

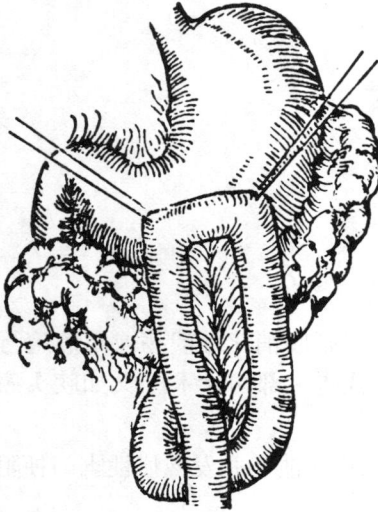

图 99　将空肠经横结肠
前方拉向胃前壁

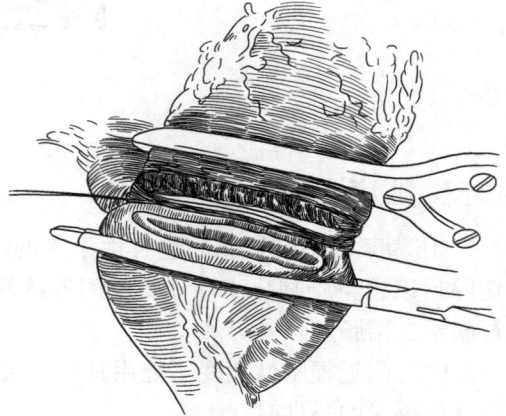

图 100　吻合口后方外层缝合后相继切开空
肠和胃的浆肌层,结扎横贯切口的血管,接着
切开胃肠的黏膜层

7. 缝合吻合口后壁内层　用一长中线作后壁全层连续扣锁缝合(图 101)。缝合从吻合口中部开始,第一针打结时,使结两侧线段长度基本相等,便于分别向两端进行缝合。此层缝合时,应保证缝针由一侧黏膜面进,同侧浆膜面出,再进对侧浆膜面,后由对侧黏膜面出。缝合进行中,还应随时拉紧缝线,便于发挥其止血作用。

8. 缝合吻合口前壁内层　后壁扣锁缝合至吻合口两端时,将缝针由黏膜穿至浆膜面,继而改用全层连续内翻褥式(Connell 法)缝合法吻合前壁内层(图 102)。此时缝针由一侧浆膜面进,同侧黏膜面出,再由同侧黏膜面进,后由同侧浆膜面出,下一针则在另一侧进行同样的缝合。缝至最后,两线尾在吻合口前壁中部两侧浆膜面会合打结。进行 Connell 缝合时,也应随时提紧缝线。

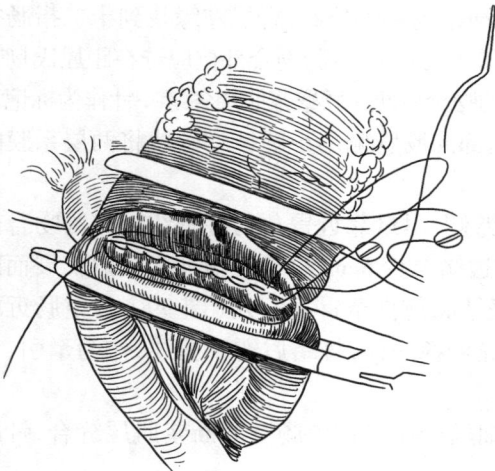

图 101　吻合口后壁内层连续扣锁缝合

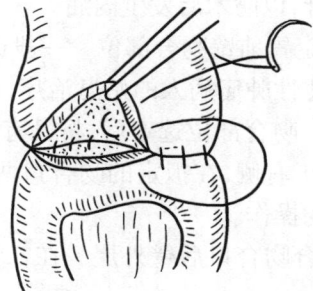

图 102　吻合口前壁内层连续内翻(Connell 法)缝合

缝合完成后,取去吻合口周围的纱布,术者用生理盐水洗双手或更换手套。

9. 缝合吻合口前壁外层　作浆肌层间断缝合(图103),以保证完善胃肠壁内翻。注意吻合口两端内翻是否满意,必要时可加强一、二针,但内翻不可过多,以免发生梗阻。吻合口两端缝合的操作应特别细致,此处最容易发生漏或梗阻。至此,吻合完成(图104)。

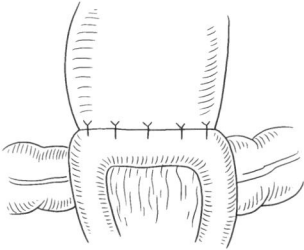

图103　吻合口前壁外层间断浆肌层(Lembert)缝合

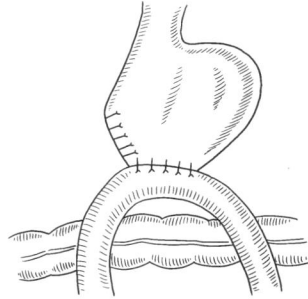

图104　已完成位于横结肠前方的胃空肠吻合

10. 吻合后处理　检查肠袢有无扭曲,吻合口是否通畅,一般以容纳三横指为宜,空肠输入口和输出口以容纳拇指通过为宜。为降低吻合口两端张力和避免该处空肠折角过锐而发生梗阻,在吻合口两端以外有时可加一、二针胃肠壁浆肌层缝合。

最后清点器械和敷料,吸去腹内可能有的积液,逐层缝合腹壁切口。

（二）结肠后吻合

体位、切口同前。进腹后,提起横结肠,在其系膜根部,脊柱左侧找到十二指肠空肠曲后,在屈氏韧带以下6~8cm处选定空肠吻合部位,如前缝上两针作为标记。然后在结肠中动脉左侧横结肠系膜无血管区剪一长6~7cm的裂孔,将空肠经此裂孔向上牵拉靠拢胃(图105),用与结肠前吻合相同的方法使空肠与胃后壁吻合。吻合后,把吻合口牵至结肠系膜下方,将横结肠系膜裂孔边缘与离吻合口1cm处胃壁作浆肌层间断缝合,以避免术后发生内疝。

结肠前吻合术,适用于横结肠系膜短、不易在横结肠系膜找到适当的“无血管区”、横结肠与空肠或胃有粘连、胃远端癌肿导致阻滞需作较高部位的吻合以及可能需行二次手术者。此法操作比较简便,但空肠输入袢(屈氏韧带与吻合口之间的空肠段)因需绕过横结肠和大网膜而较长,容易引起胆汁、胰液和肠液的潴留。结肠后吻合术最大优点是输入袢短,但步骤较繁。如需施行二次手术,则困难较大。

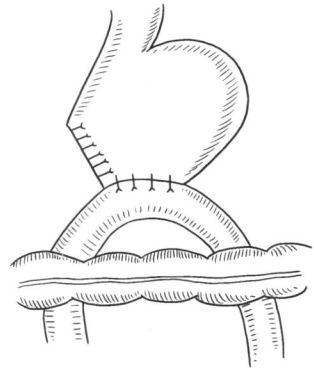

图105　位于横结肠后方的胃空肠吻合

四、注意事项

1. 选择吻合口部位时,应尽量距幽门近些,以减少并发边缘(吻合口)溃疡或空肠溃疡的机会。但输入袢太短可能导致吻合口两端空肠折角而引起梗阻或横结肠受空肠压迫而梗阻(见于结肠前吻合法)。在胃侧,吻合口应尽量靠近胃大弯,这样更利于胃的排空。

2. 输出口不要高于输入口,以免引起排空障碍。

【实习】

用犬按上述步骤作一结肠前胃空肠吻合。

（黄伟光）

第十八章

气管切开术

一、适应证

1. 解除各种原因所致喉部严重水肿、痉挛或梗阻引起的呼吸困难。

2. 昏迷或其他原因所致下呼吸道分泌物不能自主排出或排出困难而有窒息危险者,气管切开术便于吸痰、给氧、熏气以减少或治疗肺部并发症。

3. 颌面部、咽部或颈部手术及昏迷病人,为保证手术安全和呼吸道通畅,常行气管切开术。

二、手术步骤

(一)常规切开

1. **体位** 患者仰卧,切勿侧偏,肩下垫枕,使颈呈过伸位而气管向前突出(图106)。

2. **麻醉** 局部浸润麻醉。

3. **切口** 自环状软骨下缘下方至胸骨上凹正中切开皮肤2~3cm,或在胸骨上凹上两横指处作横切口(图107)。切开颈浅筋膜后,中线切开颈深筋膜,用血管钳分开两侧颈前肌肉及气管前筋膜,即可显露气管。小心将甲状腺峡部向上推开,如峡部过宽,可予以剪断,但需彻底止血。

4. **切开气管** 用尖刀在正中刺穿气管前壁,刀刃向上挑开第三、四气管软骨环(图108),也可在此将软骨部分切除,使气管切口呈圆形,以利于插入套管。切忌刺入过深而损伤气管后壁,导致气管食管瘘;切开时刀刃向上是为了避免损伤胸膜和颈部静脉。切开偏高可造成拔管困难,偏低容易损伤血管。

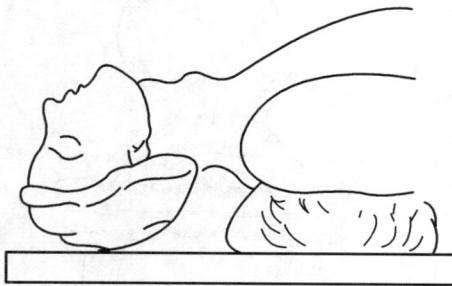

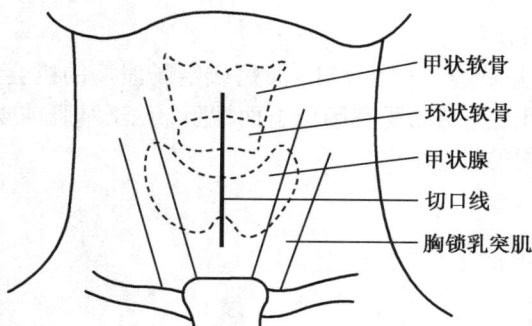

图106 气管切开体位

甲状软骨
环状软骨
甲状腺
切口线
胸锁乳突肌

图107 气管切开切口

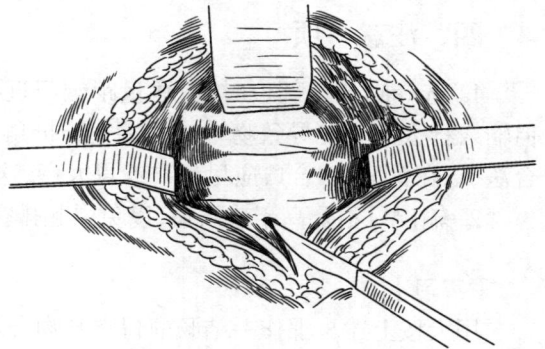

图108 尖刀刺挑切开

5. 插入套管　以弯血管钳或气管扩张器(图 109)撑开切开之气管,尽快吸除气管内分泌物,选用大小适宜的气管套管插入气管内,并迅速拔出导管内芯。此时若有分泌物自管口咳出,说明套管确已插入气管,或用少许纱布纤维置于管口,观察是否能随呼吸而飘动。

6. 缝合切口　确认无出血后将套管上下方皮肤切口稀疏缝合。

7. 固定气管套管　放好内导管及纱布垫,将套管系带绕颈在颈后打结,使套管固定于颈部防止由气管脱出(图 110)。

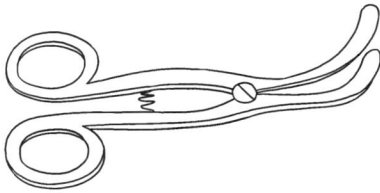

图 109　气管扩张器

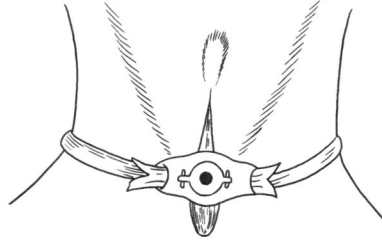

图 110　气管套管就位

（二）紧急切开

在紧急情况下,为抢得瞬息时间,甚至可不消毒,利用随手可得的任何小刀,也不用麻醉,将病人置于仰卧位,头后仰,迅速在颈前作一长 2~3cm 的横切口,切开环甲筋膜后,用左手拇、示二指固定气管迅速切开其前壁,插入气管套管或任何类似管道,尽快解除梗阻建立通气途径,恢复呼吸后才作常规气管切开处理并清创缝合紧急切开的创口。

【实习】

按以上方法作狗的常规气管切开术。手术结束后,可将气管套管拔出,以纱布盖创口,轻轻按摩创口片刻,不必进行缝合。

（曾晓华）

第十九章

胸腔闭式引流术

胸膜腔是一个密闭潜在的腔隙,腔内压力不论在呼气或吸气时,均低于大气压而呈负压(吸气时 $-5\sim-3cm\ H_2O$,呼气时 $-10\sim-5cm\ H_2O$)。此负压结合肺的弹性回缩力是维持肺通气量的重要保证。一旦因伤、病而负压消失或呈正压,则受累侧肺将萎缩而失去呼吸功能甚至在吸气时因两侧胸腔压力不平衡而使纵隔被推向健侧,导致健侧肺部分萎缩而更为严重地影响肺通气。胸腔闭式引流术的目的是用手术确保胸腔恢复并维持其负压。此法是向胸腔置入一引流管,管的外端接连一位置低于胸腔不少于 50cm 而盛水之玻瓶,管端持续置于水面之下,使呼气时,胸内空气能经管排出,而吸气时,空气受水的阻隔而不能进入胸腔。因此胸内气体愈来愈少而再建胸内负压。胸腔闭式引流的关键是利用盛水的"水封瓶"。

一、适应证

1. 严重的外伤性血胸、气胸。
2. 急性脓胸需持续排脓者。
3. 脓胸并发支气管胸膜瘘者。
4. 胸内手术后。

二、手术步骤

1. 麻醉　局部浸润麻醉。
2. 准备引流管　取一内径约 8mm 之引流管,在邻近其前端的管壁上剪孔数个(有利于加强引流通畅度)备用。
3. 切口　胸部外侧沿第七、八肋间方向作长约 1.5cm 之切口(气胸时,宜作锁骨中线与 2 肋间交点切口),切开皮肤,用血管钳钝性分开皮下组织、深筋膜及肋间肌,最后刺破胸膜。
4. 置入引流管　直血管钳夹闭式引流管尾端。用弯血管钳夹持其前端,经皮肤切口及胸壁戳孔将引流管置入胸腔。然后将尾端接至水封瓶玻璃管。松钳观察引流管是否通畅。必要时酌情调节引流管之位置。
5. 缝合切口　一般只需缝合皮肤一针,打结后即用此线缚住引流管,使之固定而不致滑落(图 111)。

三、注意事项

1. 观察玻璃管内水柱是否随呼吸上下波动,管端是否排液、排气。不波动表示不通,此时应检查引流管是否扭曲折角。如管的前端确在胸内,有时可借变换引流管位置或挤压引流管使之通畅。

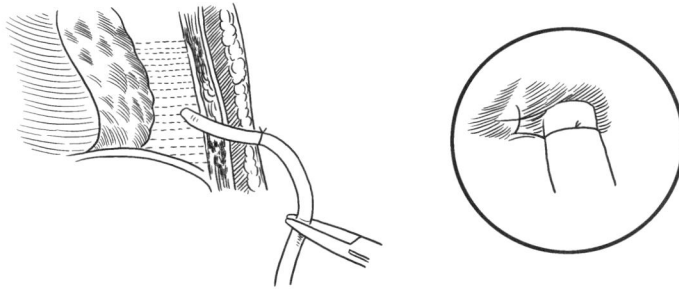

图 111　插入引流管后,用皮肤缝合线缚扎固定引流管

2. 连接引流管的玻璃管下端必须持续保持在水面下 3~4cm(图 112),使其不与大气相通。水封瓶塞常另插一短玻璃管,其下端应远离水平面,与大气相通。

3. 管道各接头处必须牢靠,防止漏气或滑脱。

4. 水封瓶应低于胸腔至少 50cm。

5. 拔出引流管　不需要继续引流时,一手持纱布及油纱布,另一手在吸气终末时拔除引流管,迅速盖住胸壁引流孔,略行按摩后固定敷料。

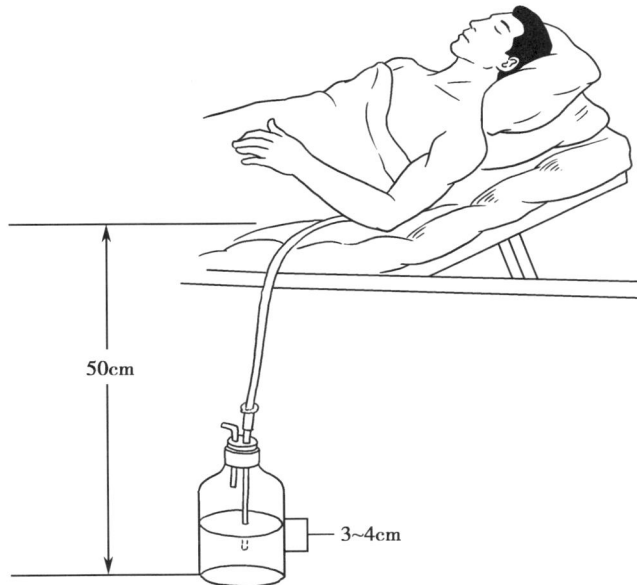

图 112　引流管接水封瓶

【实习】

犬仰卧,确定第七肋间及腋中线交点位置后,按上法,施行胸腔闭式引流术。确认其有效性后,拔去引流管。

（朱　冰）

附录

手术记录和术后首次病程
记录的书写要求

手术记录是指手术者书写的反映手术一般情况、手术经过、术中发现及处理等情况的特殊记录，应当在术后 24 小时内完成（危重病人即时完成）。特殊情况下由第一助手书写时，应由手术者审查并签名。术后首次病程记录是指参加手术的医师在患者术后即时完成的病程记录。

一、手术记录的书写要求

1. 手术记录应当另页书写，内容包括一般项目（患者姓名、性别、年龄、科别、病房、床位号、住院病历号）、手术日期、术前诊断、术后诊断、手术名称、手术者及助手姓名、麻醉师、麻醉方法、手术经过、术中出现情况的处理等。

手术经过、术中出现的情况及处理应记录以下内容：

（1）术时患者体位，皮肤消毒方法，消毒巾的铺盖，切口方向、部位、长度、解剖层次及止血方式。

（2）探查情况及主要病变部位、大小、与邻近器官或组织的关系；肿瘤应记录有无转移、淋巴结肿大情况。如与术前临床诊断不符合时，更应详细记录。

（3）手术的理由、方式及步骤，应包括离断、切除病变组织或脏器的名称、范围，修补重建组织与脏器的名称，吻合口大小及缝合方法，缝线名称及粗细号数；引流材料的名称、数目和放置部位；植入物及各种特殊物品的名称、型号、数量、厂家等。必要时手术方式及步骤绘图说明。

（4）术毕敷料及器械的清点情况。

（5）送检化验、培养、病理标本的名称及病理标本的肉眼所见情况。

（6）术中患者耐受情况，失血量，术中用药，输血量，特殊处理和抢救情况。

（7）术中麻醉情况，麻醉效果是否满意。

（8）如改变原手术计划，术中更改术式、需增加手术内容或扩大手术范围时，需说明理由。

2. 手术者（主刀医师）仅限 1 人，手术记录由手术者书写并签名；特殊情况下由第一助手书写时，必须由手术者审阅签名（包括请院外专家手术时）。

3. 一台手术需由多个科室、多名手术者完成时，由手术者分别书写所做手术的手术记录，不能由一名手术者全部书写。

二、术后首次病程记录的书写要求

术后首次病程记录是指参加手术的医师在患者术后即时完成的病程记录。内容包括手术时间、麻醉方式、手术方式、手术简要经过、术后诊断、术后处理措施、术后应特别注意观察的事项等。

（李 明）

Fundamentals of Surgical Operation

Second edition

Revisor	Yu Jiefei
Chief editors	Wu Kainan, Kong Lingquan
Associate editors	Huang Weiguang, Li Hongyuan, Zeng Xiaohua
Editors	Wang Zhongliang (Children's Hospital of Chongqing Medical University)
	Wang Xuehu (The First Affiliated Hospital of Chongqing Medical University)
	Wang Ruijue (Children's Hospital of Chongqing Medical University)
	Kong Lingquan (The First Affiliated Hospital of Chongqing Medical University)
	Li Hongyuan (The First Affiliated Hospital of Chongqing Medical University)
	Ran Liang (The First Affiliated Hospital of Chongqing Medical University)
	Zhu Bing (The Second Affiliated Hospital of Chongqing Medical University)
	Liu Jiashuo (The First Affiliated Hospital of Chongqing Medical University)
	Li Ming (The First Affiliated Hospital of Chongqing Medical University)
	Li Hao (The First Affiliated Hospital of Chongqing Medical University)
	Li Fenghe (The First Affiliated Hospital of Chongqing Medical University)
	Li Yingcun (Children's Hospital of Chongqing Medical University)
	Wu Kainan (The First Affiliated Hospital of Chongqing Medical University)
	Zou Baoshan (The First Affiliated Hospital of Chongqing Medical University)
	Xu Zhou (The First Affiliated Hospital of Chongqing Medical University)
	Huang Weiguang (The Second Affiliated Hospital of Chongqing Medical University)
	Zeng Xiaohua (Choingqing University Cancer Hospital)
	Wei Yuxian (The First Affiliated Hospital of Chongqing Medical University)

人民卫生出版社

Introduction

In the field of surgery, surgical operation is one of the chief means for the treatment of diseases. The first edition of this textbook was published in 2003 and had been approved by readers. According to the suggestions of the students and teachers, some contents of the second edition of this book have been revised to adapt the English medical teaching.

In this course we are going to learn the principles as well as to practice the basic techniques of surgical manipulations in experimental animals. The main contents in this textbook include aseptic techniques (such as surgical scrubbing, gowning, gloving, carrying and passing of aseptic instruments and articles, etc.) and fundamental operative manipulations (such as incision, exposure of operative field, hemostasis, ligation, suturing, etc.). The students are required to master the former strictly and the latter familiarly. The experimental animals should be treated conscientiously and carefully as our patients by executing aseptic techniques and principles strictly, avoiding unnecessary injury of living tissue, so as to develop a sound foundation of good medical technique and style for ourselves.

It is a bilingual (Chinese-English) textbook for Fundamentals of Surgical Operation, which written by some specialists who major in long term medical teaching and clinical working with sound Chinese-English basis, as well as some excellent young teachers. Grateful acknowledgements should be made to professor Yu Jiefei, the famous senior surgical specialist of our country, for his great efforts in appropriately revising this book.

This textbook is written for medical students of various educational system (7-grade, 5-grade, etc.) and specialists or clinicians who are required to learn or interested in the proper use of the English terms for the fundamentals of surgical operation. There is no denying the fact that it is hard to avoid some of the defects, even mistakes. We are ready to hear criticism and suggestions from our readers and colleagues for further revision of the second edition.

Wu Kainan & Kong Lingquan
March, 2018

Contents

Chapter 1

Requirements in Operating Room and Surgical Asepsis

Section 1   Basic requirements of Operating Room

Operating room is the site that ensures surgical operation to be carried out safely and successfully. As the aseptic techniques are the basic techniques of prime importance, all aseptic regulations must be complied with in the operating room strictly.

Those who have got upper respiratory infection or other suppurative infections are not allowed to enter the operating room. Visitors in one operating unit should not exceed three. They should put on clean clothes, shoes or slippers, cap and mask supplied by the operating room, same to the surgical staff, and obey the supervision and guidance of the working personnel to comply with the aseptic principles strictly and conscientiously. The operations should be arranged in sequence according to the degree of possible contamination: strict aseptic operation should be arranged before possibly contaminated ones in the aseptic units, while patients having pyogenic infection are arranged in units only for infected cases. After each operation, the operating unit should be cleaned to get rid of dirty fluids, badly contaminated materials are discarded, instruments and relatively clean drapes and dressings may be collected for washing and sterilization. Each operating unit should be cleaned at the end of every working day, with every thing clean and put in order. In addition, the operating unit should be thoroughly cleaned once a week.

The air in the operating room should be sterilized at regular intervals, by lactic acid or ultraviolet ray. 12ml of 80% lactic acid can be used for every 100m³ of the operating unit by vaporizing the acid through heating by an alcohol burner. The door and windows should be closed for 30 minutes during lactic acid sterilization and opened for ventilation afterwards. A 30 watts ultraviolet ray generator can be used for every 10–15m² of the floor 1 hour and the generator is put at a level 1.5m above the floor.

After an operation for patient with pyocyanic infection, the air in the operating unit should be sterilized with lactic acid vapor for 1 to 2 hours, then clean all the subjects in the room with 0.1% bromogeramine and the doors and windows are opened for ventilation for 1 hour.

After the operation for a patient with tetanus or gaseous gangrene, the operating unit can be sterilized by the vapor produced by adding 2ml of 40% formaldehyde into 1 gram of potassium permanganate for each m³ space of the unit. The windows are opened for ventilation 12 hours afterwards.

After the operation for an HbsAg positive patient, the floor and the operation table can be sprinkled with 0.1% hypochlorous acid 30 minutes before cleaning.

Section 2   Preoperative Preparations for Members of the Operating Team

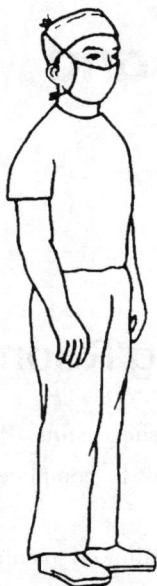

1. General preparation

After entering the operating room, first put on clean clothes, shoes or slippers, cap and mask in the dressing room to avoid carrying dirt outside into the operating room (Fig.1). Hairs, nose and mouth should be well covered. The cuff of the upper underclothes should be leveled over the superior 1/3 of the upper arm and the lower parts of it should be put inside the waist of the pants. The fingernails should be shortened before disinfection of arms. Those who have got upper respiratory infection or suppurative infection and those have their hands or arms injured should be refused to join the team.

Fig.1   Put on clothes, cap and mask supplied by the operating room

2. Disinfection (surgical scrubbing) of the hands and arms

Bacteria lie extensively over human skin including its wrinkles and deep parts as hair follicles, sebaceous glands and sweat glands.

It is found that there is about 40,000 bacteria over $1cm^2$ of skin surface and 38 hundred millions in 1g nail dirt. By surgical scrubbing, the superficial bacteria are easily to be eradicated but those deeply seated may be protected by the sebum, and may migrate from the deep parts to the superficial accompanying the secretion of sebum and sweat during operation, therefore, it is required to put on sterile gloves and gown for further protection from the contamination of the operating field.

There are several forms of surgical scrubbing for members of the operating team. The traditional one is scrubbing with soap and running water. It is practiced in many hospitals in our country, but in western countries, it is displaced gradually by simpler, less irritative and equally efficient methods.

The commonly used disinfection methods for hands and arms are introduced as follows:

(1) Scrubbing with soap and running water: the first step is to have a preliminary wash of the hands and forearms with soap and tap water for simple cleaning of sebum and dirt, then take an aseptic brush to brush these parts vigorously and orderly with sterile liquid soap, from the finger tip up to a level about 10cm above the elbow. The brushed area can be divided into three overlapping segments, i.e., fingertip to wrist, wrist to upper 1/3 of forearm and middle forearm to above elbow level. Brush orderly from the distal parts to the proximal. You can brush one side first and then the other, or brush the corresponding segments of both sides orderly. Brush evenly without missing any small area. Pay special attention to those easily neglected areas like fingertips, nail grooves, interdigital areas and the ulnar side of the forearm. Remember that the number of strokes and the vigor of brushing is far more important than the time you spent. After each turn of brushing which usually lasts at least for 3 minutes, rinse the brushed area with water from finger to elbow. Don't allow the water to flow back from elbow to the hand by keeping the hands at a higher level than the elbows. The amount of liquid soap should be large enough to have foams and suds. Repeat the brushing for three rounds, totally taking ten minutes. Then a piece of sterile towel is used to dry one arm by blotting or short strokes, still

in a direction from hand to elbow orderly. Any stroke in opposite direction is forbidden. After that, fold the towel and allow the other surface of it to dry the other arm in the same way (Fig.2).

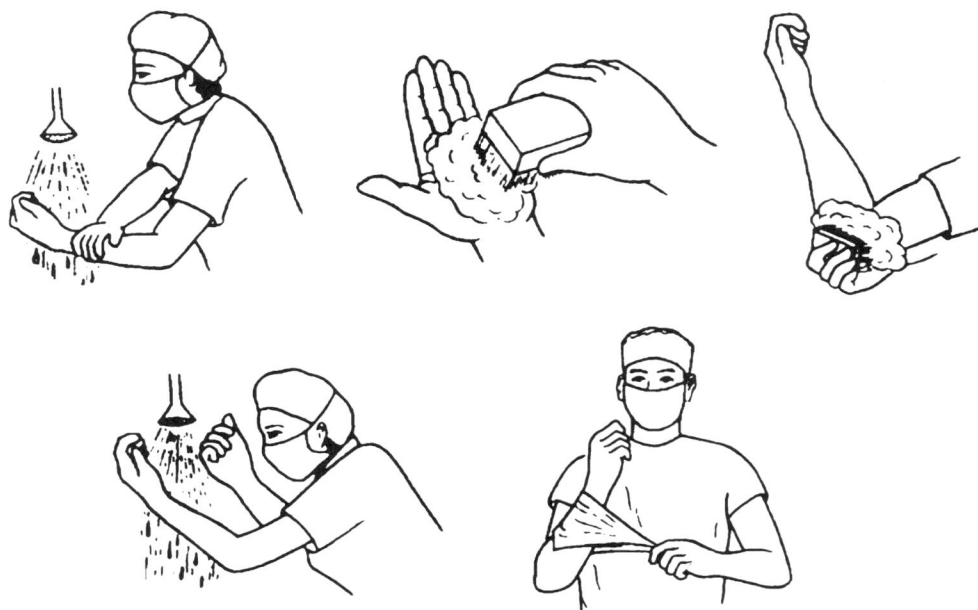

Fig.2   Scrubbing and blotting

The second step is to immerse the scrubbed limbs in antiseptic solution for 5 minutes. The commonly used antiseptic solutions include 75% alcohol, 0.1% bromogeramine and 0.1% chlorhexidine. Immerse the two upper limbs in a tub filled with antiseptic solution up to the level 6cm above the elbow for 5 minutes. During immersion, the germicidal effect will be greatly increased by rubbing the hands and forearms with a towel in the tub. Withdraw the limbs out of the tub and crook the arms with the hands up and forward, so that the solution over the limbs will drip back to the tub from the elbow. Now, beware of not touching any non-sterilized thing, or rescrubbing should be required.

(2) Scrubbing together with chlorhexidine sterilization: This is a newly developed method in our country. Use an aseptic brush to brush the arms with 15% liquid soap vigorously, just same as scrubbing with soap and water method, but brush for one round only about 3 minutes, then dry the arms with sterile towel, and rub the arms with a piece of gauze soaked with chlorhexidine solution or chlorhexidine foam from finger tip to a level 6cm above the elbow.

(3) Scrubbing together with povidone iodine (PVP-I) sterilization: This method is more commonly used in western countries. It may be used to sterilize arms of members of the operative team as well as the skin over the operating field of the patient. Preparations of PVP-I from different pharmaceutical factories contain same effective bactericidal integrant—free iodine, but high concentration of PVP-I doesn't mean necessarily high bactericidal power because more iodine is in combined form instead of free. The desirable concentration of PVP-I in surgical scrubbing is 0.1%–0.5%.

Brush the arms just like that in scrubbing with soap and water method for only one round too. Rub the hands and arms with a piece of gauze soaked with 0.5% PVP-I for 2 to 3 times, then you are ready for gowning and gloving.

By comparing the above mentioned methods of scrubbing, it is found that scrubbing with chlorhexidine and PVP-I are more convenient and time saving than that simply by soap and water method, though they have similar effects. It is believed that PVP-I is still superior to chlorhexidine, because the concentration of chlorhexidine available in the market is somewhat lower for sound surgical disinfection; in addition, chlorhexidine is a cationic scavenger while soap is an anionic one, any remnant of soap, iodine or alcohol will lower the efficacy of chlorhexidine in the process of sterilization.

(4) Surgical hand antisepsis with waterless antiseptic agent

1) Remove ornaments (such as rings, watches, and bracelets) before beginning the "surgical hand scrub" and prune the nails in accordance to requirements (nail length should not exceed the fingertips).

2) Washing hands: While cleaning your hands, pay attention to clean the dirt under nails and palm skin folds. Rinse thoroughly with flowing water and dry with a sterile towel. During the whole process, the hands should be positioned at the level of chest and above the elbow, in order to let the water flow to the elbow. Take the appropriate amount of hand sanitizer and follow the steps below to wash your hands (Fig.3):

A. Rub the palms facing one another with the fingers kept close together.

B. Rub the palm along the back of the hand and vice versa for another palm.

C. Rub your palm facing each other with fingers interlaced.

D. Bend your fingers, so that the joints can rotate and rub in the palm of another hand.

E. Rotational rubbing of the thumb clasped in another palm and vice versa.

F. Rotational rubbing of the palm with fingers of another closed palm and vice versa.

G. Annular rubbing the wrist to the inferior 1/3 of the upper arm with another hand and vice versa.

H. Wash with flowing water over hands, frontal side and inferior 1/3 of upper arm, then dry the hands and arms with sterile towels.

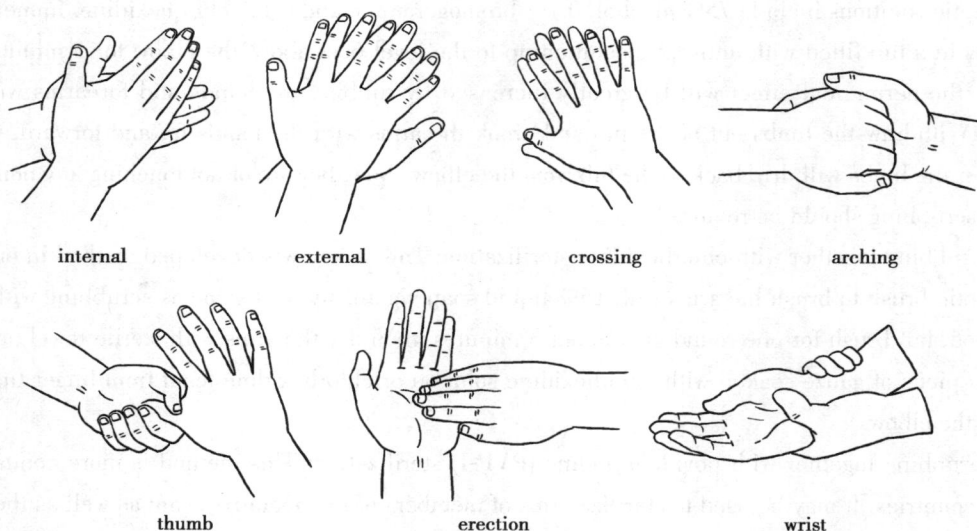

internal   external   crossing   arching

thumb   erection   wrist

Fig.3   Handwashing steps

3) hand disinfection: Take appropriate amount of disinfectant and apply over the parts of both hands, the front wall and 1/3 of upper arm, and carefully rub each other until the disinfectant gets dry. The amount of hand disinfectant liquid, rubbing time and the method of usage should be in accordance with the user's product guideline. For the whole process, both hands should be kept at the level of chest and above the elbow. Take appropriate amount of the disinfectant and follow the steps below to disinfect your hands for two times:

A. Rub the palms facing one another with the fingers kept close together.

B. Rub the palm along the back of the hand and vice versa for another palm.

C. Rub your palm facing each other with fingers interlaced.

D. Bend your fingers, so that the joints can rotate and rub in the palm of another hand.

E. Rotational rubbing of the thumb clasped in another palm and vice versa.

F. Rotational rubbing of the palm with fingers of another closed palm and vice versa.

G. Annular rubbing the wrist to the inferior 1/3 of the upper arm with another hand and vice versa.

4) Hand disinfection is completed, maintain the hand position (hands away from the chest, arms should not drop), wear sterile surgical clothing and sterile gloves.

(5) Scrubbing methods in emergency: in managing a life-threatening patient, the above mentioned routine scrubbing methods are not practical because they are time consuming. To seize every minute and second, the following methods may be used to rescue the patient:

1) Put on a pair of sterile gloves, wear a sterile operative gown and then put on another pair of sterile gloves. After that, the operation may be preceded.

2) Simply rub the hands and arms with a piece of PVP-I gauze for 2 to 3 times before gowning, gloving and operation.

3) Rub the hands and arms with a piece of 3%–5% tincture iodine gauze. After drying of the tincture, deiodinize with 70%–75% alcohol. Then proceed to gowning, gloving and operation.

3. Gowning and gloving

The operative gown and gloves are sterilized in steam autoclave by which all the microorganisms are expected to be killed; while the hands and arms are disinfected mechanically and chemically which can't eradicate all the bacteria over the skin completely. Thus, gowning and gloving provide a further protection for asepsis.

(1) Gowning: grasp the collar of a gown from the operating table and unfold it to its full length with its inner surface facing you in a spacious area. Don't keep the arms too low, nor too close to your chest to avoid touching of the gown with non-sterile areas. Make sure where the entrances of the sleeves are. With a quick and harmonized movement to lift the gown a little bit up and loose your grips on its collar, insert your arms into the sleeves momentarily. Don't keep the arms too high or overstretched. Keep the gown suspended on your outstretched arms until a running nurse behind you has caught the posterior parts of the gown to help you to put the gown in place (Fig.4). When your hands have passed out of the cuffs, cross your arms and pick up a tape at waist level of opposite side by each hand and hold them backward until the running nurse catches the tapes and ties them together. Don't roll up the sleeves if they are too long. The naked hands are not allowed to touch the outer surface of the gown. After the gown is put on, the hands should always be kept forward and a little bit raised. Don't place your hands below the level of the belt and over the level of the shoulder.

(2) Gloving: after gowning, select a pair of gloves that fit your hands. The scale of glove is the distance from the transverse wrist fold to the tip of middle finger in inches. Make sure which glove is the right or left one. Pick up both gloves with their ends everted and hold steadily. Don't touch the outer surface of the gloves by your naked hands. While holding the gloves by your right hand, the left hand is inserted into the glove first with fingers spreading slightly and worked into the glove. Then pick the right glove with fingers of the left gloved hand in the fold of the everted cuff and insert the fingers of the right hand into the right glove. Adjust the gown cuffs and make their ends reach the wrists and roll back the everted ends of gloves to cover the gown cuffs completely (Fig.5).

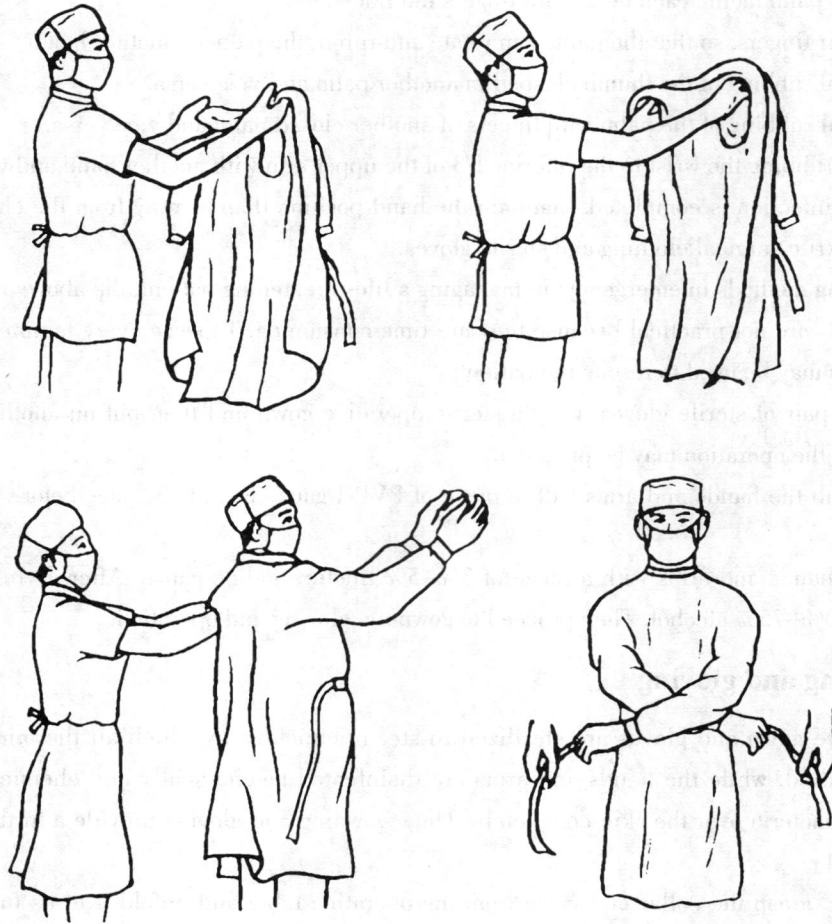

Fig.4   Gowning

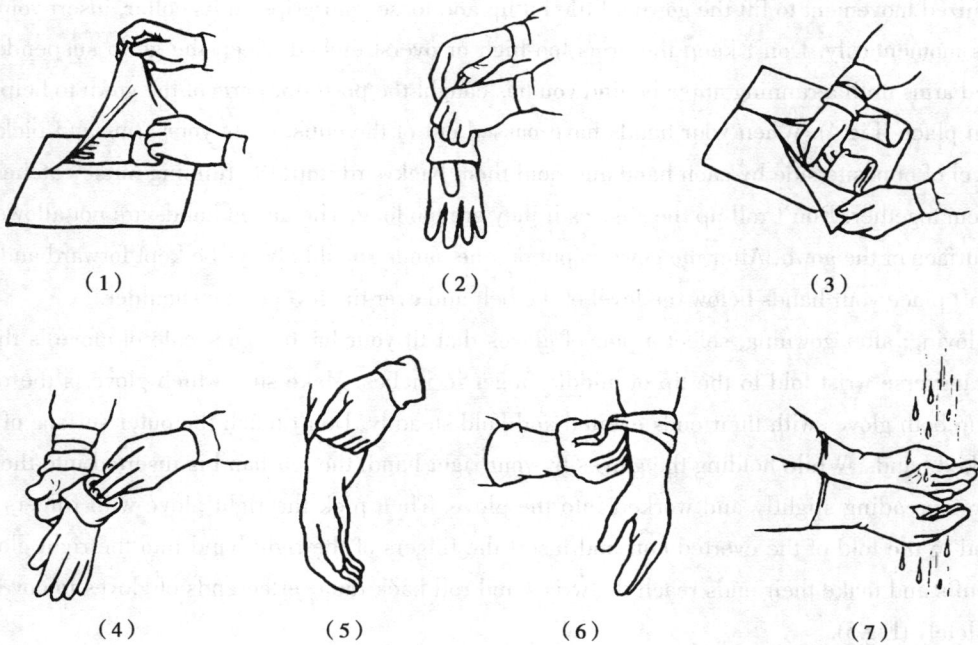

（1）   （2）   （3）

（4）   （5）   （6）   （7）

Fig.5   Gloving

After gowning and gloving, your upper limbs, the front and lateral side of your trunk and lower limbs, except feet, are all separated from the aseptic environment. During gowning and gloving, the most important point is that the scrubbed but naked hands and arms are not allowed to touch the outer surfaces of the sterile gown and gloves.

Section 3   Preparations of Patient on Operating Table

1. Posture of the patient

The patient on the operating table should be placed in a proper position to facilitate easy approach to the diseased part and good exposure of it, thus you may expect to perform the operation smoothly. However, you have to consider the convenience of the anesthetist, the patency of patient's air passage and blood circulation and the patient's comfort. Don't exert compression or over traction upon vascular and nerve trunks. To ensure a stable posture and to avoid undesirable movements of the patient during operation, some parts of the patient's body may be padded and restricted.

Most surgical operations are performed with the patient lying on the operating table. The most common postures are supine, prone and lateral positions.

Supine position is used in operations for the ventral parts of the body, especially abdominal operations (Fig.6). Some minute adjustments may be made if needed. For example: In operations over anterior cervical region, a pillow may be placed under the shoulders of the patient, thus the patient's head is extended, making the anterior part of the neck more prominent (Fig.7); for operations over the lateral part of face or neck, turn patient's head to the contralateral side (Fig.8); For perineal, anal and certain urogenital operations, a so called "lithotomy position" may be used, i.e., flex and abduct patient's both hips and put his or her knees on attached stands of the operating table (Fig.9).

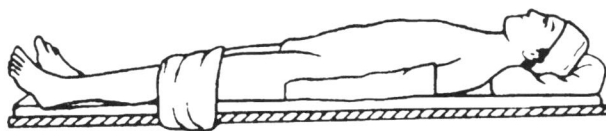

Fig.6   Supine position

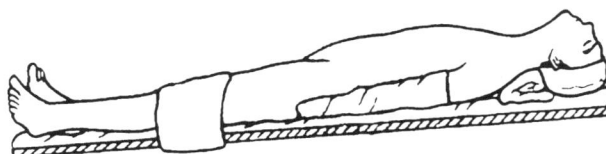

Fig.7   Supine position with prominent cervical region

Fig.8   Supine position with the head turned to the opposite side

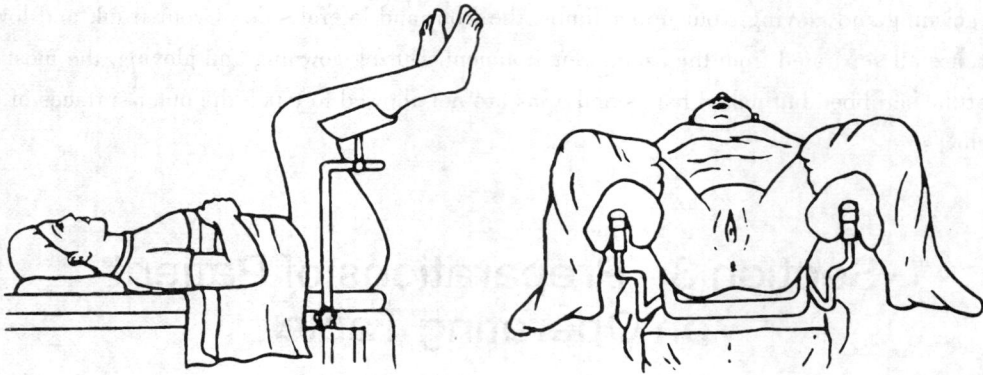

Fig.9　Lithotomy position

Prone positionis used in operations over the dorsal side of the body like back, sacrococcygeal region, anal region and buttocks (Fig.10). For anorectal operations, the operating field may be put in a more prominent situation by flexing both hips (Fig.11).

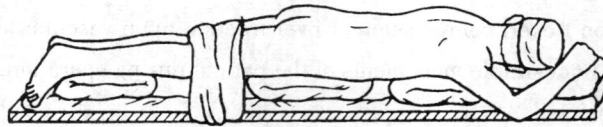

Fig.10　Prone position

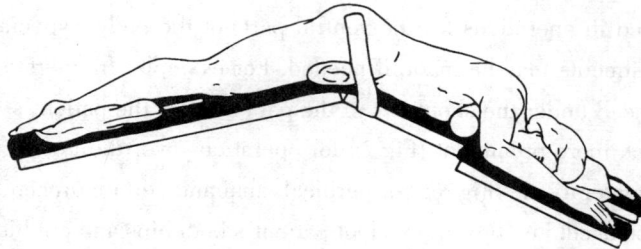

Fig.11　A prone position for anorectal operations

Lateral positionis common in thoracic and urological operations (Fig.12). It is sometimes used in operations of combined thoracoabdominal approach too. The degree of rotation of patient's body differs according to different requirements.

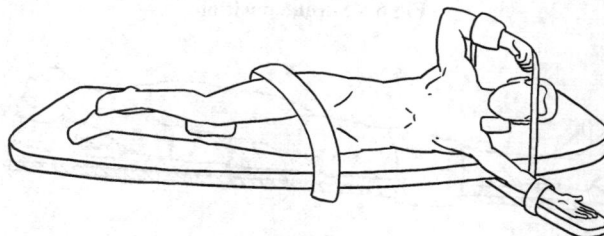

Fig.12　Lateral position

2. Preparation of the operative area

(1) Cleaning of the operative area: this is done in the day before operation, except in emergency. The hairs of the operative area should be shaved because they shelter dirt. Hairs over pubic area, ipsilateral armpit

and head should be shaved in abdominal surgery, chest surgery and cephalocervical surgery respectively. Shaving should be done carefully without injuring the skin. After shaving, use soap and water to clean the skin, then disinfect with 3% tincture iodine and 75% alcohol successively. After that, the skin is protected by sterile towel. This process is stricter, sometimes requiring 3 times in 3 successive days, in orthopedic surgery. In this laboratory for animal surgery, we first cut the long hairs with scissors, then eliminate the remnant hairs with depilatory agent, or shave after smearing with soap water. Depilatory agent is strongly corrosive to skin, so the depilated skin must be washed with profuse amount of water.

(2) Disinfection of skin over operating area on operating table: this is performed by the first assistant of the team (usually before gowning) and cooperated by the instrument nurse of the team. Rub the skin by sponges (held by ring forceps) soaked with 3.5% tincture of iodine and 75% alcohol successively, or PVP-I may be used for 2 turns instead. For mucous membrane and delicate skin like those over face, perineum, external genitalia and infant skin, diluted PVP-I or 0.1% bromogeramine may be used, each for 2 turns. Points of attention:

1) The first stroke of the sterilization of skin of operating area starts at the proposed line of incision as the center. Subsequent strokes are applied progressively apart from this center and each stroke is required to overlap the previous one (about 1/4-1/3). In disinfection of abdomen, squeeze a little amount of disinfectant solution into the umbilicus, suck the solution away at the end of disinfection.

2) In case tincture iodine and alcohol are used for disinfection, iodinization is not started until the tincture iodine is dry. The alcohol sponge is held by another sponge forceps other than that hold the iodine sponge.

3) In infectious or dirty operating area like anus and perineum, disinfection should start from the relatively clean periphery progressing to the more dirty or infectious area.

3. Draping

After skin disinfection, drapes should be applied surrounding the proposed incision for more perfect asepsis. A towel with hole or 3-4 small towels are enough for draping in minor operations, while in moderate or major operations, especially those having a deep operating field, a large sheet with a hole is further draped to cover the whole body of the patient and the operating table and only exposing that part the surgical incision is to be made. It is usually performed by the first assistant of the team and helped by the instrument nurse. Sometimes, the small sterile towels can be replaced by a sheet of disposable adhesive plastic membrane to cover the operating area. The common processes of draping are described as follows, taking abdominal operation as an example (Fig.13).

(1) Use four towels or a towel with hole to drape the operative area, only exposing the incisional site. The sequence of draping is to drape the caudal side first, then the cephalic side, the opposite side and the operator's side. If you drape the operative area after gowning, then the sequence is changed into: the operator's side, the caudal side, the cephalic side and the opposite side.

(2) Towels should be laid over the desired region exactly. Any migration after being laid from the periphery toward the central area is forbidden. If it is not laid exactly, discard it and drape with another towel.

(3) The towels should be draped with one edge folded. This edge is placed close to the center of the operative area. After draping, fasten the towels with towel clips at the four corners. Beware of the skin, don't hurt it with the clips.

(4) In performing a major operation, a large sheet with a hole such as abdominal sheet or chest sheet is draped with the hole opposite to the proposed incision. The sheet covers the whole operating table. It is usually draped by the members already gowned and gloved.

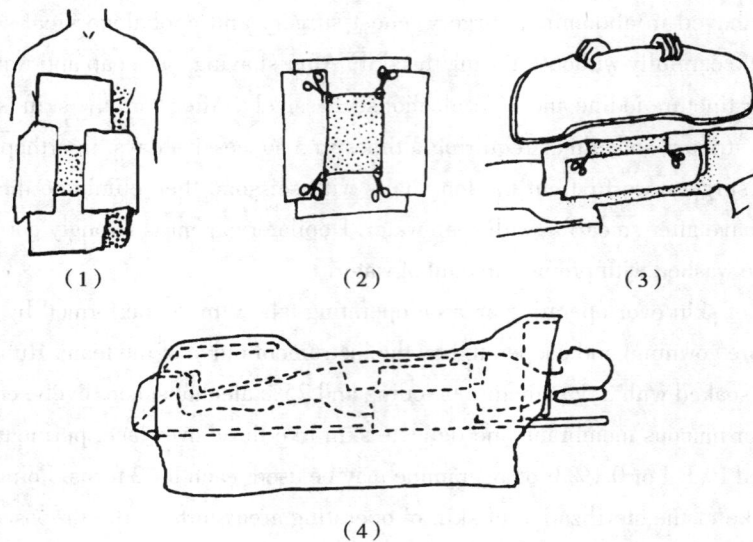

Fig.13 Draping for abdominal operation

(1) Draping with four towels ; (2) Fasten the towels with towel clips;

(3) Abdominal sheet is draped with the hole opposite the proposed incision; (4) Unfold the abdominal sheet

Section 4　Aseptic Principles
during Operation

As all the instruments and supplies have been sterilized, the surgical staffs scrubbed, gowned and gloved, and the operative area disinfected and draped, any violation of the aseptic regulations during operation may contaminate the instruments and operating area, leading to postoperative infection or even failure of the operation threatening the patient's life. Therefore, all the members, participating in the operation, have to comply with the following aseptic principles or regulations strictly and conscientiously. They should mention each other any breaks in the aseptic principles promptly without hesitation.

1. Keep solemn and quiet, out of sport and noise during operation.

2. From the right beginning of scrubbing, your arms and hands are not allowed to touch any non-sterile object. After gowning and gloving, areas above your shoulders, below the waist and your back are not considered aseptic. You are not allowed to touch the draped sheet hanging below the edges of the operating table too.

3. The number of gauze and instruments must be counted and checked by two team members and recorded before operation. Small pieces of gauze are not allowed to be brought into the operating area in operations with deep operating field like chest or abdomen. Before closing the incision at the end of operation, make sure that the number of gauze and instruments must coincide with that counted before operation, any foreign body left in the wound will lead to serious complications.

4. During operation, don't touch the disinfected but naked skin of the patient by your gloved hand, except the skin is covered by a sheet of sterilized adhesive plastic membrane. If necessary, you should hold a piece of sterile gauze and it is discarded after manipulation. After making incision, the edges of the cut wound are protected by 2 small towels to avoid the naked skin edges being exposed. Fix the towels with clips. If a sheet

of adhesive plastic membrane is used, towel protection is more necessary. The surgical knife and forceps, used in making skin incision, are discarded and not allowed to be used again.

5. In preceding the operation, instruments should be passed at a low level above the operating table and under the operator's arms when passing across him. It is not allowed to pass anything behind any team member. Any instrument which drops below the level of the edges of the operating table should not be used any more.

6. If necessary, members of the team in the same side can exchange their positions back to back during the operation.

7. Sweat on head of team member may be wiped away by running nurse when turning the head aside.

8. Once a glove is torn or contaminated, it should be changed immediately. If the sleeve of the operative gown is contaminated, put on an oversleeve to cover it. The moistened drapes should be covered with dry towel or sheet.

9. Avoid unnecessary talking during operation. If necessary, don't talk, cough or sneeze facing the operating field.

10. Before opening a hollow organ, gauze pads should be placed around it to prevent contamination of the surroundings by its contents. After the hollow organ is closed, the gloved hands should be rinsed with sterile water, and the pads as well as the instruments should be changed.

11. Observers should neither stand close to the team members nor stand too high. They are not allowed to walk around frequently to lessen the chance of contamination.

12. If a team member is going to perform another operation after finishing an aseptic operation without rupture of his gloves, take off the gown and gloves (the ungloved hands should not touch the gown and the outside of the glove), immerse the arms in 75% alcohol for another 5 minutes, or rub the arms with chlorhexidine pharmaceutics or povidone iodine solution for 1 turn, then he is ready for further gowning and gloving to perform the second operation. If the first operation is not aseptic or the gloves once ruptured during that operation, the operator is required to scrub his hands again.

(Li Hao   Kong Lingquan)

Chapter 2

Common Surgical Instruments and Supplies

To learn the structural characteristics and essential functions of the instruments is the key to master and manipulate them skillfully.

1. Scalpel

(1) Different forms of scalpels: a scalpel or surgical knife is composed of a blade and a handle marked with scales. There are different shapes and sizes of blades and handles (Fig.14) for different purpose. Scalpel is used in cutting and sometimes in isolation of tissues. Large round blade is commonly used to cut skin and ordinary tissues, small round blade is used in fine or delicate cutting and blade with pointed tip is commonly used for pricking tissues or drainage of an abscess.

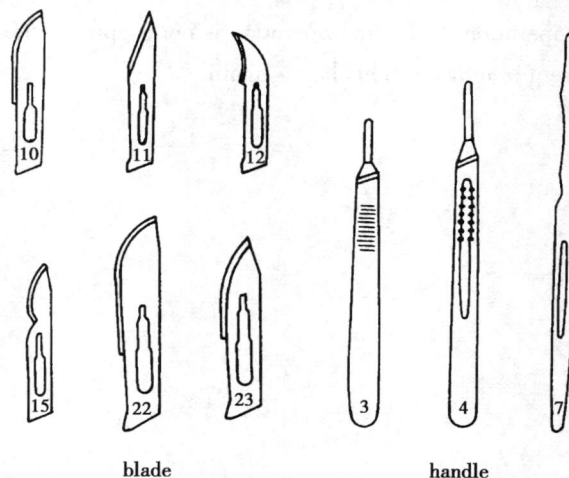

blade   handle

Fig.14   Different shapes and parts of a scalpel marked with scales

(2) Combination and detachment of blade and handle: to fix the blade to a handle, hold the back part of the blade by a hemostatic clamp or needle holder, insert the tip of the handle into a gap of the blade so as to fit the oblique border of the blade to that of the handle. To detach the blade from its handle, you can catch the end of the blade with the clamp and raise it a little and push forward to separate the two parts (Fig.15).

(3) Handling of scalpel: There are usually four forms to hold a scalpel (Fig.16).

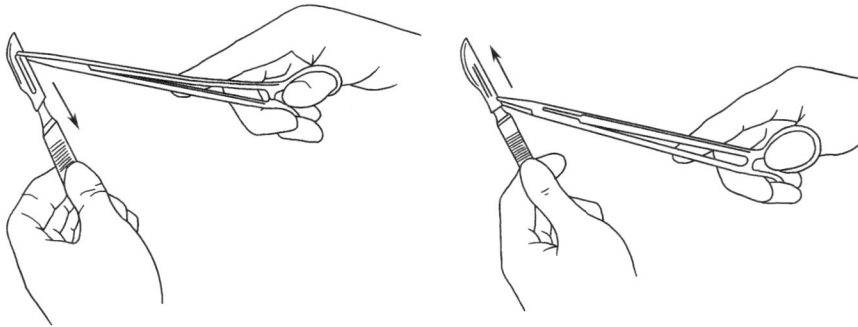

Fig.15   Fix the blade to the handle and detachment of it

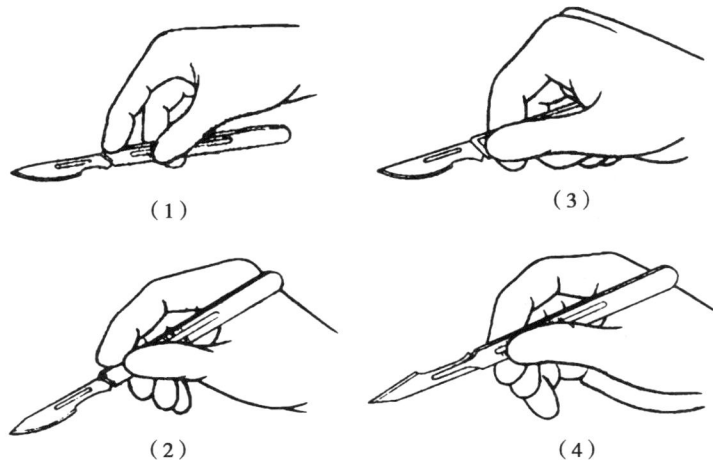

Fig.16   Handling of scalpel

(1) bow holding form; (2) pen holding form; (3) grasping form; (4) scalpel holding for pricking

1) The knife can be held as handling a violin bow by extending the index finger and pressing it on the back of the blade. This is common in making a long cut or to cut tough tissues.

2) The knife can be handled just like holding a pen. This is mainly used in making a fine and delicate cut, as in dissection and isolation of blood vessels and nerves.

3) The knife can be held by grasping, which is mainly used in making long cut or cut of very tough and thick tissues, like cut of thick muscle in amputation.

4) Hold the knife like holding a pen with the cutting edge of the knife facing upward. This is used to avoid injury of deep tissue during cutting, such as in pricking of wall of common bile duct or drainage of an abscess.

In passing a scalpel during operation, the instrument nurse is required to grasp the back of the neck of the handle, and pass the handle, instead of the blade, to the operator (Fig.17). This is to avoid accidental hurt to the operator.

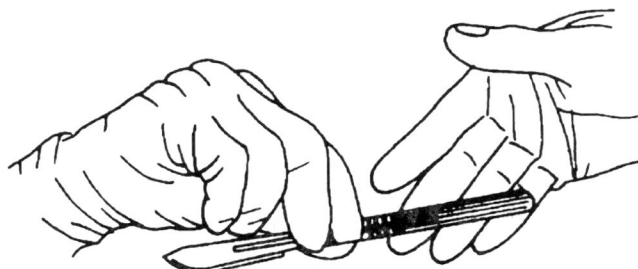

Fig.17   Passing scalpel

2. Scissors

Scissors are usually divided into two types, i.e, dissecting scissors and suture scissors (Fig.18). Dissecting scissors have different sizes and shapes, straight or curved. They are used to divide, dissect or cut tissues. The tips of their blades are relatively small and blunt. One or both tips of suture scissors are pointed, they are used to cut dressings and suture materials, usually after ligation of bleeders or suturing of tissues. In holding the scissors, put your thumb and ring finger into the rings of the scissors separately with your index finger at the joint of the scissors for stabilization (Fig.19).

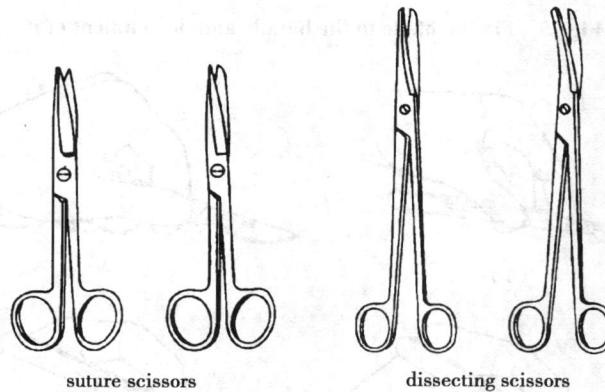

suture scissors   dissecting scissors

Fig.18   Scissors

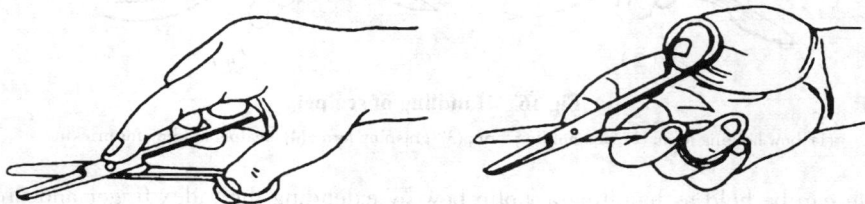

Fig.19   Method of holding scissors

3. Forceps

This is used to stabilize the tissues to be divided, cut or sutured. There are smooth forceps and teeth forceps of different shapes, sizes and lengths used in different situations (Fig.20).

(1) Teeth forceps or tissue forceps: the tips are hooked. The teeth forceps may be used to hold tough tissues steadily, like skin, fascia, aponeurosis, scar, etc. But there may be certain damage to the tissues to be held.

(2) Smooth forceps: the tips are smooth with transverse streaks but no hock. It is used to hold delicate tissues like gastrointestinal tract, peritoneum, mucous membrane, blood vessel, and nerve. There is little damage to the tissue. To hold the forceps, the 2 arms of it are held between your thumb and other fingers in opposition softly and steadily.

4. Hemostatic clamp

(1) Different kinds of hemostatic clamps: different sized hemostats have their blades straight (straight clamp) or curved (Kelly clamp), tips of the blades hooked (Kocher clamp) or not hooked. The inner surfaces of the blades of a hemostat may bear fine transverse streaks over the anterior halves of the blades or completely (Fig.21). These streaks act to prevent slipping away of the clamped tissues.

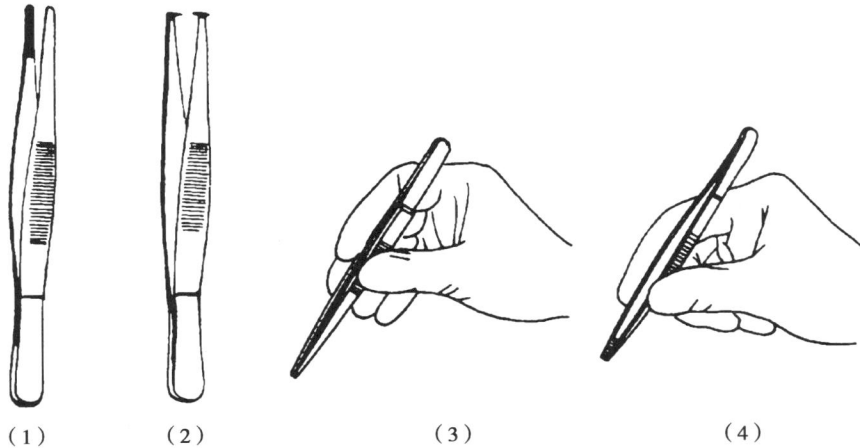

Fig.20　Smooth forceps and teeth forceps and the way to hold them

(1) smooth forceps; (2) teeth forceps; (3) right way of holding; (4) wrong way of holding

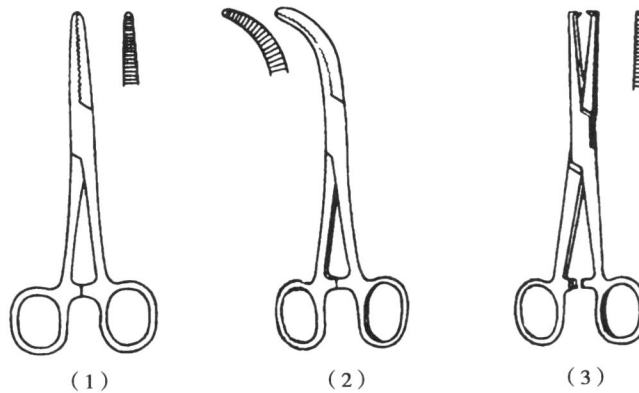

Fig.21　Hemostats

(1) straight clamp; (2) Kelly clamp; (3) Kocher clamp

Ordinary straight and Kelly clamps are 14cm in length, the former is usually used in manipulations in relative deep layers. In case of very deep manipulations, longer clamps, and 20cm or even longer, are used. The main functions of hemostatic clamps are to check bleeders but they are also used in blunt dissection of tissues. Straight clamp in the hand of first assistant of the team helps to draw needle when the operator is making sutures. Hemostat is not allowed to catch skin or hard substances to avoid damage to the tissues or the clamp itself.

Mosquito clamps are small sized hemostats usually 12.5cm long. Blades of mosquito clamps may also be straight or curved. They are used in fine and delicate manipulations.

Kocher clamps are more solid and strong than ordinary straight and curved hemostats. They have paired hooks at tips and deep transverse streaks over the inner surfaces of their blades, which will hold tissue more steadily. They are commonly used to hold tough tissues or obliterate intestinal lumen before severing an intestinal loop.

(2) Manipulating a hemostat: hemostatic clamp (hemostat) is commonly used in operation for catching tissues and bleeders to control bleeding. To hold a hemostat, like that in holding scissors, put your thumb and ring finger into the rings of the handles of the clamp separately with your index finger placed at the joint of the clamps for stabilization (Fig.22). After the bleeder is caught, the clamp is locked by approximating the 2 rings of the clamp. During the ligation or suture of the bleeder, the clamp should be unlocked. Hemostat is unlocked by approximating the rings and twisting the handles (Fig.23).

correct   wrong

Fig.22   Way of handling a hemostat

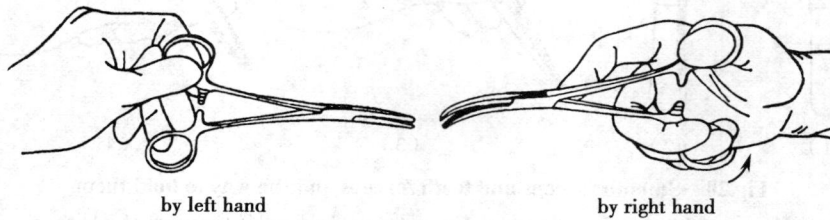

by left hand   by right hand

Fig.23   Ways of unlocking a hemostat

5. Allis clamp

Tips of an Allis clamp are curved with fine shallow teeth, which will do little damage to the tissues and be more effort-saving and stable than using forceps (Fig.24). It is used to hold skin, fascia or tough tissue for traction.

6. Towel clips

The anterior part of a towel clip is composed of 2 curved and pointed claws (Fig.25). It is mainly used to grasp and fix towels, which cover the skin surrounding the incision. Sometimes, it is also used for holding tough tissue, like skin flap without damage.

7. Sponge forceps

The tip of each blade of a sponge forceps (ring forceps or oval clamp) is a teethed or smooth ring (Fig.26). The former is used to hold gauze pledget in skin sterilization and the latter is occasionally used to hold and tract delicate tissue like intestinal loop. A ring forceps may be reserved in a container with antiseptic solution and used by a running nurse to pass instruments, dressings or materials of provisional need of the operating team. In such cases, remember that: the cephalic end of the sponge forceps should always be kept lower than its handle side to prevent back flow of the sterilizing solution.

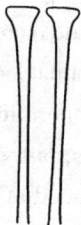

Fig.24   Allis clamp   **Fig.25   Towel clip**   **Fig.26   Sponge forcep**

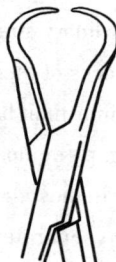

8. Needle holder

Needle holder is used to hold a needle, usually a curved one, for suturing (Fig.27). It is similar to a hemostat in shape, but it is more solid, and the distance between the fulcrum and its tip is short, so that the needle is caught more steadily. A needle should be caught at the junction of its middle third and the eyed third with its long axis perpendicular to that of the needle holder. The threaded suture should be properly overlapped (about one fourth of its whole length for interrupted suture) and is put aside the needle and in the gap between the tips of the needle holder. The needle holder may be held in the same fashion as holding a hemostat. But it is better to be grasped in the palm, the latter will make suturing more convenient.

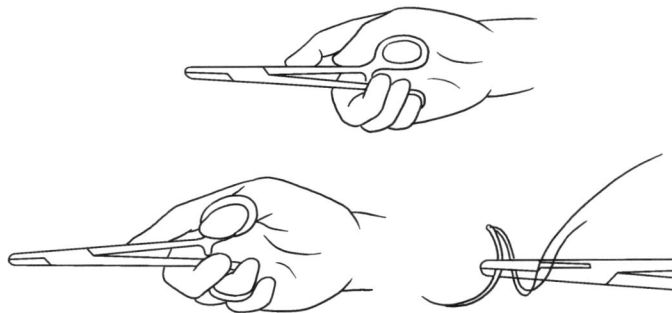

Fig.27   Needle holder and way of holding it

9. Retractors

Retractors are used to expose the operative field better by keeping off its surrounding tissues or organs. There are self-retaining and hand holding retractors of different shapes, depths and breadths. The commonly used retractors include thyroid retractor, appendix retractor, abdominal retractor, Dever's (deep curved) retractor, rectangular retractor etc (Fig.28). Don't pull the retractor too vigorously to avoid injury to tissues retracted. Gauze pads may be put between the retractor and the tissue or organ in tracting delicate structures, such as liver, intestinal loop and other viscera.

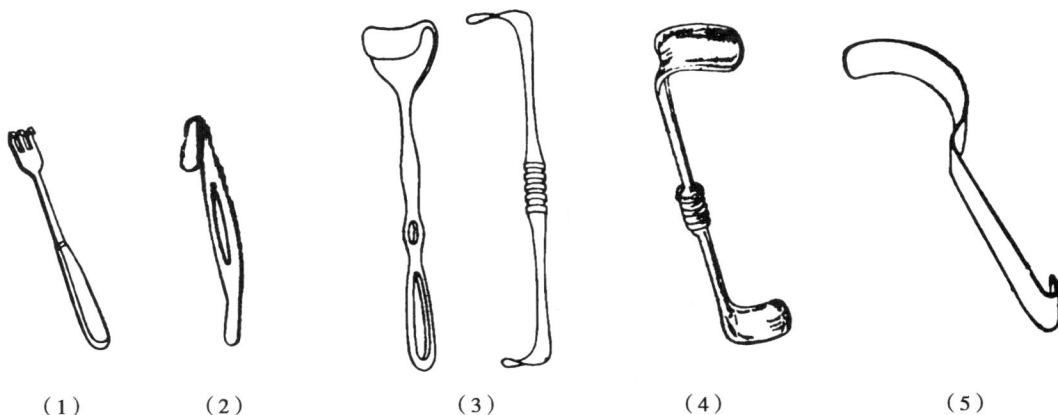

(1)   (2)   (3)   (4)   (5)

Fig.28   Common retractors

(1) cutaneous retractor; (2) thyroid retractor; (3) appendix retractor;

(4) plain abdominal retractor; (5) "S" shaped retractor

10. Probe

Ordinary probe is a flexible solid metallic wire used to explore a tract, sinus or fistula. Both ends of it are blunt to avoid damage to the tissue or creating a false tract in exploration.

A grooved probe is used to guide a scalpel in cutting a fistula or sinus or to drain an abscess (Fig.29).

11. Suction canula

This is usually a set of metallic or disposable plastic double-barreled tube used to get rid of fluids in operative field. The external barrel bears many pores that will prevent the front opening of the inner canula from blockage during suction. The other end of the inner canula is connected by rubber tube to an electric motor of the suction apparatus (Fig.30).

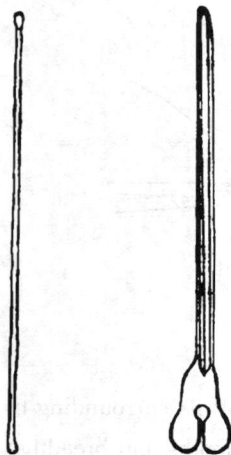

Fig.29   Ordinary and grooved probe

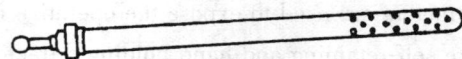

Fig.30   A double barreled suction canula of suction apparatus

12. Needle and suture materials

A needle used in suturing tissues may be straight or curved, round or cutting (triangular in cross section of its pointed half), with different lengths and sizes. Cutting needle has sharp edges and can penetrate tissue easily, so it is used for suturing tough tissues, like skin, cartilage, mammary capsule and scar, but it does more damage to them. In ordinary sutures, round needles are used. Curved needle is more easily manipulated in deep part of the operative field and straight needle is used in manipulation in superficial parts (Fig.31).

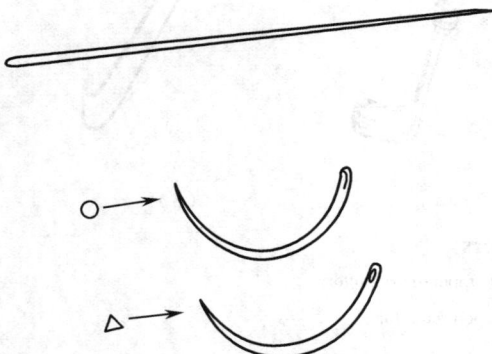

An atraumatic needle has no eye and the suture material is embedded directly into the tail of the needle. There is no need of threading the needle and doubling the suture material after threading, so the damage of tissue during suture is lessened.

Suture materials used in operation fall primarily into 2 categories, absorbable and non-absorbable. They are made of natural or synthetic materials, monofilamented or polyfilamented.

Fig.31   Needles

(1) Non-absorbable suture materials: silk is the most

commonly used natural non-absorbable suture material with advantages of yielding negligible tissue reaction, low cost, offering enough tensile strength and secure ligation, requiring relatively fine needle and thus bringing less damage to the tissues. The major disadvantage of silk suture is its non-absorbability leaving a permanent foreign body in the tissue. Sometimes it may work as a stone core when it is retained in the mucous membrane of biliary tract or urinary tract. Furthermore, under septic condition, bacteria may invade and hide in the interfibrillary spaces of the silk leading to persistent infection or formation of sinus or fistula, which are difficult to be cast off.

Common synthetic non-absorbable suture materials are high polymers, like nylon, dacron, prolene etc, of which, the commonest one is nylon. Nylon suture bears high tensile strength and yields negligible tissue reaction. However, it is relatively stiff and the knot made after suturing is easy to loose or slip. To overcome this disadvantage, it is required to tie 5 to 6 times successively and leave the remnant longer in cutting the thread.

(2) Absorbable suture materials: the most common natural one is catgut, which can be gradually digested by proteinase in the body, while the more widely accepted synthetic material is that made of polyglycolic acid, which will be hydrolyzed in the tissue postoperatively.

Catgut may be plain or chromic acid treated. The former may be digested in tissues within 5 to 10 days, while in the latter; the absorption may be postponed to 1 or more weeks later, according to different forms of chromic acid treatment. Catgut in tissues may be totally digested and absorbed without leaving permanent foreign body, however, being a foreign protein, it may provoke pronounced tissue reaction before being absorbed. In addition, it is less strong than other suture materials. To fulfill enough tensile strength, more thick catgut is used thus requiring thicker needle and bringing more damage to the tissue during suturing. Furthermore, early digestion of the gut may lead to loosening of the suture knot before sound healing of the tissue is established. Thus, it is nearly discarded nowadays.

Of the synthetic absorbable suture materials, polyglycolic acid (Dexon) treated is the commonly used one. It will be perfectly absorbed in 60 to 90 days. Other advantages of it include satisfactory tensile strength, easy manipulation and minor tissue reaction but the suture knots are still easy to loose. Although it may be used in suturing deep tissues, it is mainly used for the suture of skin and subcutaneous tissue.

Suture materials are scaled according to their tensile strength and diameter. Those scaled with bigger positive number are thicker and stronger; and those labeled with more "0" are thinner.

13. Drains and drainage tubes

Oil gauze: gauze soaked with vaseline or paraffin oil is mainly used to protect the wound with no epidermis or to fill the abscess cavity to keep it unblocked.

Rubber sheet drain: this is a rubber strip clipped from a rubber glove. It is usually placed in the subcutaneous layer to drain oozed blood or exudates after thyroid, scrotum or breast operations.

Cigarette drain: this is made by wrapping a gauze roll with a rubber sheet and it looks like a cigar. A cigarette drain is commonly used to drain actual or possible oozing of blood, exudates or even purulent fluids in abdominal cavity following an operation.

Drainage tube: latex, silica gel or plastic tubes are used to drain deeply situated fluid or blood collections.

T tube: this is a latex, silica gel or plastic tube of "T" shape used to drain common bile duct.

Urinary catheter: there are different sized and shaped urinary catheters, which can be used for instant drainage of urine through urethral catheterization or retained for continuous drainage of urinary bladder (through urethra or through cystostomy), stomach (through gastrostomy) or drainage of hydropneumothorax (through thoracostomy). Mushroom shaped or balloon bearing catheters can prevent the indwelling catheter from sliding out of the hollow organs. Balloon bearing catheter may sometimes be used to press the raw surface left behind prostatectomy to check the oozing of blood from the wound (Fig.32).

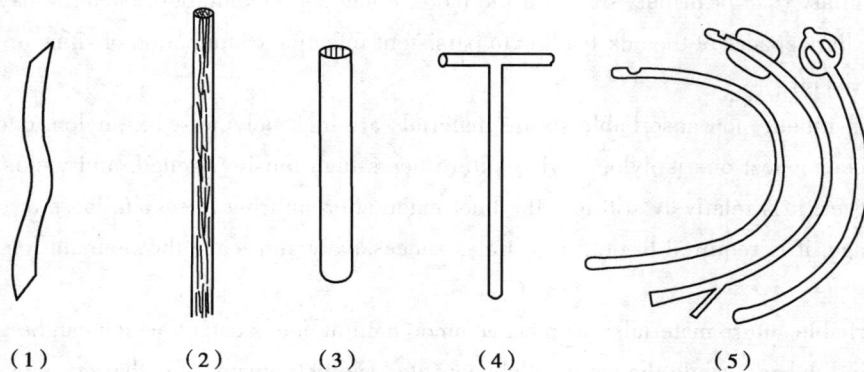

Fig.32   Several types of drain and drainage tubes
(1) rubber sheet drain; (2) cigarette drain; (3) drainage tube; (4) T-tube; (5) urinary catheter

Double barreled drainage tube: it contains two cannulas, an inner and an outer. There are many pores over the front part of the outer tube and a pore at its posterior end. The inner tube is relatively longer than the outer one and it may be connected to the drainage system with negative pressure or used for temporary or continuous perfusion. Posterior part of the outer tube is blocked against the inner one to maintain negative pressure in the suction system. This drainage tube is mainly used to drain deep parts of the abdominal cavity like pelvic cavity or subdiaphragmatic area. The double barrel design can prevent the inner tube from blockage during suction with negative pressure.

(Xu Zhou   Kong Lingquan)

Chapter 3

Fundamental Operative Techniques

Section 1   Tissue Cutting

1. Basic principles of making incision

(1) An incision should expose the operating field satisfactorily for a smooth operation.

(2) It should bring least damage to the tissues. For example, make an incision as close the lesion as possible, don't make unnecessary long incision, and use sharp scalpel or scissors in cutting to reduce the damage of tissue.

(3) It should be made with least disturbance to physiologic function. For example, make the incision in line with natural wrinkle of the skin, don't make an incision at weight bearing area (e.g. heel) and a longitudinal incision across a joint. The damage to major blood vessels, nerves and glandular ducts should be avoided.

2. Skin cutting

In making a long incision, the operator and the first assistant press their four fingers of their left hands on two sides of the proposed incision separately to make the skin tense before cutting (Fig.33). In making a small incision, the surgeon may use his own thumb and index finger to press the skin on both sides of the incision without the help of the first assistant.

The skin is incised with the scalpel perpendicular, parallel and perpendicular again to the skin surface. Hold the scalpel steadily and cut with even strength. It is desired to accomplish the cut of full thickness of the skin in one move.

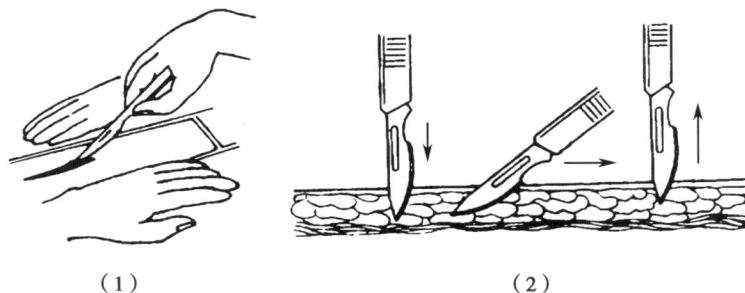

(1)   (2)

Fig.33   Skin incision

(1) make a skin incision cooperated with the first assistant; (2) method of scalpel holding

3. Fascia and aponeurosis cutting

Usually a small opening is first made by a scalpel, then through the opening of the fascia, put in a pair of scissors (or Kelly clamp), by spreading the blades of the scissors (or Kelly clamp) the fascia is detached from its underlying from its underlying tissue which allows further cutting of the fascia to an extent as desired.

4. Muscle cutting

To expose spaces beneath a muscle, it is better to split the muscle bluntly along the direction of its fibers without cutting. This will result in less bleeding. If muscle cutting is not avoidable, apply 2 Kocher clamps alongside the proposed line of cutting and cut the muscle cross its fibers between the 2 clamps. Bleeders are ligated by ligatures. If an electric cautery (electrotome) is ready, use it to cut the muscle and there will be less bleeding resulted.

Section 2   Tissue Dissection and Isolation

The purpose of dissection of tissues, normal and pathologic, is to expose or isolate the diseased tissue or organs satisfactorily for its management.

1. Sharp dissection

Sharp dissection made by scissors or scalpel is more accurate and sharp with less tissue trauma. Sharp dissection should be preceded under direct vision at areas of clear anatomic relationship. Don't use scissors or scalpel blindly to avoid unnecessary damage to vessels, nerves and tissues.

2. Blunt dissection

This form of dissection is to strip loose tissues by hemostat, tissue scissors, scalpel, swab or even operator's fingers following natural tissue plane or cleavage. In proceeding blunt dissection, exert appropriate force and don't be rough, otherwise it may cause laceration of the vessel, nerve or viscus.

Combined sharp and blunt dissection can be done conveniently. The dissection is made layer by layer along the anatomical cleavage. Insert the tips of scissors, with blades closed, into the potential space beneath the tissue to be cut, then widen the blades a little bit to free the tissue. Cut the freed part of the tissue when you are sure that no important structure (blood vessel, nerve or any other) is nearby. Repeat the above manipulations until you complete the dissection.

Section 3　Hemostasis

1. Hemostasis by Pressure

This is the most commonly used method of hemostasis in bleeding from small vessels, especially veins. Pick a piece of gauze in your hand and press upon the broken vessel. It will slow down the blood flow, facilitate coagulation process and lead to hemostasis. In case of relative profuse bleeding when urgent hemostasis is required, you can stop the bleeding temporarily by holding the bleeding tissue in your fingers or pressing the proximal segment of the broken vessel, then you can search for the injured site of the vessel. Hot saline gauze packing may further promote the process of coagulation by heat. It is commonly used in pressure hemostasis to stop oozing from wound tissue.

Occasionally, there is bleeding or oozing difficult to be controlled, gauze or gauze tape packing to exert pressure is effective for hemostasis. The packing is drawn segment by segment 5–7 days postoperatively.

2. Hemostasis by ligation

(1) Ligation following clamping: the bleeding point should be clamped before ligation (Fig.34). It is caught by the tip of a hemostat clamp together with as little surrounding tissue as possible. In making ligation, raise the hemostat and wind a segment of suture around the bleeder. Keep the suture tight and begin to tie. Loose the hemostat at the moment the knot is tightened. Make sure that the knot is secure, and then a second knot is made to complete the ligation. Sometimes a third knot is required in ligating a relatively large bleeder. In tightening a knot, the 2 force points of your fingertips should be in line with the ligating point, otherwise, the ligated tissue may be torn or the knot is not tight. If a vessel is to be severed, you may dissect it first at the part to be severed, then clamp it by 2 hemostats and sever it between the hemostats. Ligate the 2 severed ends separately.

Fig.34　Hemostasis by clamping and ligation

(2) Hemostasis by transfixion suture or figure of "8" suture: this is a more secure method of hemostasis, which is commonly used for ligation of relatively large vessel to prevent slipping of ligature. Clamp the vessel by 3 hemostats first, then sever the vessel between the proximal 2 and the distal 1 hemostats. The proximal stump is ligated with a triple knot proximal to the proximal clamp first and then ligates the distal stump. A transfixion (figure of "8") suture is made proximal to the middle clamp eventually (Fig.35). In ligation of severed tissue, which contains relatively large vessel, a transfixion suture may also be used. In such case, be sure that the needle is only allowed to pass through the avascular part of the tissue instead of through the vessel itself. Otherwise, bleeding or hematoma formation may result.

3. Hemostasis by cautery

High frequency current may coagulate tissues (too high intensity current will liquefy tissues instead). When the cautery tip contacts with a hemostat clamping the bleeder, it may stop bleeding by tissue coagulation if bleeders are small (Fig.36).

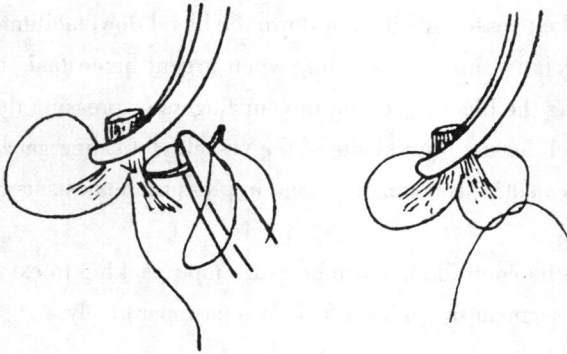

Fig.35   Transfixion suture

Fig.36   Hemostasis by cautery

Hemostasis by electro-coagulation is easy to handle and time saving. There is no foreign body left behind. It can also be used to check remote bleeding through an endoscope, while hemostasis by ligation is not possible to accomplish remotely. Electro-coagulation is dangerous if it is used to check bleeding from a relatively large blood vessel, because the coagulated vascular wall may slough postoperatively leading to massive bleeding.

4. Materials promoting hemostasis

Local hemostatic materials may be used for bleeding or oozing difficult to control like those from wound of liver or broken bone end. The commonly used ones are gelatin sponge, fibrin foam, oxidative cellulose, collagen filament and bone wax.

5. Hemostasis by metallic clips

Clips are used to check deeply situated bleeders with unsatisfactory exposure. In addition to hemostasis, the clips serve as good markers in postoperative x-ray examination. It is also used in hemostasis in endoscopic operations like those through laparoscope or thoracoscope; and to check bleedings from delicate tissues like brain. The clips are usually made of tantalum or silver.

Section 4   Ligation

Ligation is a basic and important technic in performing surgical operations. There are numerous bleeders requiring ligation encountered in an operation; in addition, suturing of different tissues requires ligation too. Qualified manipulations and proper selection of suture material are keys to make secure and quick ligation.

1.　Different forms of knots (Fig.37)

(1) Square knot: square knot is the basic and most commonly encountered knot surgically. It is composed of 2 single knots in opposing directions, and is commonly used in ligating small vessels and after tissue suturing. If manipulated properly and correctly, this knot is secure and not easy to loose.

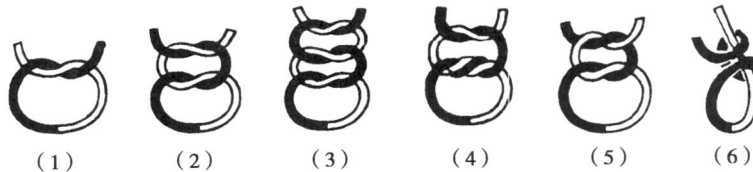

Fig.37　Different forms of common knots

(1) single knot; (2) square knot; (3) triple knot; (4) surgical knot; (5) granny knot; (6) slippery knot

(2) Surgical knot: the only difference between surgical knot and square knot is that one segment of the thread is thrown through the loop of the other segment twice instead of once in making the first single knot. Surgical knot is more secure and reliable than square knot because the friction between the 2 segments is increased, but it will take more time to perform. It is usually used to ligate large vessel and tissues with high tension.

(3) Triple knot: a triple knot is made of 3 single knots, i.e., to add a third simple knot to a square knot. The direction of the third is same as the first. It is used to ligate large artery and tissues with high tension because the knot is tight and not easy to loose. Knots made by nylon or catgut suture are difficult to ligate tightly, in such cases, triple knots are desirable. The disadvantage of a triple knot is that it leaves more foreign body in the tissue.

(4) Granny knot: if the 2 single knots are made in a same direction, a granny (false) knot will result, which is easy to slip and should be abandoned in surgical operation.

(5) Slippery knot: if the force exerted by your 2 hands are not even in making a "square" knot, the result is a slippery knot, i.e., one segment of the thread winds around another straightened segment twice (Fig.38). This is not safe and should be abandoned in surgical operation.

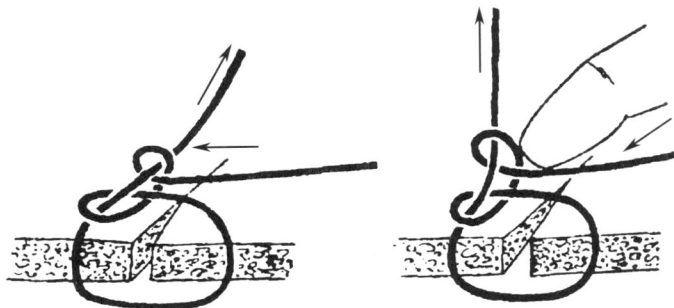

Fig.38　The formation of slippery knot

2.　Tying a knot

(1) One hand method of knot tying: the one hand method is most frequently used for its simplicity and convenience, but if not properly manipulated, it will lead to a slippery knot. The manipulations are shown in Fig.39.

（1）　　　　　　　　　　　　　　（2）

（3）　　　　　　　　　　　　　　（4）

（5）　　　　　　　　　　　　　　（6）

（7）　　　　　　　　　　　　　　（8）

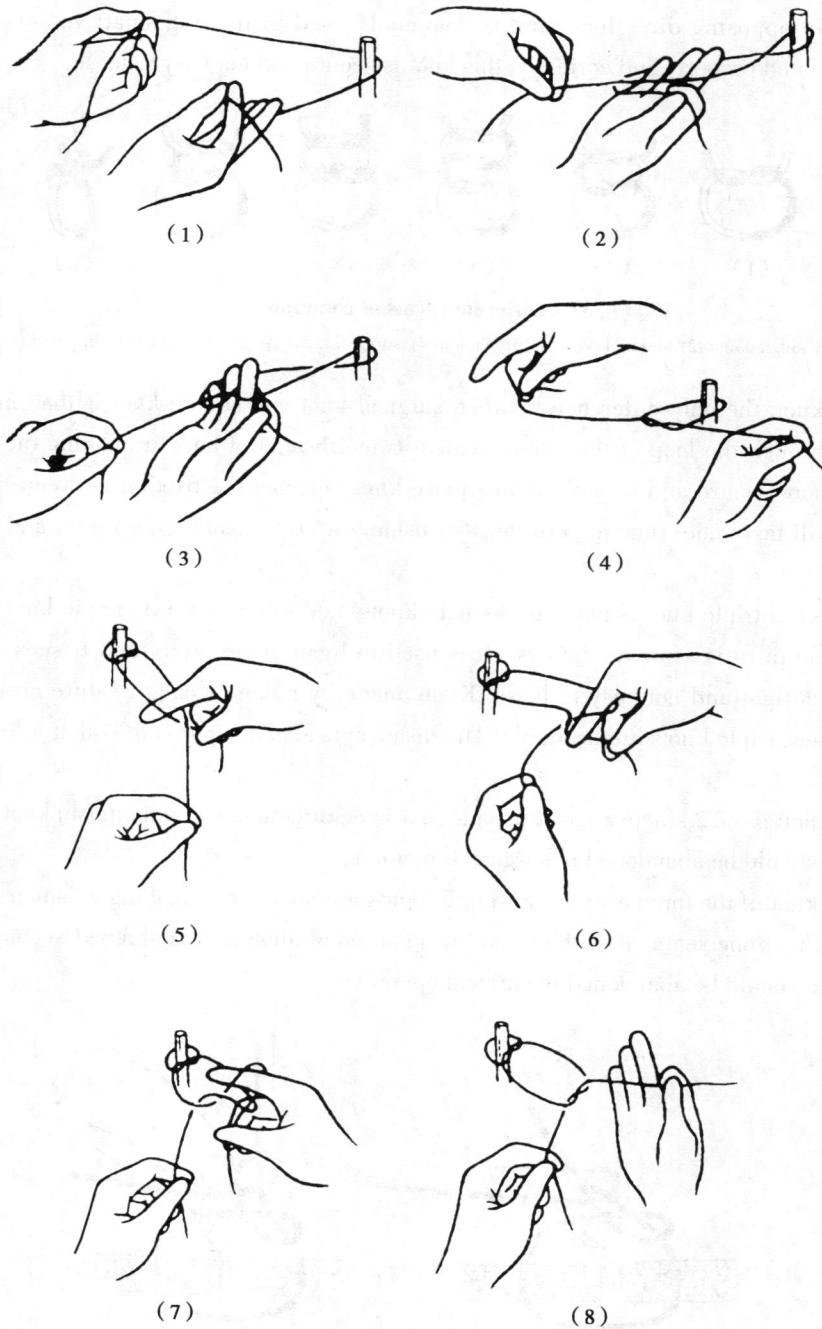

Fig.39　One hand method of knot tying

(2) Two hands method of knot tying: besides to be used in ordinary ligation, it is more commonly used in the ligation of deep tissues or tensile tissues because of its security and reliability (Fig.40). In addition, it is easier to make a surgical knot in two hands knot tying.

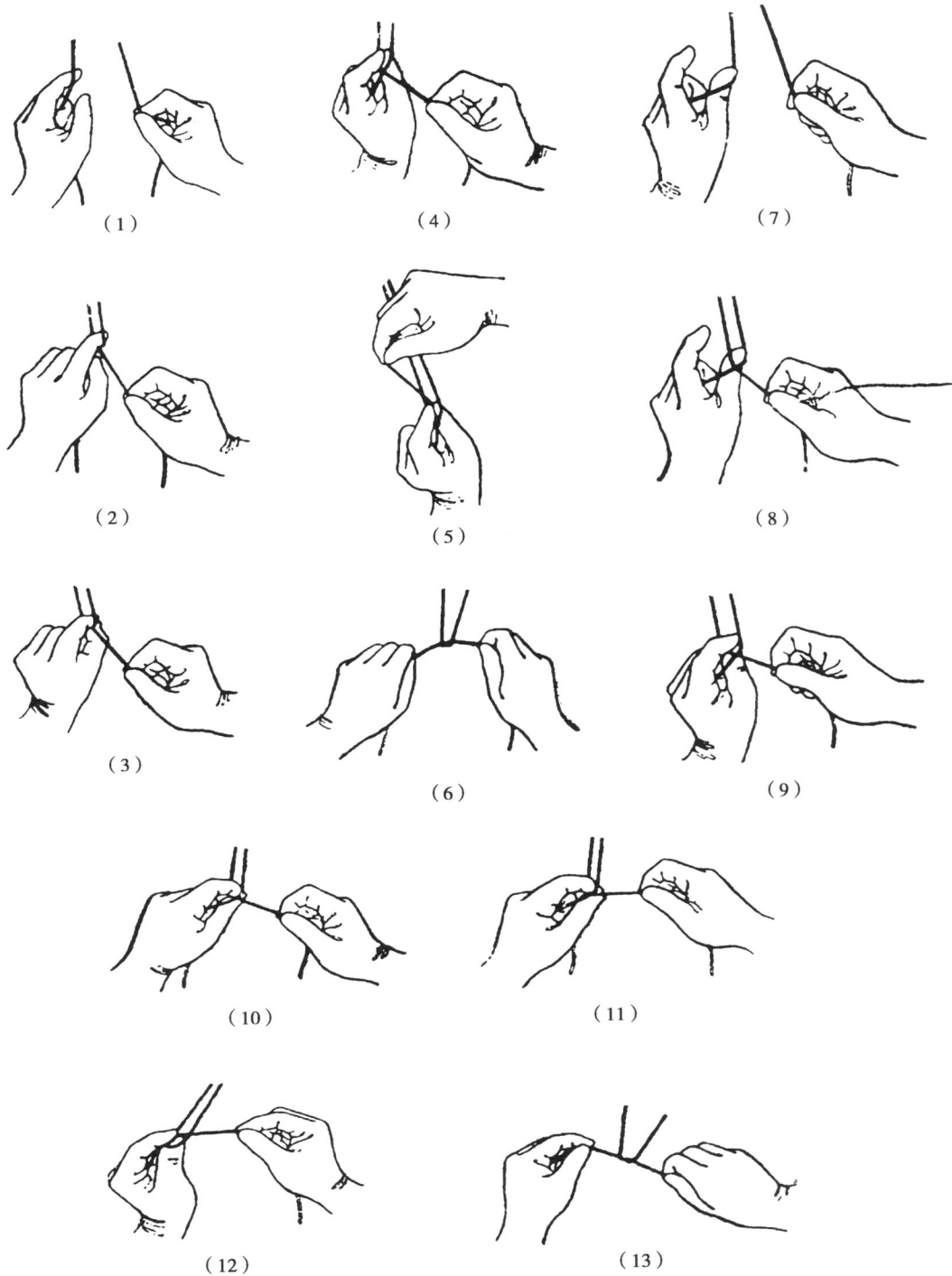

Fig.40　Two hands method of knot tying

(3) Instrument method of knot tying: the instrument method saves a lot of suture material and decreases the number of needle threading (Fig.41).

(4) Ligation in deep part of operative field: to ligate the deep tissues or important vessels deeply seated, take a long segment of thread, catch its one end by a hemostat, bring it to the deep field to loop over the tip of the hemostat that catches the tissue to be ligated, then go ahead to make ligature, better by two hands method of knot tying (Fig.42).

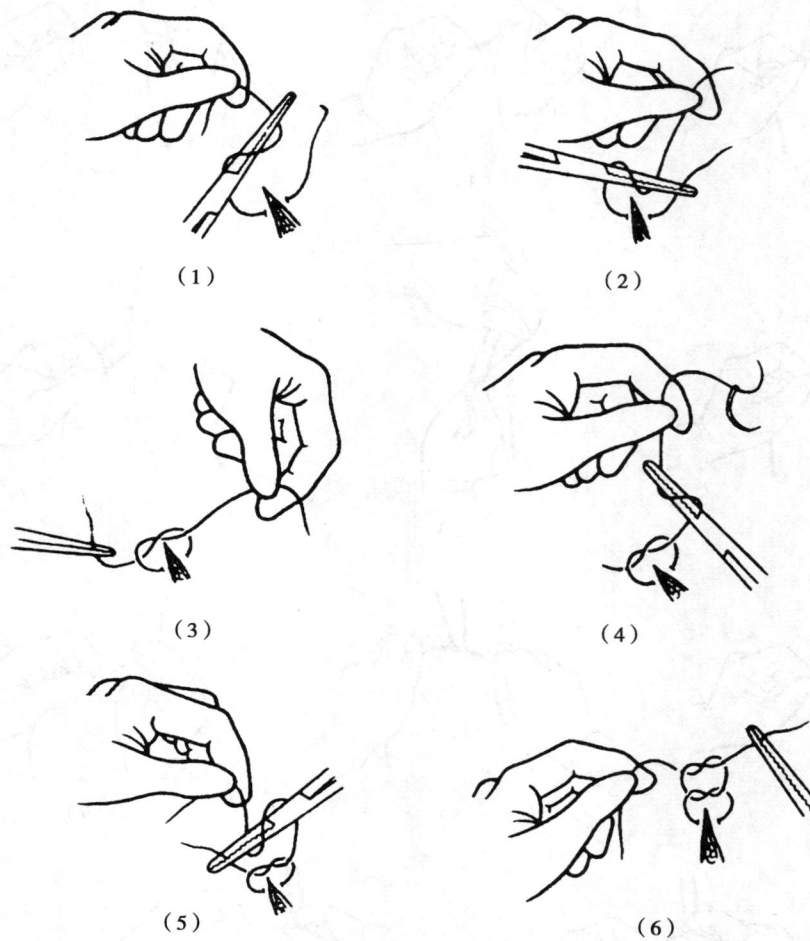

Fig.41   Instrument method of knot tying

3. Points of attention in knot tying

(1) When tying the knot, 3 points (two force points and the ligating point) should be in the same line, otherwise the ligated tissue may be torn or the knot is not tight.

(2) The two simple knots must be opposite to each other in square knot.

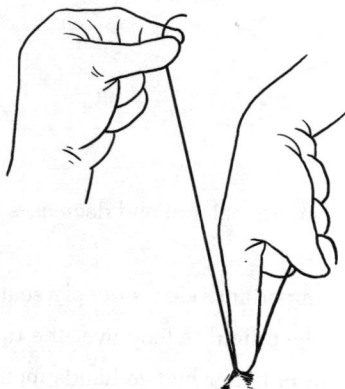

(3) In tightening the 2 simple knots, you have to cross your hands in one of them.

(4) Force exerted in two hands during manipulation should be even in making square knot.

(5) In tying a knot, the action should be gentle and the force used should be even. The ligature is tightened slowly to avoid rupture of the ligature resulting in rebleeding even massive hemorrhage.

(6) Qualified and proper sized suture material should be selected for ligation. If you soak the suture material in saline before ligation, the friction and the tensile strength will be increased making the ligature more secure.

Fig.42   Ligation of tissues in deep field

Section 5   Tissue Suturing

1. Basic principles of tissue suturing

(1) Tissues should be accurately identified and approximated layer by layer, interdigitating approximation will aggravate their dysfunction after healing.

(2) Approximate the tissues accurately. Distances between every 2 stitches should be even and appropriate and the strength used in tying should be moderate. Unduly wide or deep suture will lead to inversion of the edges of sutured tissue and uneven width or depth of sutures will result in improper approximation so as to affect sound healing. The width, depth and stitch distance of sutures are determined according to the thickness and toughness of the tissues and suture method selected.

(3) The tissues to be sutured should be able to bear the traction of sutures. Skin, muscular layer of mucosa, fascia, pleura, peritoneum, nerve sheath are strong enough to hold stitches while fat and muscle are usually weak and unable to hold stitches steadily.

(4) Don't tie sutures too tightly to prevent inhibition or cut of blood supply leading to delayed healing or even necrosis of the sutured tissues.

(5) Dead space should be avoided by secure approximation during suture. A dead space makes not only the edges of wound apart from each other, but offers a space for fluid collection which sometimes may lead to infection. All these will delay the healing of the wound. Don't suture the edges of a deep wound in a whole thickness manner instead of layer by layer. This is the best way to prevent dead space formation.

(6) Selection of suture materials used in different tissues depends on the nature of the tissue concerned. In tissues with little or no contamination, non-absorbable sutures are desirable. If there is marked contamination, it is better to use absorbable ones. Absorbable sutures are not used in ligation or suturing a large sized blood vessel to avoid possible postoperative bleeding following unexpected early absorption of the suture. In making sutures passing through mucosa of biliary tract or urinary bladder, absorbable ones are used to avoid stone formation in their lumens. Sutures in gastrointestinal wall are usually made for 2 layers, the inner layer of sutures that pass through the mucous membrane will not exist there for long time as the sutures will detach together with the inner layer of gastrointestinal wall which will slough down in few days; and therefore, non-absorbable sutures are not abandoned.

2. Suture methods

There are a lot of suture methods used in different situations. They are primarily subdivided into interrupted and continuous ones.

(1) Simple interrupted suture: it is the most common suture used to suture tissues like skin, subcutaneous tissue and fascia. Unduly wide or deep suture will lead to inversion of the edges of sutured tissue and uneven width or depth of sutures will result in improper approximation so as to affect sound healing (Fig.43).

(2) Double interrupted suture (figure of "8" suture): it may be used to suture strong tissues like aponeurosis, tendon, and

Fig.43   Simple interrupted suture

ligament. There are two kinds of double interrupted suture, in which the cross of "8" may appear superficial or deep to the sutured tissues (Fig.44).

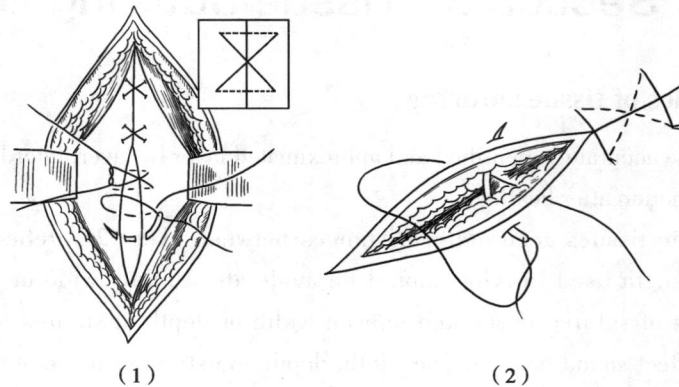

Fig.44   Figure of "8" suture
(1) cross of "8" situated superficially; (2) cross of "8" situated deeply

(3) Simple continuous suture: this is most commonly used in peritoneal suturing (Fig.45). It has the advantage of time saving, close approximation of tissues and bearing some hemostatic effect; but it leaves too much foreign body in the tissue, and the wound may totally disrupt once the suture is broken at one point in early postoperative period.

(4) Lock suture: it is similar to the simple continuous suture except that each stitch should be locked, i.e., passing the needle through the thread loop during suturing (Fig.46). The suture, when being pulled tightly, may have satisfactory hemostatic effect even superior to that of simple continuous suture. It also helps to prevent undesirable inversion of the wound edges during suturing.

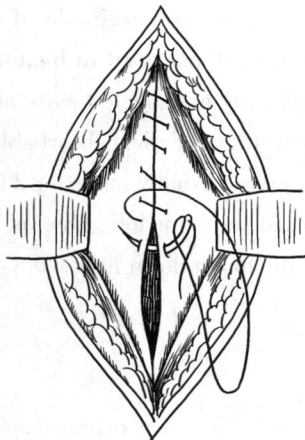

Fig.45   Simple continuous suture

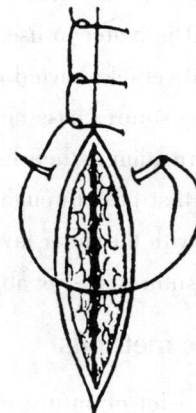

Fig.46   Lock suture

(5) Tension suture (retention suture): when an abdominal incision is closed under high tension or the patient's general condition is poor, 2–3 tension sutures are used to prevent possible disruption of the incision. Nylon and thick silk sutures are usually used to hold the whole layer of the abdominal wall (except peritoneum) on both sides of the incision together (Fig.47). A small rubber tube or a small role of gauze is padded under the ligature before ligation to prevent cutting of the skin by the suture when high tension appears. In addition, don't make the suture under high tension to prevent inhibition of blood supply.

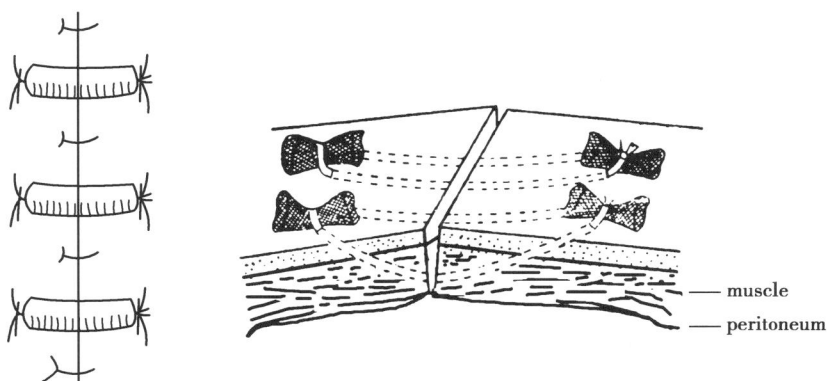

Fig.47   Tension suture

(6) Inverting sutures: the walls of gastrointestinal tract and urinary bladder are composed of several laminae or strata. The innermost stratum, the mucosa, refuses to heal when being approximated to each other. Therefore, inverting sutures are used in suturing gastrointestinal wall or bladder wall to prevent eversion of mucosa and to ensure sound healing of the wound. Otherwise, leakage of gastrointestinal content or urine (fistula formation) may result. A lot of inverting sutures will be recommended in the chapter of "Fundamental Principles of Gastrointestinal Operation".

(7) Everting sutures: this kind of suturing method is to evert the edge of the tissue to be sutured to keep its inner surface smooth. It is commonly used in repair or anastomosis of blood vessels to keep the inner surface of the vessel (intima) smooth and lessen the chance of thrombus formation (Fig.48). In suturing skin, which is loose and lack of elasticity, like scrotal skin, everting sutures may prevent inversion of the skin edges after suturing (Fig.49).

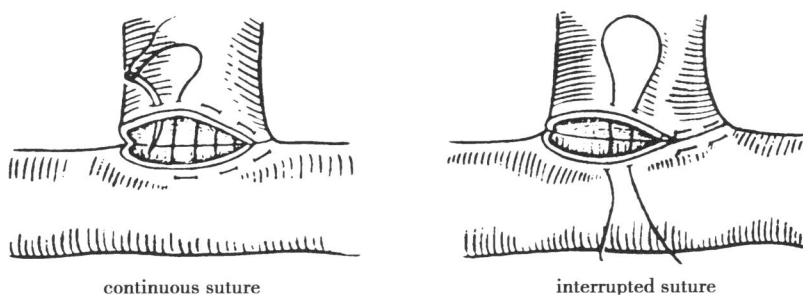

continuous suture   interrupted suture

Fig.48   Everting sutures in anastomosis of blood vessel

3. Points of attention in suture

(1) Any suture material, including the absorbable, is a foreign body to the tissue, which should be left in the tissue as little as possible. Use the least thick suture material, which is able to bear the tissue tension. Remnants of ligatures should be as short as possible. Use more interrupted sutures rather than continuous.

(2) There will be some inflammatory reaction in sutured tissues due to ischemia of the ligated tissue and the stimulation of

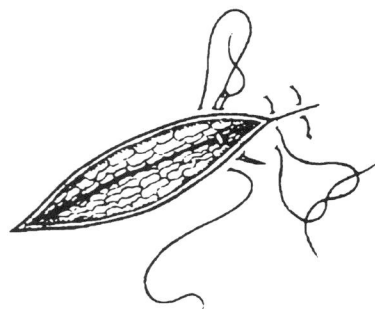

Fig.49   Everting sutures for wound of scrotal skin to prevent inversion of skin edges

suture material. Therefore, don't catch too much tissue during suturing.

(3) Approximate the tissues layer by layer accurately without dead space left which favors fluid collection, leading to delayed healing or even secondary infection.

(4) Ligate too tightly will inhibit blood supply and leading to delayed healing or even necrosis; while loose ligation will result in poor approximation of tissues and affecting sound healing too.

(5) Approximate tissues of the same stratum and of same nature accurately. Interposition of other tissues may lead to malunion and improper healing.

Section 6   Suture Cutting

1. Cutting after ligation

The length of the suture ends left after cutting, which depends on the quality and thickness of sutures, should be as short as possible without causing the knot to slip. It is better to leave the remnant of the suture about 1–2mm long for silk suture and 3–4mm for absorbable suture. In case of ligation of relatively large amount of tissues, large vessels or ligature bearing high tension, it is better to leave a longer remnant, for example, 2–3 mm in silk ligature.

After ligation, hold the double strands straight, slide the scissors down with one blade against the strands until it meets the knot and then rotate for an angle of 10°–45°, followed by cutting the strands (Fig.50). The remnant of the suture cut in such a way would usually be about 1–2mm long, it would be longer if the rotation angle is larger. To adjust the length of the remnant, you can, of course, to cut the suture at any point you desire under direct vision. Skin sutures are ordinarily removed several days postoperatively, a longer remnant about 1cm long is left for easier handling later.

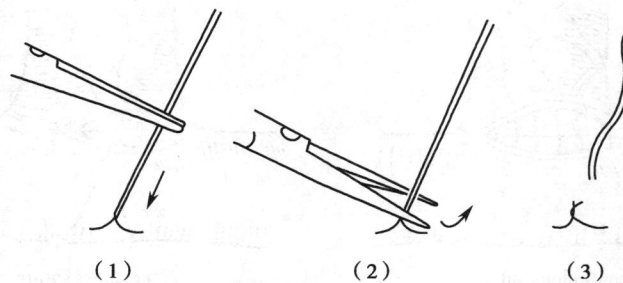

（1）   （2）   （3）

Fig.50   Cutting suture after ligation

2. Removal of skin suture

After healing of the wound, the skin sutures are removed routinely. The time of stitch removal depends on the systemic condition of the patient, healing capacity of the tissue, tension born by the wound and the nature of the suture material. Ordinary silk sutures are removed 4 to 5 days after operations for head, face or neck, 7 days after operations for abdomen and chest, 9 to 12 days after operations for limbs and 14 days for tension sutures. In aged, debilitated, malnourished patients, and operations at sites of poor blood circulation or periarticular area, stitch removal is usually postponed to at least 10 to 14 days after operation. Sometimes, the stitches may be removed at intervals. If there are signs of inflammation or infection, the stitches should be removed earlier or the wound is open for drainage when there is collection of pus.

The principle of removal of skin stitches is that the exposed segment of the suture is not allowed to be drawn into the skin to prevent from contamination.

Remove the dressings to expose the wound. The wound and the stitches are disinfected. Then, the remnants of the suture are picked and lifted up by forceps held in the left hand to show its imbedded part. Cut the imbedded part of the suture with a pair of scissors under the knot and then withdraw the suture out (Fig.51). The wound is disinfected once more and protected with sterile gauze.

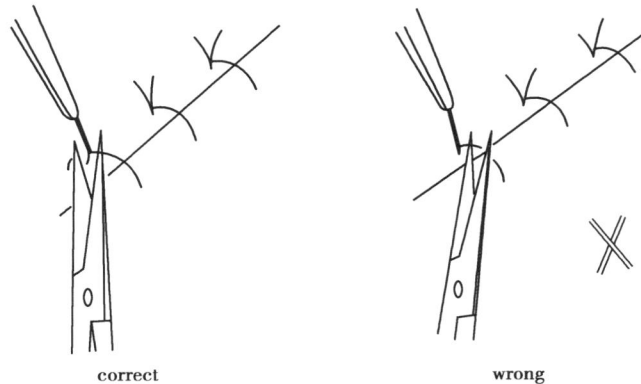

correct   wrong

Fig.51 Removal of skin stitches

Section 7 Dressing change

1. Introduction of dressing change

Dressing change is the generic term for further management of the wounds undergone preliminary treatment. This procedure includes evaluating and cleansing the wound properly, and replacing new dressings. It is an essential surgical technique for preventing and controlling infection of wounds, reducing the potential factors impacted on wounds repairing, hence promoting the wounds healing.

2. Purpose of dressing change

(1) Evaluating of the wounds: to clarify the necessity of further special treatment.

(2) Cleaning the wounds: to elicit the pus, necrotic tissues, exudates and foreign body, and keep the drainage tube open.

(3) Shortening the course of treatment: to initiate the regenerated epithelium and granulation tissue, thus accelerate the wounds healing and relieve the hypertrophic scars.

(4) Protecting the wounds: to wrap and fix the wound with fresh dressing to prevent progressive injury and contamination.

3. Indication of dressing change

(1) Take out stitches after wound healing.

(2) Loosen or remove the drainage tube.

(3) Remove exudate and stop bleeding from wounds.

(4) Remove the old dressing soaked by exudates, drainage and blood.

(5) Re-examine and evaluate the wounds.

4. Interval for dressing change

(1) Change dressing every 2–3 days for aseptic incision and wounds with primary suture.

(2) Change dressing 1–2 times per day or whenever necessary for heavy contaminated wounds or those with excessive exudates.

5. Steps of dressing change

(1) Preparation includes: wearing operating cap and mask, washing hands with soap thoroughly and preparing related items (i.e. fresh dressing, gloves, forceps, gauze, scissors, etc.)

(2) Remove old dressing

1) Tear the adhesive tape gently and remove it with external dressing.

2) Use aseptic forceps to remove drainage tube and internal dressing along the longitudinal axis of wounds (Fig.52). If adhesion occurred between internal layer and wounds, sterile physiological saline can be used to moisten the dressing first. Press one side of the wounds lightly with forceps and wet cotton ball sometimes may be helpful for removing the adhesive internal dressing.

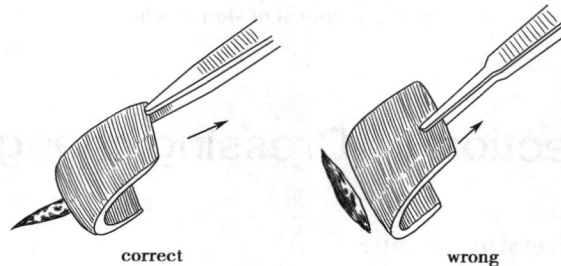

correct   wrong

Fig.52   Method of dressing removal

(3) Disinfection of the local skin around the wounds: use disinfection solution (75% medical alcohol or 5% povidone iodine solution) to disinfect the skin twice from inside to outside, to be sure not to flow the solution into wounds (Fig.53). The extent of disinfection should exceed the gauze covered on the wounds. The operator can absorb or remove it by sterilized dry cotton ball before skin disinfection if too much pus present.

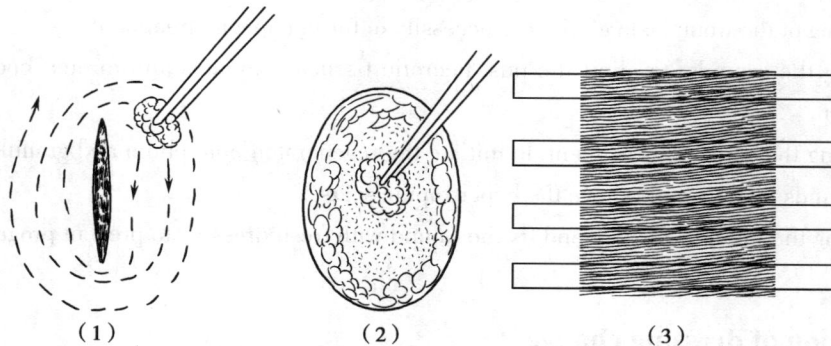

(1)   (2)   (3)

Fig.53   Dressing change

(1) Disinfection of the local skin around the wounds; (2) Clean the the wounds;
(3) Cover the wounds & fix the dressing

(4) Clean the wounds

1) Clean and remove the liquefied products, exudates, necrotic tissues gently on the surface of the wounds

with sterilized cotton ball and physiological saline (do not clean it roughly in order to prevent regenerated epithelium and granulation tissue from injury) (Fig.53); too much solution in cotton ball may lead to local skin contamination due to pus flow-out instead of cleaning the exudates effectively; do not clean the internal side of wounds with the cotton ball used for the skin.

2) Avoid dropping of cotton ball into those large and deep wound cavities.

3) Wash the wound cavity with 3% hydrogen peroxide solution, 0.1% bromogeramine and sterile physiological saline orderly.

4) Remove the liquefied metabolites, necrotic tissues, exudates and foreign body thoroughly.

5) Cover the wounds with either vaseline gauze, anti-inflammatory ointment or sterile saline drainage strip after re-disinfection of the skin according to the wound condition (Fig.53). The thickness of the dressing depends on the conditions of wound stages, amount of exudates and environmental temperature, usually at least 8 layers.

(5) Use adhesive tape or bandage to fix the dressing with low pressure (Fig.53). Adhesive tape should be vertical to the longitudinal axis of body, and the length is always 2–2.5 times of dressing.

(Li Yingcun   Kong Lingquan)

Chapter 4

Requirements in Animal Experiments

By animal experiments in a dog surgery laboratory, the students are expected to experience the general concepts and principles of surgical operations as well as to practice and familiarize with the surgical manipulations. Dog is selected as the experimental animal to perform some surgical operations imitating those done in human beings.

Section 1   Requirements in Dog Surgery Laboratory

1. Put on your work gown, cap and mask before entering the laboratory. Those who join the operative team must have their hand scrubbed, and have the operative gown and gloves on. Complying with the aseptic principles or regulations strictly and conscientiously. Redisinfection must be done when contaminated.

2. Keep the operating region clean and in order, clear away the animal excreta in time. The student should be responsible for the sanitation and hygiene of the laboratory. Clean the laboratory after experiment.

3. Keep solemn and quiet, out of sport and noise.

4. Take good care of the instruments, and save supplies. The instruments should be counted before operation, washed, wiped and counted again after operation. You have to pay for any lost and damaged instruments.

5. Take good care of the animals and refrain from making fun of them. Pay attention to your safety, refrain from injury by the animal.

6. Each operative team is composed of 5–7 members, who should share out the work and cooperate with one another to accomplish the operation.

7. Before operation, the chief operator, anesthetist and first assistant in the team are responsible for anesthesia and cleaning and shaving of the skin of the operative field. After operation, they have to carry the animal to the animal house. Instrument nurse, first assistant and second assistant, if any, in the team should wash the instruments, dry them and smear with oil before returning them to the teacher on duty. The running nurse is responsible for the sanitation around the operating table.

8. The task of different members in the team during operation.

Chief operator: He is the chief manipulator standing usually on the right side of the animal. His duty is to dominate the operation, make incision and exposure, hemostasis, ligation and suturing. He or she should write an operating note after operation, which should be handed to the teacher for revisement before next experiment.

First assistant: Being a chief cooperator in the team, he or she is responsible to check the instruments and to sterilize and lay towels or drapes over the operative field right before the operation. During operation, he stands on the left side of the animal just opposite the chief operator to help him or her to make every procedure carried out smoothly, such as checking bleeding and making ligation, offering satisfactory exposure of the operative field, etc.

Second assistant: He or she occupies a position on the left side of the operator. His or her main duty is to hold the retractors to expose the operative field well, to cut excess threads following ligation and suture, and to clean off the blood in the field.

Instrument nurse: He or she stands on the right or caudal side of the animal. His or her duty is to sort and count the instruments including sutures and dressing before operation, supply them in time during operation and check them again after operation. He or she is also responsible for keeping the operating region clean and in order.

Anesthetist: He or she occupies a position at the cephalic side of the animal. He or she is responsible for keeping the animal in a satisfactory anesthetic state for smooth operation, monitoring the vital signs (pulse rate, respiratory rate, blood pressure, etc.) of the animal and manipulating the fluid infusion or transfusion.

Circulating nurse: He or she makes rounds around the operative table to supply any extra needs of the team and to communicate the team with the surrounding if necessary.

Section 2   Management of Dog for Experiment

1. Holding the dog

When you are going to perform an animal operation, a dog will be supplied by the animal center for each operative team. By the help of the laboratory technicians you can bring the animal from the animal house to the laboratory. The unrestrained and struggling animal may be controlled by the use of a steel clamp (Fig.54) or a lasso (Fig.55) to hitch it up. Under restriction, the mouth of the dog is now covered by a mouth casing (Fig.56) or bounded with a tape (Fig.57). After that, the limbs of the animal are bundled up. Now the animal is ready for anesthesia.

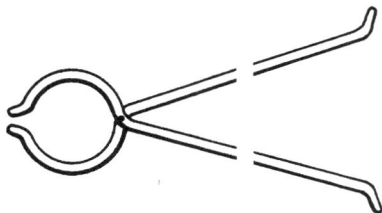

Fig.54   A clamp to hold a dog

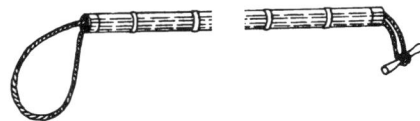

Fig.55   A case to hitch a dog

2. Anesthesia

Bring the restricted dog to the laboratory, weigh it first in a scale. If the dog is restless making the weighing difficult, it is better to weigh it with some person together. The dog's weight can be obtained by subtracting that person's weight from the total reading. After weighing, calculate the amount of anesthetics required and give it to the animal through the route you select.

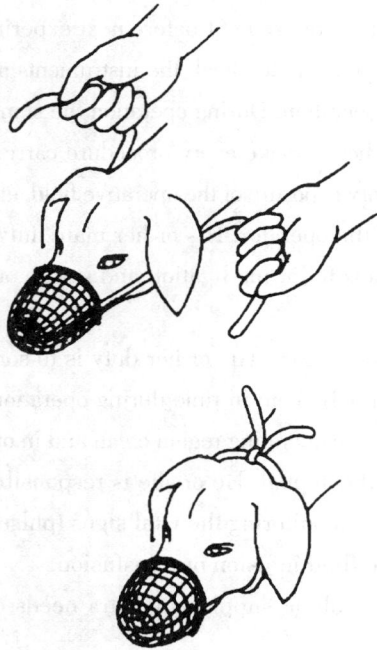

Fig.56   The dog's mouth with a
          mouth casing on

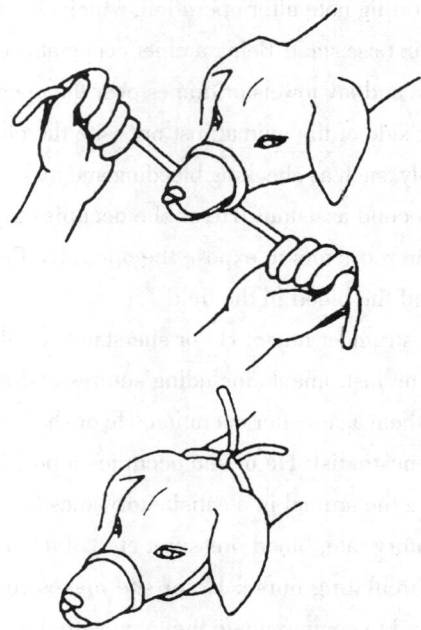

Fig.57   The dog's mouth bounded by tape

For dog operation, general anesthesia is better used. There are a lot of anesthetic agents to be used, our first choice is 2.5% sodium pentobarbital solution, given intraperitoneally, intravenously or intramuscularly in a dose of 25–30mg/kg body weight. The animal will be narcotized in 10–15 minutes after intraperitoneal injection and the anesthesia will last for 3–4 hours by a single dose of the drug. 2.5% sodium pentothal in a dose of 25mg/kg body weight by similar routes is another choice. If given intravenously, its narcotizing effect appears more quickly, but the effect last only about 45 minutes. It can be used as a supplement to pentobarbital anesthesia when the effect of the latter is over before the operation is finished.

If you give the anesthetics intravenously, you can inject it into the cephalic vein or saphenous vein of the dog. The former is situated over the anterior aspect of its fore limbs (Fig.58), and the latter over the lateral aspect of its hind limb (Fig.59). Inject 2/5 to 1/2 of the narcotics first and then give it slowly. Stop your injection when signs of narcosis begin to appear.

After narcosis, the dog is placed on the operative table, pull its tongue out of its mouth to keep air passage free. The anesthetist begins now to monitor its physiological status.

If supplementary narcotics are required, it can be given through the veins over the tongue of the animal.

3. Preparation of skin over the operative field

The hairs over the skin of he operative area should be removed after the animal is under anesthesia by shaving or the use of depilatory agent.

(1) Shaving: though old fashioned, it is effective when properly manipulated. It is important that shaving should be done carefully without injuring the skin. The animal is fixed on the operating table with the operative area well exposed. The long hairs are cut with a pair of scissors first. Don't pick up the hairs during cut; otherwise, the skin may be injured because it may be lifted by pulling the hairs, as the subcutaneous tissue is loose. Remnants of hairs are then soaked with soap water and shaved.

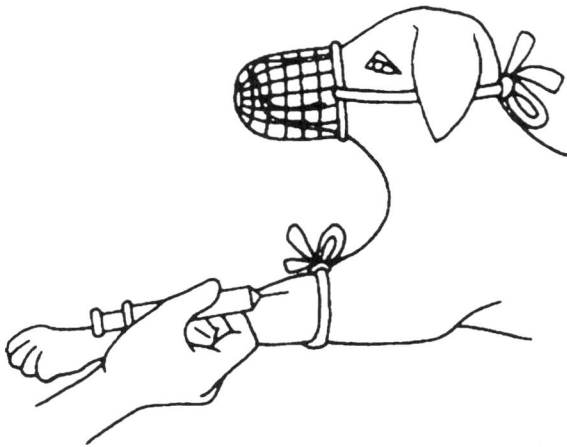

Fig.58   Cephalic vein injection in fore
limb of the dog

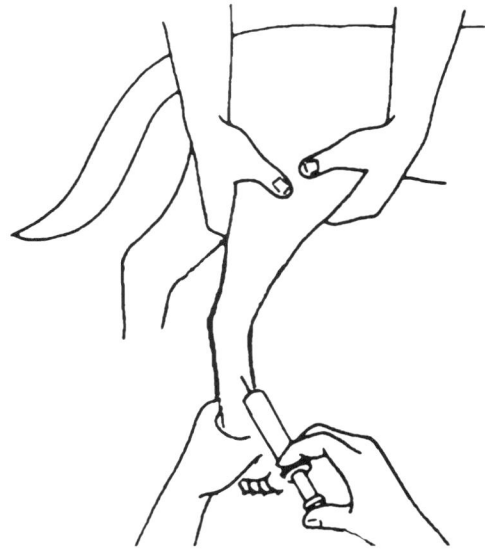

Fig.59   Saphenous vein injection in hind
limb of the dog

(2) Removal of hairs by depilatory agent: this is easy to manipulated, complete depilation is usually accompanied with no injury to the skin, but the solution is foul and offensive. If improperly manipulated, it may lead to injury of the skin.

The commonly used depilatory agents are sodium sulfide, barium sulfide and arsenic sulfide, of which sodium sulfide is the most common one with high solubility. A 15% solution is prepared with hot water of 50℃ right before using. Use a sponge forceps holding a pledget of gauze soaked with this solution to smear the skin of operating area, one or two minutes later, the hairs will turn sticky and detach from the skin. Wipe the detached hairs with a piece of gauze. Finally, the skin is rinsed with large amount of water and dried.

In addition to the above mentioned management before operation, there are some after care you have to perform. At the end of the operation the skin should be carefully sutured. There is no need to pack or cover the wound with gauze for the animal will reject all the dressings when anesthesia is over. Bring the animal back to the animal house and you are required to follow the postoperative course of the animal as frequently as possible in early postoperative period. Be familiar with your animal and bring the same animal to the laboratory later for further experiments.

(Li Hao   Kong Lingquan)

Chapter 5

Venesection

1. Indications

(1) When a patient requires emergent infusion of fluid while there is difficulty in venepuncture, for instance, in case of shock, severe dehydration and profuse bleeding with superficial veins collapsed.

(2) It is desired to keep a fluent infusion passage for a relatively long duration as in major operation.

(3) A patient is expected to have repeated or persistent intravenous drip, like hemodialysis and parenteral nutrition by intravenous drip.

(4) When certain diagnostic or therapeutic procedures performed through veins, like cardiac catheterization and measurement of central venous pressure, are expected.

2. Selection of veins

Nearly all superficial veins of human limbs may serve for venesection, of which great saphenous vein is most commonly selected, for its relatively constant anatomical relation. Others like cephalic vein and basilic vein are also selected frequently. Infusion of long duration, hypertonic glucose or certain drug may irritate the intima of vein leading to aseptic phlebitis or even venous thrombosis and resulting in venous occlusion. Therefore, it is suggested to select the distal segment of a vein in priority so that the proximal part of it can be used if another venesection is required.

3. Surgical procedures (take great saphenous vein as sample)

(1) Search for the great saphenous vein at the anterosuperior aspect of the medial melleolus of ankle. Sterilize the operative field with tincture iodine and alcohol, followed by draping an aseptic towel with a hole over it.

(2) After being anesthetized locally, a longitudinal incision about 1.5cm to 2.5cm is made close to the vein.

(3) After opening the skin, dissect the subcutaneous tissues to expose the great saphenous vein with a mosquito or small curved hemostat along the vessel and a segment of it about 1.5cm long is isolated from the surrounding tissues (Fig.60).

(4) Two segments of No.4 silk suture are passed under the isolated vein with a clamp. Tie the distal segment of suture to occlude the vein. Don't cut the silk after tying, for it can be used to tract the vein in the following procedure. Leave the proximal segment of silk alone without tying it temporarily (Fig.61).

(5) Pull the distal segment of suture to stabilize the vein and make a small oblique incision on the vein proximal to the ligation. To prevent cutting through the vessel, an injection needle is allowed to pass through the vessel transversely and then cut the vascular wall against the needle. Connect a plastic tube with beveled

tip to a syringe filled with physiological saline. Insert the tube, with the bevel of its tip facing downward, into the vein through the cut opening on its wall. A back flow of blood followed by free infusion of the saline without resistance and leakage suggest that the intubation is successful (Fig.62 and Fig.63).

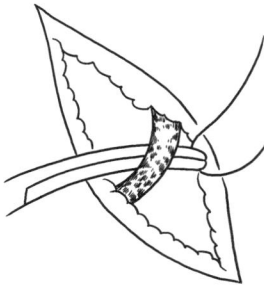

Fig.60　Isolation of great saphenous vein

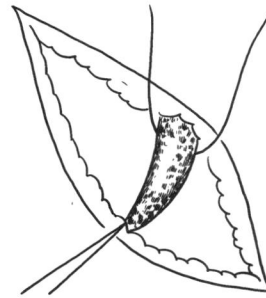

Fig.61　Ligation of the distal part of the isolated vein

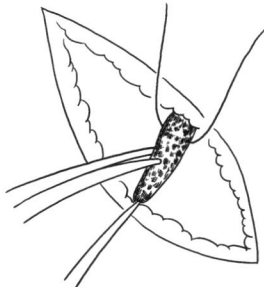

Fig.62　Making a small cut on the wall of the vein

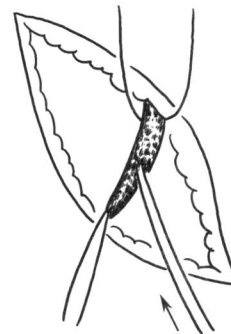

Fig.63　Inserting a plastic tube into the vein

(6) The proximal suture laid under the vein previously is tied now tightly to snare the vein containing the plastic tube (Fig.64).

(7) Disconnect the syringe and the end of plastic tube is connected to the infusion system as quickly as possible to start the infusion without air entering into the system.

(8) Suture the skin with cutting needle interruptedly. One of the sutures is allowed to encircle the exposed plastic tube to prevent it from sliding away.

(9) Adjust the rate of infusion.

4. Points of attention

(1) After intubation, if the saline doesn't flow or flow unsmoothly, the following conditions should be considered:

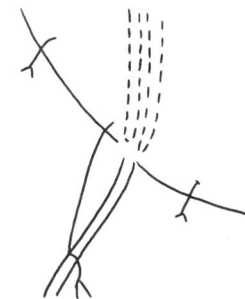

Fig.64　Ligation of the proximal part of the incised vein and suture of the skin

1) The proximal suture around the tube is too tight. Cut it and repeat the ligation.

2) The plastic tube is inserted into the dissecting wall of the vein, so the saline is infused with resistance or leakage. It requires reintubation.

3) The vein may show spasm by irritation of the tube, it can be relieved by hot compress or infusion of 1−2ml of 0.25% procaine.

(2) When leakage appears, the following conditions should be considered:

1) The proximal suture of the vein is not tight enough. Ligate it again.

2) The tip of plastic tube in the vein penetrates vascular wall. Make another venesection at a more proximal site.

5. Postoperative treatment

(1) Plastic tube may slip out of the vein for patient's restlessness. Secure fixation of the tube after operation is required.

(2) At the end of infusion, cut the fixation suture and withdraw the tube out of the vein accompanied by pressing the wound for 1 to 2 minutes.

【 Practice 】

Fix a dog on the operating table in supine position with its both hind limbs stretched to same side. Search for the saphenous vein in the lateral side of the leg and make a venesection by the above mentioned procedures and principles of incision and suture. Attention: Dog has only one set of saphenous vein over each leg.

(Kong Lingquan)

Chapter 6

Deep vein catheterization

1. Indication

(1) When the patient requires long time infusion and the peripheral vein is difficult to be punctured.

(2) A patient is expected to have repeated or persistent intravenous drip, such as high concentration, high stimulus parenteral nutrition and chemotherapeutic solution.

(3) The critically ill patients require rescue, such as shock patient needs large amount of infusion, vasoactive agent and blood sampling.

(4) To monitor the central venous pressure.

(5) A patient requires hematodialysis and plasmapheresis.

(6) Using as the way for interventional operation.

(7) Contraindication: thrombogenesis in the proximal or distal part of the vein for puncture or infection in the puncture area.

2. Selection of veins

(1) Internal jugular vein.

(2) Subclavian vein.

(3) Femoral vein.

3. Surgical procedures (femoral vein catheterization)

(1) Communication between doctors and patients, get the agreement for the procedure. Essential preoperative examination, such as: blood coagulation function test, blood routine test for platelet evaluation, etc.

(2) Preparation of perineal skin.

(3) Relevant material preparation, such as caps, gown, masks, gloves, catheter insertion devices, disinfectant, 2% lidocaine, heparin sodium solution, injector, needle and aseptic dressing, etc.

(4) Selection of insertion site (Fig.65).

Position: keep the thigh in abduction and external rotation of 30° –45° .

Punctual point: 2–3cm below the inguinal ligament and 1–2cm inside to the femoral artery with palpated pulse.

The angle between the needle and skin: 30° –45° (Fig.66).

The punctual direction: toward to the umbilicus.

The depth of puncture: about 2–4cm and different with the degree of the patient's obesity.

(5) Sterilize the operative field with povidone-iodine or tincture iodine and alcohol, followed by draping with an aseptic towel.

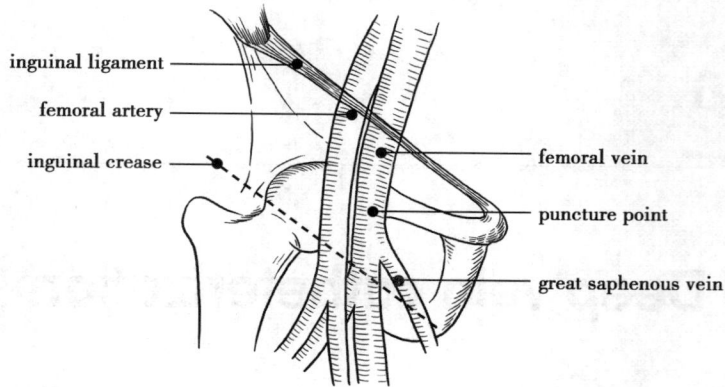

Fig.65   The anatomy of femoral vein

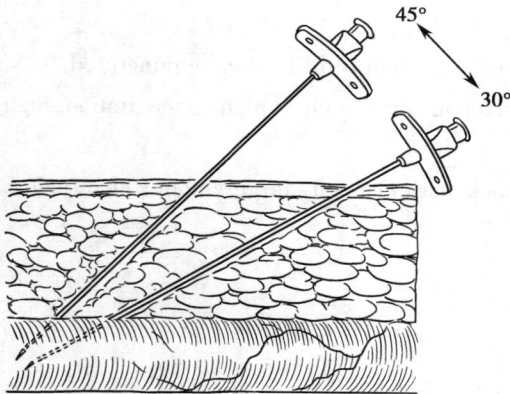

Fig.66   The angle in the procedure of puncture

(6) Local anesthesia and positioning: using 2% lidocaine; while injecting the lidocaine, the procedures are as follows: inject-withdrawing (no blood)-inject-withdrawing (dark red blood, means the tip of needle in the vein), and the next puncture step can be done through the above direction and position.

(7) Following the key point which is indicated as above. An incision about 2mm in length is made in the puncture area of the skin. Slowly advance the needle while gently withdrawing plunger of the syringe. While the puncture is being done, the plunger must be kept with negative pressure. When needle is inserted into the venous wall, the feeling of break-through can be felt. Then, move away the injector. It suggests that the needle is in the artery when sprays out bright red blood, and in the vein when drip out dark red blood.

(8) When the needle is confirmed to be inserted into the vein, send the guide wire into the vein about 20cm through the needle. Then move away the needle, and set the catheter into the vein along the guide wire (Seldinger technique).

(9) After that, pull out the guide wire. Then the catheter can be fixed and covered by sterile gauze.

4. Points of attention

(1) All the operation must be performed in sterile.

(2) It indicates that the needle is in the artery when sprays out bright red blood. The needle must be pulled out and the puncture point must be pressed over 5 minutes.

(3) More than 3 times repeated puncture should be avoided. If there is difficulty, the puncture should better be done under the guidance of ultrasound.

(4) After puncture, X-ray should be used to confirm the location of the catheter.

(Wang Xuehu)

Chapter 7

Débridement

1. General considerations

Every traumatic wound is inevitably contaminated by bacteria and pathogens in the environment. It may contain foreign bodies and sometimes some of the damaged tissues may be devitalized. These may lead to infection of the wound. The severity and variety of infection differ from different environments and conditions of the trauma. The purpose of débridement, the primary surgical management of a traumatic wound, is to get rid of the contaminated tissues, foreign bodies and devitalized tissues to prevent the patient from developing infection of his wound. A débrided or cleaned wound is usually sutured to promote healing of the wound by first intention. Heavily contaminated wounds and those débrided unsatisfactorily are better left open without suturing them. Wounds already infected are not subjected to débridement. Otherwise, infection will spread.

2. Principles of surgical treatment

(1) Preoperative treatment: examine the patient carefully, quickly and comprehensively to learn whether there are any severe or compound injuries which have to be managed in priority.

(2) Pay special attention to prevent and treat shock, bleeding, dehydration or other major complications.

(3) Débridement should be performed as early as possible after injury if the patient's condition allows. Bacteria in the contaminated wound proliferate quickly and will invade the surroundings even the distant tissues after few hours. Therefore, the earlier the wound is débrided, the better will be the result. We commonly perform débridement within 6–8 hours after injury. By so doing, most of the fresh wounds will heal by first intention instead of getting infected, because there are only limited amount of bacteria localized in the wound, instead of invading the surrounding tissues. After that time limit, the chance of wound infection will increase progressively, and the operation is abandoned. However, débridement may be done in certain exceptional occasions after 6 to 8 hours; for examples, wound in craniofascial region where the blood circulation is excellent, cut wound by very sharp instrument leaving few devitalized tissue, relatively clean environment with little contamination, early administration of preventive antibiotics after injury. In these occasions, débridement can be done in 8 to 12 hours after injury. On the contrary, if the wound is heavily contaminated or the bacteria are highly virulent, infection may develop in 4 to 6 hours. Under these conditions, only simple cleansing of the wound is done instead of débridement. Whether a wound is sutured after débridement depends on several factors. Suturing can be done for wounds of short duration, without heavy contamination or satisfactorily debrided; otherwise, leave the wound open without suturing. When you are facing a difficult choice, you may suture the deep tissues only, while postpone the suture of the skin and subcutaneous tissue or you may suture the wound but leaving a drain in it.

War wounds are usually treated as infected wound, especially deep ones, because they are usually severely contaminated and easy to develop anaerobic infection; in addition, the injury is usually extensive and patient's systemic condition is usually poor.

3. Procedures of débridement

(1) Cover the wound with aseptic gauze and shave the surrounding hairs with gloved hands. Scrub the shaved skin with an aseptic brush and liquid soap gently. The scrubbed area should be large enough. After that, wash the scrubbed skin with profuse amount of saline but prevent the water flowing into the wound. If necessary, change another aseptic gauze to cover the wound, rescrub and wash the surrounding skin once more.

(2) Take away the gauze covering the wound, rinse the wound with sterile saline or 1 : 1000 bromogeramine, and take away any free foreign body located superficially at the same time. If there is active bleeding in the wound, ligate it or catch it with a clamp temporarily. Dry the wound and the surrounding skin with dry gauze.

(3) Change another pair of gloves and sterilize the surrounding skin of the wound with tincture iodine and 75% alcohol or 1 : 1000 bromogeramine (attention: tincture iodine and alcohol are not allowed to touch the wound). Aseptic towels are draped after sterilization.

(4) Examine the wound carefully to find its extent and the structures damaged. Clear away foreign bodies and blood clots in the wound again. Rinse it again with normal saline.

(5) A stripe of marginal skin about 0.2–0.5cm in width around the wound and all the contaminated, crushed or contused, or devitalized tissues, superficial and deep, should be removed. In cutting with a scalpel, it is suggested to keep one side of the blade always facing the contaminated tissues and the other side facing the healthy. To manage a deep wound, the wound can be extended or the deep fascia can be cut to offer a better exposure. Tissues are considered devitalized when they are dark red or grayish white and do not bleed when being cut. The devitalized muscles don't contract when they are stimulated. If there is a tract in damaged tissue, open it and clear away all the blood clots and nercotic tissues. Neglected tract may serve as a focus of infection later.

(6) A contaminated tendon or nerve should never be cut, but the surrounding connective tissue or the overlying sheath can be cleared away. If broken or sectioned, it should be repaired or anastomosed. In case the contamination is severe or the defect (or gap) is too large making the primary anastomosis difficult, you can leave a segment of silk to each broken end as a mark for recognizing the broken structure in a secondary operation later. Minor blood vessels can be ligated when ruptured, while injured major blood vessels should be repaired or anastomosed. If vascular grafting is required, it is performed only in cases without heavy contamination and the débridement is satisfactory. In bone injuries, small free fragments of bone can be cleared away, but large free fragments and fragments attached with soft tissues should be reserved to avoid delayed union, nonunion or malunion. Ruptured articular capsule is trimmed after clearing away the blood clots and foreign bodies. The articular cavity is rinsed with saline, and then repairs the ruptured capsule by catgut with no drainage. 200 000 to 400 000 units of penicillin and 0.5 to 1.0 gram of streptomycin should be injected intra-articularly to prevent from infection. If there is a large defect in the capsule, fix the surrounding fascia or muscles over the joint. Don't leave the articular cartilage exposed. Otherwise the cartilage may undergo necrosis and initiate joint infection.

(7) Thoroughly rinse the wound with saline once more after complete hemostasis, then close it by full thickness sutures (for superficial wound) or layer by layer (for deep wound). A drain may be left in the closed wound for 24 to 48 hours in case of imperfect débridement or unsatisfactory hemostasis. If the wound is left

open, vaseline gauze or dry gauze may be used to fill the wound cavity loosely for drainage. Finally, the wound is dressed with sterile gauze. The drain left in the wound should be removed in 24–48 hours postoperatively.

4. Postoperative management

(1) Put the wounded limb at functional position to avoid impairment of function. Raise the distal end of the limb a little higher to help the venous back flow and to lessen or prevent the swelling of the limb.

(2) Observe the local and systemic changes closely. Give appropriate systemic treatment to those heavily wounded.

(3) Infection should be prevented and treated energetically. Be alert to the development of tetanus and gas gangrene. Inject 1500 units TAT intramuscularly routinely to prevent tetanus. Systemic antibiotic treatment should be given to patients with their wounds severely contaminated.

In short, the purpose of débridement is to lessen the chance of wound infection and to promote healing by first intention. Therefore, débridement must be done carefully with least operative trauma and functional impairment.

【 Practice 】

A dog is fixed in its lateral position on the operating table. After the teacher makes a wound on its buttock or thigh, proceed to perform débridement according to the above principles and procedures.

(Kong Lingquan)

Chapter 8

Incision and Drainage

As a kind of common surgical disease, abscess can result from many reasons like infection. Incision and drainage for abscess is a basic surgical operating technique.

1. Indications

(1) After the abscess has formed, obvious fluctuation of enclosed mass can be found on palpation on its surface. And the pus can be proved to be existent in superficial abscess through puncture, while further puncture or ultrasound is needed in deeper abscess.

(2) Abscesses in special sites, such as cellulitis, infection of hands and abscesses in other special sites, need to be drained and decompressed actively even when the fester abscess has not formed obviously to reduce infection and risk.

2. Surgical Procedures

(1) Disinfection and draping:

Areas of disinfection: abscess area and at least 10–15cm from the edge of abscess.

Orders of disinfection: inside-out in concentric disinfection for unruptured abscess; out-inside in centrifugal disinfection for ruptured abscess, finally to the ruptured area. Use iodine tincture and alcohol for regular disinfection, and then drape with aseptic towel.

(2) Anesthesia: Make local infiltration anesthesia along the planned incision with 0.2%–0.5% of lidocaine (Fig.67).

(3) Abscess puncture: the needle may be kept in the abscess cavity as an incision mark if the abscess is deep and difficult to be positioned after extracting the pus through local puncture. The pus should be routinely sent for cultivation and drug sensitivity test.

(4) Incision and drainage: generally, incise the area with obvious fluctuation. The incision should be parallel to the directions of vessels and nerves, which should be kept away in case of injury. Find the abscess after incising skin and subcutaneous tissue, then make a vertical cutting at the wall of abscess, or use hemostatic forceps to dissect it to eliminate the pus. Then put finger into the deep cavity to separate the fibrous septum and enlarge the incision to make the drain unobstructed. (Fig.68–Fig.71).

(5) Set drainage: vaseline gauze or cigarette drain may be used to drain according to the size and length of the abscess (Fig.72). Make a contra-aperture drainage at both sides of the abscess if the abscess cavity is large and deep. Active bleeding site should be ligated. For oozing of blood or unobvious bleeding, vaseline gauze should be used to tamp the cavity tightly in certain order, and then further controlled by compression bandage. Take out the vaseline gauzes within 2 to 3 days after operation, and then change them with saline

gauze. Gradually pull out and cut the drainage in accordance with the reducing of pus and the narrowing of abscess cavity, until complete healing of the wound.

Fig.67　Local anesthesia

Fig.68　Making an incision

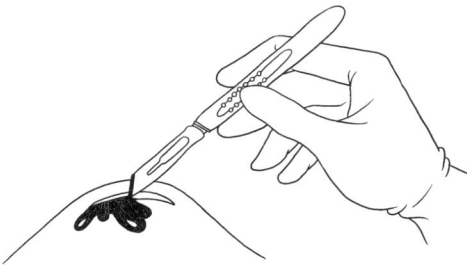

Fig.69　Open the abscess incision

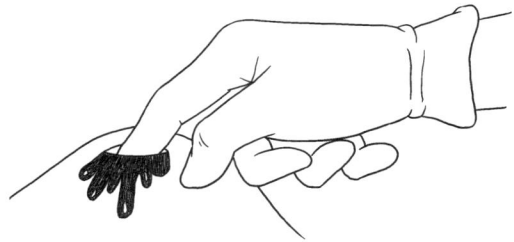

Fig.70　The finger explores the abscess cavity and separates the septa

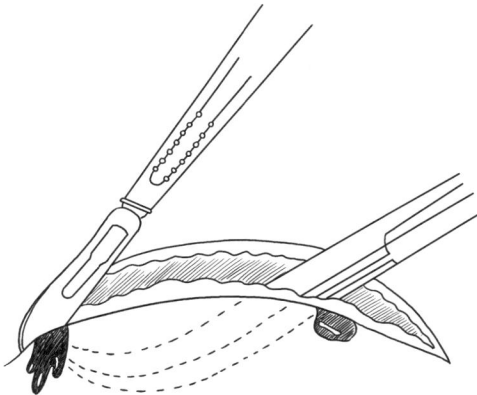

Fig.71　The full-length open of the abscess

Fig.72　Cavity filled with gauze

3. Points of attention

(1) Incise the area with obvious fluctuation, and never dissect forcefully in the cavity, in case of vessel, nervous tissue or other organ injury.

(2) Puncture should be done to confirm the position and depth before incising deeper abscess.

(3) In order to make unobstructed drainage, the incision of abscess should be long enough and in lower place.

【Practice】

After anesthesia, fix the rabbit on the operating table. Firstly the teacher inject 20–30ml of 30% fat emulsion to the dorsal site of the rabbit subcutaneously. Then the students operate according to the above steps.

（Ran Liang　Kong Lingquan）

Chapter 9

Nail Removal

1. Indications

(1) Empyema below the nail, ingrown toe with infection, traumatic hemorrhage under the nail or the nail separated from its bed, intractable nail fungus.

(2) The adjuvant therapy for hemangioma under the nail, the periungual wart and the subungual exostosis.

2. Contraindications

(1) The patient with bleeding tendency.

(2) The patient with serious visceral disease.

(3) The patient with scar diathesis.

(4) The patient with psychosis.

(5) The patient with inflammatory skin diseases such as chronic radioactive dermatitis, purulent skin disease, recurrent herpes simplex, acne in acute inflammatory stage, dry skin pigmentation disease, etc.

(6) The patient with vitiligo in the active stage.

3. Anesthetization

Nerve block anesthesia is performed in the root of finger or toe. Firstly, inject the needle intracutaneously and transfuse a little amount of 2% lidocaine to form a hillock in the dorsal of the finger or toe root, then penetrate vertically to phalanx and inject 0.5ml of 2% lidocaine, then to both insides of the finger with each injection of 0.5–1ml of 2% lidocaine, to make the local soft tissue swelling (Fig.73).

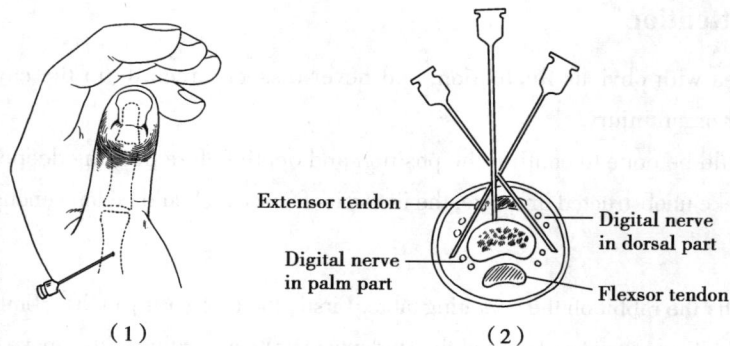

Extensor tendon
Digital nerve in dorsal part
Digital nerve in palm part
Flexor tendon

(1)   (2)

Fig.73   Nerve block anesthesia in fingers or toes root

(1) Position where the needle penetrates; (2) Direction in which the needle injects.

4. Surgical procedures

(1) Sterilize the hands or feet to wrist or ankle with tincture iodine and alcohol in conventional way and drape an aseptic towel with a hole over it, then anesthesize according to the above method.

(2) Tie up the root of finger or toe with rubber band which is clamped by the hemostatic forceps to prevent bleeding and prolong the anesthesia effect (Fig.74).

(3) The performer holds the tip part of the suffering finger or toe with his left thumb and index finger to fix it so as to manipulate it easily, and to control bleeding at the same time. Stab the sharp knife into the interface between nail and skin in the nail root, then separate the skin from the nail, and make a longitudinal incision of the skin on both sides of the nail root.

(4) Then stab the sharp knife to the interface between nail and its bed to separate the nail from its bed along the nail inner side.

(5) After the nail is seperated completely, clamp the nail side with hemostatic forceps and scroll the nail to the other side to remove the nails from its bed.

(6) After making sure that there is no nail residue, cover the nail bed with vaseline gauze and dress the finger or toe with a sterile gauze (Fig.75).

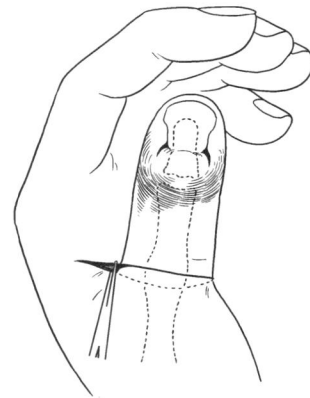

Fig.74 Tying up the finger root with rubber band clamped by hemostatic forceps

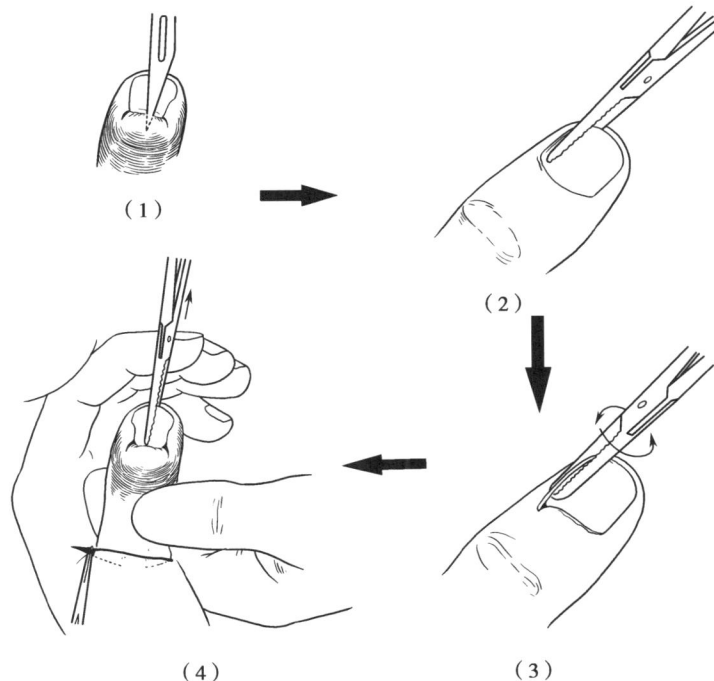

(1)

(2)

(3)

(4)

Fig.75 Nail removal steps

(1) fixing the finger; separate and cut the skin of nail root; (2) separation of the nail from its bed;

(3) scrolling the nail; (4) pulling out the nail and checking whether the residual is left.

5. Postoperative treatment

(1) Dressing change should be done daily until the wound healing for the infective wound and after 5 to 7

days for aseptic wound.

(2) The patients suspicious for a bacterial infection around the nail should be administrated antibiotics for 5 to 7 days postoperatively.

6. Points of attention

(1) No adrenaline should be added to lidocaine, otherwise it may cause the finger or toe arteriospasm which can lead to the necrosis of the finger or toe.

(2) When tying up the root of finger or toe with rubber band to prevent bleeding, the rubber band should not be looped in the finger or toe root in order to prevent its failure removal postoperatively which will cause the necrosis of the finger or toe.

(3) When separate the skin from nail in the nail root with a sharp knife, attention should paid not to make the skin damage to avoid the nail deformity born from the eponychium in the future. When separation of nail bed surface, the blade should be close to the nail, pointing to the back of the nail, to prevent damaging the nail bed. After pulling the nail, if the nail bed is not flat, it should be scraped flat gently by the blade to avoid a rugged newborn nail in the future.

(4) To prevent injury to the nail bed, the nail can also be seperated by inserting the mosquito hemostatic forceps in the interface of the nail and its bed, then splitting it after separating the edge of the nail bed with a sharp knife.

(5) Because the nail with onychomycosis is so brittle as not to scroll it, it can be pulled out directly after separating it from skin and its bed.

(Wang Zhongliang)

Chapter 10

Diagnostic Peritoneocentesis (Abdominal Paracentesis)

Diagnostic peritoneocentesis is an important supplementary diagnostic measure in surgical practice when there is difficulty in making diagnosis and decision for treatment in certain abdominal conditions. It helps in diagnosis by observing the nature of fluid (clear or turbid, transudatory or exudative, bloody or purulent, etc.) aspirated from the abdominal cavity through a trocar. The aspirated fluid can be studied in a laboratory too, e.g., amylase for pancreatitis, cultures for microorganisms, etc. Diagnostic peritoneocentesis is safe and easy to manipulate. The reliability rate of it reaches as high as 90% or even higher.

1. Indications

(1) To establish or approach a diagnosis for patients with acute abdomen of unknown origin, especially those having signs of shock, signs of peritoneal irritation and signs of rapid declination of red cell counts in short duration.

(2) To ascertain the state of intestine in intestinal obstruction, strangulated or not.

(3) To make sure of the presence of suppurative peritonitis, usually caused by pathologic or traumatic rupture of hollow organs.

(4) To make certain of the presence of visceral trauma in closed abdominal injury and the nature of the organ involved, solid or hollow.

2. Contraindications

Patients with certain intra-abdominal tumor (especially abdominal aneurysm), marked abdominal distension, and diffuse abdominal adhesions are contraindicated for a diagnostic peritoneocentesis. In addition, don't proceed to perform it in an irritative, restless or uncooperative patient.

3. Surgical procedures

(1) Order an aseptic package ready for abdominal paracentesis.

(2) Put the patient in supine position, sterilize and drape the puncture area which is usually the McBurney point on the right side and the symmetrical area on the left side. Sometime the puncture is made at the cross point of a horizontal line passing through the umbilicus and the anterior axillary line (Fig.76).

(3) Anesthesia: local infusion anesthesia is used.

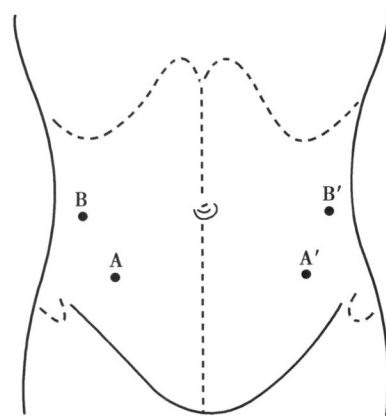

Fig.76 Puncture points for peritoneocentesis

(4) Incision: make a small incision about 1cm long at the site of puncture selected. The puncture trocar is slowly stabbed into the peritoneal cavity through subcutaneous tissue, muscular layers and peritoneum. There is a sensation of sudden release of resistance when the trocar just ruptures the peritoneum and gets into the abdomen.

(5) Insertion of the drainage tube: withdraw the sharp stylet and then a fine plastic tube is inserted through the outer tube of the trocar into the peritoneal cavity and suck the intra-abdominal fluid. By adjusting the direction of the trocar, depth of the plastic tube or posture of the patient, you can lead the fine plastic tube to different sites in the abdomen. The trocar and plastic tube are withdrawn at the end of the procedure.

(6) Suture of incision: usually only one stitch is enough to close the skin incision.

4. Points of attention

(1) During puncture, the patient should keep quiet without moving his body and no cough is allowed, otherwise the trocar may injure his viscera.

(2) Puncture gently and slowly without vigorous impulse to prevent trauma.

【Practice】

A dog is fixed in supine position with intra-abdominal anesthesia on the operating table. The teacher first injects appropriate amount of methylene blue in saline, then make diagnostic peritoneocentesis by the above procedures.

(Wei Yuxian Kong Lingquan)

Chapter 11

Laparotomy

1. Common incisions for laparotomy

A laparotomy incision is an approach to the abdominal cavity for performing intra-abdominal operations. Such an incision is desired to expose the abdominal viscera satisfactorily, with little structural and functional damages to the handled tissues and organs. It should be easy to perform, easy to extend when in necessary and easy to recover, bearing little chance of developing undue complications. There are a number of laparotomy incisions introduced, five of the commonly used incisions are recommended here (Fig.77).

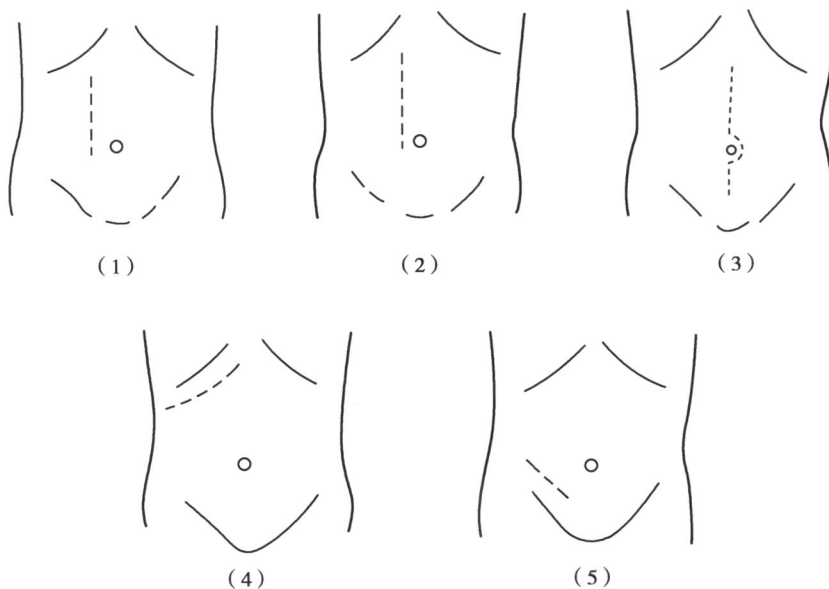

Fig.77 Common incisions for laparotomy
(1) right rectus incision; (2) right paramedian incision; (3) midline incision;
(4) right subcostal incision; (5) right iliac (McBurney) incision

(1) Rectus or rectus splitting incision: this is the most commonly used longitudinal abdominal incision passing through the right or left abdominal rectus muscle. After dividing of the anterior sheath of the muscle, the muscle is splitted to expose its posterior sheath. In splitting the muscle, all the traversed vessels and nerves are cut and bleeder ligated. Then cut the posterior rectus sheath, transverse fascia and peritoneum as a whole to enter the abdomen. This incision can be performed in short time. If necessary, it can be extended in either direction. An upward extension may sometimes transfer the incision into a thoracoabdominal incision.

Sometimes, a transverse extension may be made to form a T-shaped incision to expose the operating field better. The disadvantage of a longitudinal incision is easy to disrupt under high intraperitoneal pressure. If a rectus incision is too long, it may result in relaxation of the abdominal wall around the incision because more than 2 traversed intercostal nerves are cut.

(2) Paramedian incision: this is also a longitudinal incision. It lies 1.5 to 2.0cm from the midline. The procedures in making this incision is similar to the rectus splitting incision except rectus muscle is not splitted but the freed medial part of the rectus muscle is retracted outward. It bears the similiar advantages of the rectus splitting incision, while it does not cut the traversed intercostal nerve in addition. The manipulation of this incision is a little bit more complicated in comparison with rectus splitting incision.

(3) The midline incision: this is to open the abdomen through the midline, i.e., through the white line (linea alba) of the abdominal wall. It is simple and timesaving, and is accompanied by little tissue injury and bleeding. It bears the common disadvantage of a longitudinal incision. In addition, its major disadvantage is easy to disrupt because the white line is devoid of sufficient blood supply and muscle protection, leading to poor healing and more chance of incisional hernia.

(4) Subcostal incision: this is an oblique abdominal incision from a point 2cm below the xiphoid process to the anterior axillary line, parallel to the costal margin. All layers of the abdominal wall are divided or incised in this direction. This incision parallels approximately to the lines of force of the abdominal wall, so the sutures will bear less tension and healing will be firmer. It is sometimes used in right side for biliary tract operation and in left side for splenic operation. It will offer a good exposure of the operating field. On the other hand, it is difficult to be extended and will take more time to open and close.

(5) Oblique iliac (fossa) incision: this is an incision of the lower abdomen, leading from the upper outer part of it to the lower medial. A right-sided oblique iliac incision is the classic incision for an appendectomy, which is frequently practiced in clinical surgery and is known as McBurney incision also. It is about 6–8cm long running across a point (McBurney point) at the junction of outer and middle thirds of a line which leads from the right superior anterior iliac spine to the umbilicus. After the skin and subcutaneous tissues are cut, the aponeurosis of external oblique muscle is cut in the same direction. Then the internal oblique and transversalis muscles are splitted (instead of cut) to expose the transverse fascia and peritoneum, which are eventually opened. A left sided oblique iliac incision is not frequently used, it is occasionally used for a colostomy in left abdomen. An oblique iliac incision usually heals well because the interdigital cut and split of the different layers of muscle protect the wound from disruption or incisional hernia formation. This incision exposes a small part of the abdomen, so it leads to minimal operative disturbances to the abdominal viscera. It is difficult to extend if it happens to be necessary.

2. Practice of laparotomy taking "Splenectomy" as example

There are a number of clinical entities indicated for splenectomy. The chief indications include traumatic rupture of spleen, late schistosomiasis, kala-azar, splenomegaly caused by malaria (usually complicated with hypersplenism) and conditions of primary hypersplenism like idiopathic thrombocytopenic purpura, familial hemolytic anemia, etc.

Spleen was considered to be an organ without important function previously. But after the appearance of a number of fulminating infections after splenectomy, especially in children, it is found that spleen is an important organ in immunological system. Hence splenectomy is considered more serious in recent years than the past especially in cases of traumatic rupture of the organ. If possible, repairment of the ruptured organ, partial splenectomy, ligation of splenic vessels or retransplantation of a part of viable splenic tissue following the removal of the organ are more reasonable choices instead of total splenectomy.

Splenectomy is a major operation in clinical surgery. You are not required to learn it in this laboratory, but you will practice splenectomy in dogs, because the anatomy of dog's spleen is different from that of human spleen and the manipulation is much easier. In this operation, you will learn the fundamental surgical techniques like opening and closing of abdominal cavity, ligation of major blood vessels, etc.

(1) Make a left rectus splitting incision

1) Starting from a point 2cm below costal margin, make an 8 to 10cm longitudinal incision about 1.5cm left to the midline.

2) Cut through the skin and subcutaneous tissue, all the bleeders should be immediately clamped and ligated with hemostats and thin silk sutures, respectively. Then the skin on both sides of the incision is covered with two sterile towels with folded edges and they are fixed with towel clips.

3) Incise the anterior rectal sheath and split the muscle, the traversed intercostal nerves and vessels are cut between 2 hemostatic clamps and the cut ends ligated. Beware that there is usually a blood vessel traversed at the level of each tendinous inscription of the muscle.

4) Now the chief operator picks up the posterior rectal sheath at the middle portion of the incision by a forceps and then the first assistant picks it too with a Kelly clamp at a point just opposite operator's forceps. When it is sure that there is no intra-abdominal tissue caught by the forceps or clamp, make a cut of the sheath together with the underlying transversalis muscle and peritoneum and the peritoneal cavity is opened.

5) Enlarge the peritoneal opening by scissors both upward (cephalad) and downward (caudally). In former extension, the chief operator and first assistant are suggested to insert their index fingers through the peritoneal opening serving as a guide behind the peritoneum to be cut and to protect the intra-abdominal structures not being damaged. In making caudal extension, the operator is better to insert his index and middle fingers in as a guide of peritoneal cutting between the 2 fingers. It is important to remember don't extend the cut cephalad too much in a upper abdominal rectus incision, lest the thoracic cavity is opened which may lead to fatal result.

6) All the gauze used intraperitoneally should be moistened by saline to decrease the irritation to the peritoneum and viscera.

(2) Removal of the spleen

1) Search for the stomach first and retract it to the right side of the operating field as far as possible to show the gastrosplenic ligament and a portion of the spleen. Grasp the partially exposed spleen with hand covered with moist gauze, and try to take the whole spleen out of the abdominal cavity. Pad the spleen with moist gauze and return all other organs or tissues, which are pulled out.

2) Cut the gastrosplenic ligament by severing the paired short gastric vessels in it pair by pair. Before the severance of each pair of the vessels, isolate and apply 3 curved (Kelly) clamps to it. Cut the vessels between the proximal 2 (gastric side) and the distal one (splenic side) clamps, and ligate the proximal cut end twice and the distal once. The proximal double ligation is much more secure because postoperative gastric dilatation (a common complication of upper abdominal surgery) may push a single ligature off and result in bleeding.

3) Now the lesser omental cavity is entered and splenic mesentery exposed (there is no splenic mesentery in man). Search for splenic artery and vein in the splenic mesentery. Isolate the artery and vein separately, and 3 clamps are applied for each of them and they are individually cut between the proximal 2 and distal one too. The proximal stump is first ligated with a triple knot and then removes the most proximal clamp. A transfixion (figure of "8") suture is made between the triple knot and the second proximal clamp. The distal stump is

ligated only once. Right after the blockage of the splenic artery (i.e., before the blockage of the vein), you may find shrinkage of the splenic capsule and the organ is getting smaller because there is only outflow of blood from the spleen without inflow into it.

4) Beginning from the inferior pole of the spleen, sever the splenic mesentery by several separate cuts. Before each cut, two clamps are applied and cut between the clamps. The proximal part is ligated with triple knot. Relatively big vessels in the pedical tissue are better ligated with two triple knots in the proximal side. After the mesentery is totally divided, the spleen is extirpated.

(3) Closure of incision

1) After the abdominal cavity is checked up with no fluid (including blood) collection, no bleeding point uncontrolled and no foreign body (including gauze and instrument) left, the abdomen is ready to be closed.

2) Put two rows of hemostats on both sides including the two ends of the incision catching the innermost layer of the incision (peritoneum, transversalis muscle and posterior sheath of rectus muscle). Intestine depressor or moist gauze should be placed under the peritoneum to separate both sides of the peritoneal incision from the viscera to avoid damage to them and outward prolapse of the viscera during suturing.

3) Lift up the hemostats and close the innermost layer of incision with No.4 silk continuous (or running) suture. The first and the last suture should include the two ends of the incision without leaving any defect to avoid visceral herniation through the defect.

4) In making the continuous suture, the appropriate distance between every 2 stitches is about 0.5cm. It is important to keep the silk straightened all the time to ensure a tight closure. Take out the intestine depressor and the gauze before making last few stitches.

5) The last stitch is made beyond (i.e., distal to) the clamp catching the end of the incision. Make a tie there by doubling the silk. The final knots are made on the other side of the clamp. Cut the silk and leave a remnant of 0.1–0.2cm long.

6) Rinse the incision thoroughly with sterile saline after closing the peritoneum.

7) Suture the anterior rectus sheath with No.4 silk interrupted simple sutures, the distance between stitches still keeps about 0.5cm.

8) Take away the skin towels. Clean the skin on either side of the incision with saline and alcohol successively.

9) Close the subcutaneous tissue with No.0 silk interruptedly distance between 2 stitches is 1.0–1.5cm.

10) Use a cutting needle to suture the skin with No.0 silk interrupted simple sutures, and the stitch distance is 1.0cm.

(Kong Lingquan)

Chapter 12

Fundamental Principles of Gastrointestinal Operation

1. Gastrointestinal tract contains large amount of bacteria, especially in the lower segments (such as colon), therefore, aseptic techniques are considered of the utmost importance in gastrointestinal operations. For examples, the operative field should be well protected with moist gauze before cutting into the gastrointestinal lumen until it is closed, don't make contact with the mucosal surface of the gastrointestinal tract as far as possible by your hands, all the instruments contacted with the mucosal surface are contaminated and should be collected in an isolated container, discard all the contaminated instruments and rinse your gloves with saline thoroughly after the closure of the gastrointestinal lumen. Furthermore, in colorectal surgery, we usually give the patient peculiar preoperative preparations, including low-residue-diet and oral antibiotics for few days and cleansing enema the day before operation because there are numerous bacteria in colon and rectum.

2. The healing of gastrointestinal wound depends on the fibrinous exudates from serosa, therefore, inversion or serosal sutures are used to close gastrointestinal opening. The approximation of the serosa should be accurate for sound healing. The poorly inverted gastrointestinal wound with eversion of mucosa will result in leakage of gastrointestinal contents which is a serious postoperative complication. A gastrointestinal wound is usually closed by an inner and an outer layer to guarantee satisfactory inversion of gastrointestinal wall. Some scholars advocate suture by only one layer, this requires skillful manipulation to avoid eversion of the mucosa.

3. Don't invert the gastrointestinal wall too much, lest it will cause obstruction of the lumen of the tract.

4. Sutures for gastrointestinal tract may be whole layered or seromuscular only. The former passes through all layers of the wall and is usually used in suturing the inner layer and the latter doesn't catch the mucosal layer and is usually used in suturing the outer layer. Both of them may be interrupted or continuous. A continuous suture is more often used for inner layer suturing, it may exert a hemostatic effect on the cut edge of the tissue. The commonly used continuous suture in this occasion may be a lock-stitch suture (Fig.78) or a continuous suture (Connell suture, Fig.79). The commonly used interrupted outer layer sutures are Lembert suture (Fig.80), Cushing suture (Fig.81) and Halsted suture (Fig.82). Furthermore, the small rupture of the gastrointestinal wall may be sutured with a purse-string suture (Fig.83). Silk suture is generally the common choice for gastrointestinal tract suture, while chromic catgut may sometimes be used for inner layer suture.

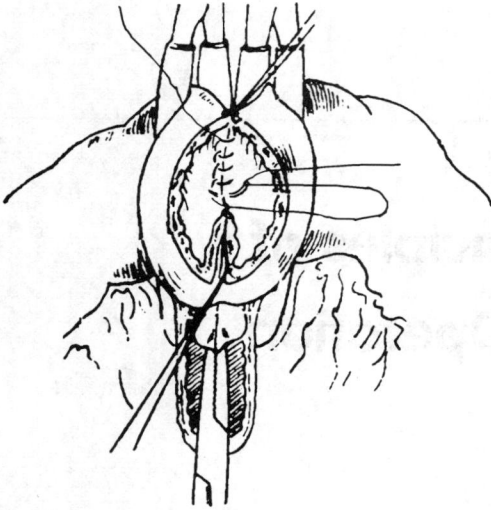

Fig.78   Whole layer lock suture

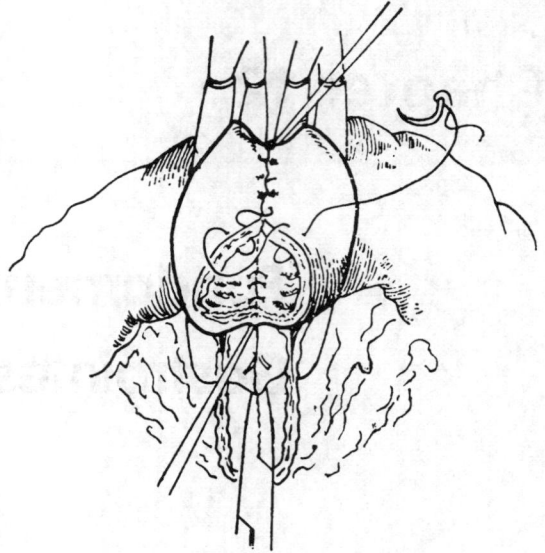

Fig.79   Continuous mattress Connell suture

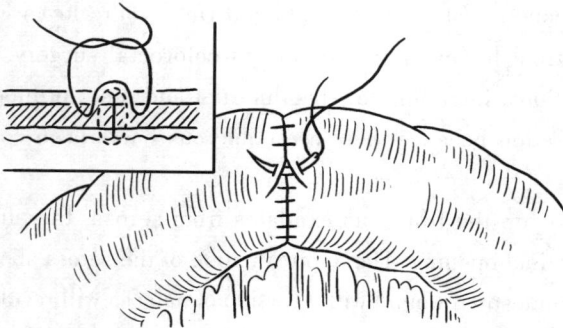

Fig.80   Interrupted seromuscular (Lembert) suture

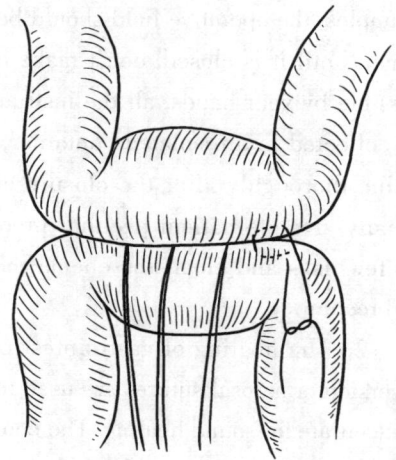

Fig.81   Interrupted mattress (Cushing) suture

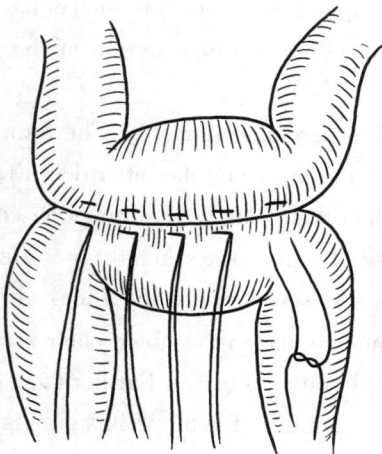

Fig.82   Interrupted vertical mattress (Halsted) suture

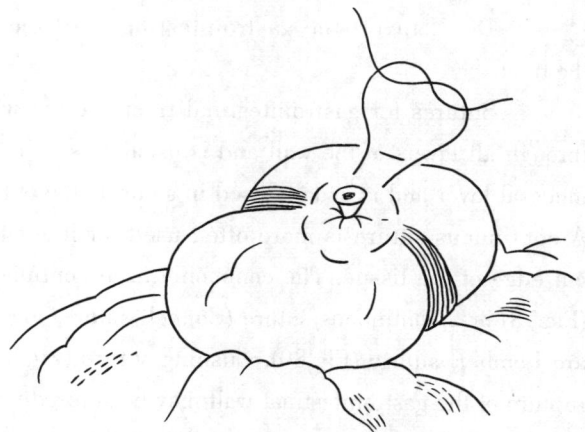

Fig.83   Purse-string suture

5. The amount of blood supply in different segments of gastrointestinal tract are different. There are many blood vessels and collaterals in stomach so it has the richest supply. The blood supply of small intestine is quite good except the duodenum and upper jejunum. The colon and rectum have fewer amounts of blood vessels and collaterals than the other segments of the tract. Blood vessels of intestine usually come from the mesentery, therefore most vessels enter the intestinal wall at its mesenteric side and end at the antimesenteric side. The direction of section of an intestinal segment is therefore somewhat oblique, i.e., more intestinal wall on the antimesenteric side is cut away than on the mesenteric side. This not only ensures the blood supply to the antimesenteric side but also reduces the possibility of anastomotic stenosis. In lateral anastomosis of intestine, it is suggested to cut the intestinal wall of the antimesenteric side to ensure the blood supply to both sides of the cut. All these operative principles are especially important in colonic surgery.

6. It is important to avoid over traction upon the sutured area or stoma of anastomosis, because hyper-traction may block the blood supply leading to poor healing and leakage of the sutured area. hyper-traction may sometimes be a result of postoperative intraluminal pneumatosis.

7. A drain, if required, should not be placed near the sutured or anastomotic area; otherwise, poor healing may be resulted as the fibrinous exudate is drained.

8. The gastrointestinal operation should be handled with especial gentleness. Don't expose too much parts of the organ. Cover all the exposed parts away from the operating area with moist gauze to prevent possible contamination and irritation by dryness. These are beneficial to the prevention of postoperative abdominal distention and adhesion formation.

9. The anastomosis of gastrointestinal tract may be performed openly or closely. In open anastomosis, the gastrointestinal lumen is exposed and sutured layer by layer with the intestinal lumen exposed. By this type of anastomosis, manipulations are convenient and less technical complications may appear; but the chance of contamination is high. In closed anastomosis, the gastrointestinal lumen is not exposed, so the manipulations are relatively complex and may result in more technical complications, however, the chance of the operating field contamination is greatly reduced. By the advances in preoperative preparations and preventive application of antibiotics, the open anastomosis has been more widely accepted in recent years. However, the above mentioned basic principles are still important and should never be neglected.

(Kong Lingquan)

Chapter 13

Repairment of Gastric Perforation (Gastrorrhaphy)

Gastric perforation may be a result of abdominal injury or a complication of acute gastric ulcer; occasionally, it is a complication of gastric cancer. There are several methods to treat gastric perforation, of which repairment of perforation is the most simple and convenient one.

【Practice】

A mimic operation is done in dog by the following steps for the repairment of gastric perforation.

1. Make a right abdominal rectus incision (refer to splenectomy).

2. Search for the stomach and expose it in the operating field. Let the teacher make a stab wound in an appropriate site of the stomach.

3. Fully expose the perforation of the stomach, cover its surrounding parts with moist gauze to prevent contamination and leakage of the gastric contents into the abdominal cavity.

4. Close the perforation by several full thickness sutures with the needle perpendicular to the long axis of the stomach (Fig.84), then make a second row of seromuscular sutures for inversion (Fig.85). For a very small perforation, only few seromuscular inversion sutures are enough.

5. If the repairment is unsatisfactory, cover it with greater omentum, which can be sutured to the perforating site to prevent leakage.

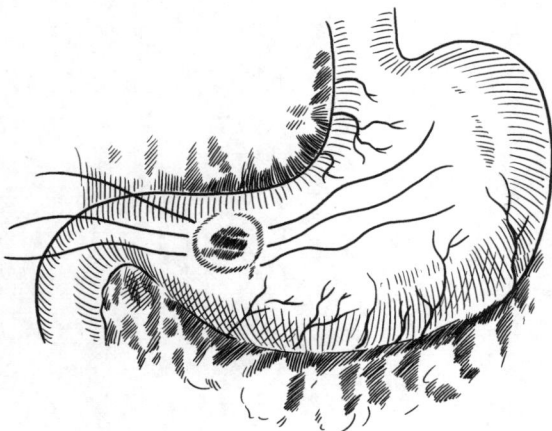

| Fig.84 Full thickness sutures for the repairment of gastric perforation | Fig.85 Seromuscular inversion sutures to reinforce the repairment of perforation |

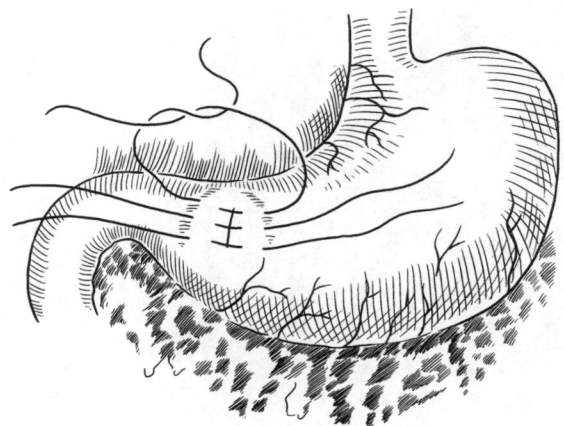

6. After repairment, the operator should rinse his gloves with saline.

7. Clean the operating field, make sure that there are no active bleeding, foreign bodies or gastric contents left in the abdominal cavity.

8. Close the abdomen, the procedure is same to that of splenectomy.

(Wei Yuxian   Kong Lingquan)

Chapter 14

Gastrostomy

Gastrostomy includes temporary gastrostomy and permanent gastrostomy, which is mainly applied to the following two situations:

1. Eating difficulty caused by all kinds of factors, such as esophageal benign stenosis, esophageal neoplasms and obstruction caused by maxillofacial trauma, etc.

2. For those patients who require long duration of gastrointestinal decompression after certain major operation of abdomen, to avoid uncomfortableness caused by the nasogastric tube; children uncooperative with nasal intubation or failure to decompress due to the thin tube; older patients vulnerable to pulmonary dysfunction; patients with portal hypertension to avoid the risk of bleeding caused by nasogastric tube and so on.

【Practice】

A mimic operation is done in dog by the following steps (Stamm gastrostomy).

1. Disinfect and drape the puncture area routinely. Make a left abdominal rectus incision (refer to splenectomy). Use the Babcock's clamp to clamp in the anterior and middle area of stomach wall, and test whether the stomach wall is easily close to the peritoneum. (Fig.86)

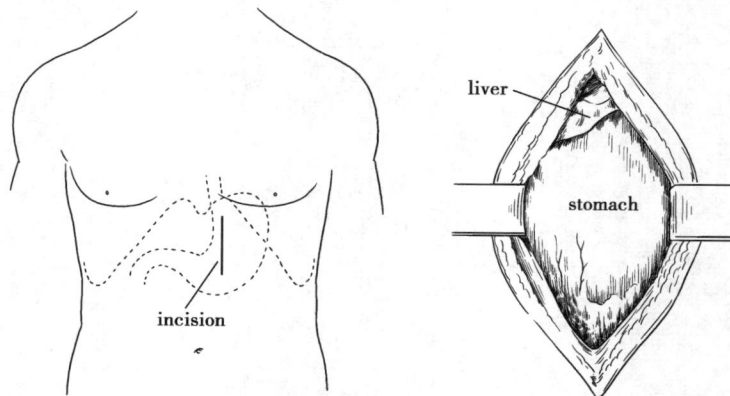

Fig.86　Make a left abdominal rectus incision

2. Make purse string suture around the stomach wall which clamped in step 1 without ligation. Cover the surrounding area with moist gauze to prevent contamination and leakage of the gastric contents into the abdominal cavity. (Fig.87)

3. Make an incision along the vertical direction of the long axis of the stomach in the middle site of the purse string suture. Suck out the gastric contents and make adequate hemostasis. Put the mushroom catheter (or the tube with side hole or Foley catheter) 10cm into the stomach and then ligate the pursue string suture. (Fig.88 and Fig.89)

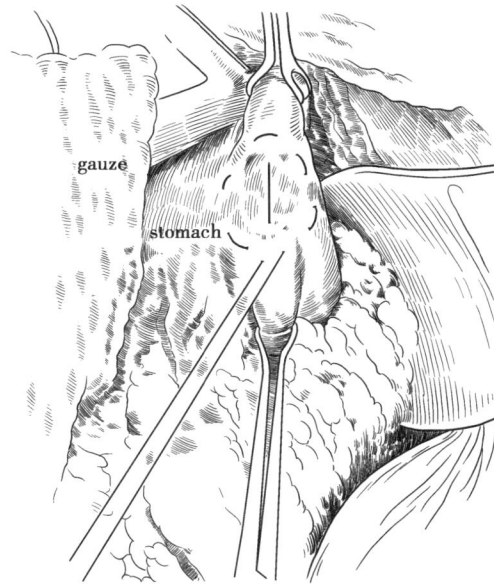

Fig.87 Make purse string suture around the stomach wall

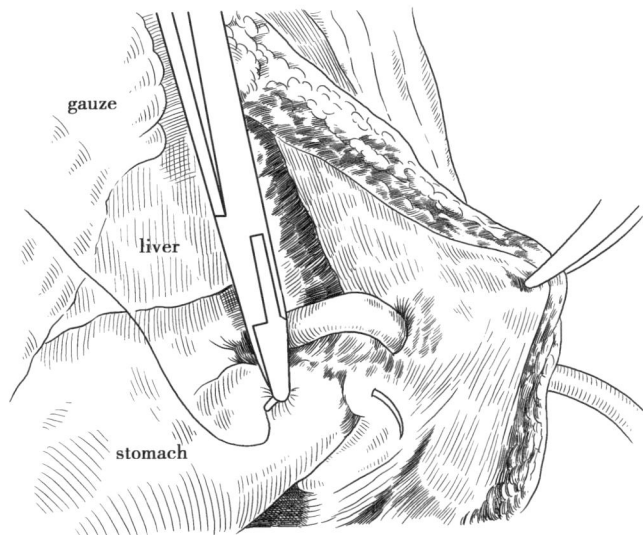

Fig.88 Put the mushroom catheter & fix

4. Make the second layer of purse string suture ligation, 1cm from the original purse string suture. If necessary the third one can be made 1cm from the second string suture. (Fig.88 and Fig.89)

5. Draw the catheter out of the greater omentum and lateral abdominal wall with the fistula covered with the greater omentum. After checking the drainage unobstructed, fixe the gastric wall surrounding the fistula to the peritoneum and then fixe the drainage tube on the skin. (Fig.88 and Fig.89)

6. Clear the operating field to make sure that there is no active bleeding, foreign bodies, and then closes the abdomen.

(Wang Ruijue Kong Lingquan)

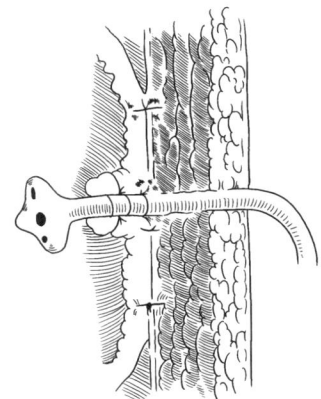

Fig.89 Closure of the abdomen

Chapter 15

Appendectomy

Acute appendicitis is the most common acute abdominal disease in man and appendectomy is the most commonly performed operation in general surgery.

【 Practice 】

Dog has no appendix, while its cecum is similar to human appendix, but thicker and longer. Therefore, you may practice appendectomy (imitating human appendectomy) by excision of dog's cecum by the following procedures.

1. Make a McBurney incision

(1) The point at the junction of outer and middle thirds of a line leading from the umbilicus to right anterior superior iliac spine is called McBurney point which is the surface marking of appendix on the abdominal wall in man. Cross the McBurney point, make a 5cm long incision perpendicular to the above mentioned line with one third of the incision above that line.

(2) After the skin and subcutaneous tissue are cut, incise the aponeurosis of external oblique abdominal muscle in the same direction.

(3) The internal oblique and transversalis muscles are splitted by the chief operator and the first assistant alternatively and the peritoneum is now exposed.

(4) Cut the peritoneum as described previously and the peritoneal cavity is entered. The margin of the peritoneal opening is fixed to the towels aside the skin incision by towel clips or Allis clamps to prevent contamination of the operative field during dissection of cecum.

2. Search for cecum

Search for the ascending colon in the right abdomen. Small intestine is relatively thin with smooth surface and it is usually collapsed, while colon looks tubular and is relatively thick with longitudinal muscular streaks on its wall. Trace the ascending colon retrogradely to find the ileocecal junction and cecum. You may find the cecum by tracing the terminal ileum too. There is a blood vessel about 4–6cm long running along the antimesenteric border of terminal ileum in dog. This is a peculiar anatomical feature in dog favoring the identification of terminal ileum. You can find the cecum after the terminal ileum is identified.

3. Isolation and resection of cecum

(1) Pull out the cecum, pad the surrounding operating field to prevent from contamination. Isolate and ligate the mesenteric tissues (human cecum has no mesentery) in its medial part carefully to free the cecum.

(2) No.4 silk is used to make a purse string suture around and about 0.5cm apart from the base of cecum. Don't tie the suture temporarily.

(3) Crush the base of the cecum with a hemostat and ligate it at the crushed part with No.4 silk. The stump of the ligature is caught with a mosquito clamp.

(4) Clamp the cecum with a straight hemostat about 0.3cm distal to the ligature, then cut the cecum close to the hemostat and take it away. Before cutting through the cecum, a piece of moist gauze is placed around the base of the cecum to avoid contamination. Treat the stump of the cecum with phenol, alcohol and saline successively. The phenol should only be painted onto the mucous membrane of the stump and the stump should be painted with alcohol and saline from its periphery toward the center. The stump of cecum is pushed into the purse string by the previously placed mosquito clamp catching the stump of the ligature, then tighten and ligate the purse string so as to invert the stump of cecum. The purpose of using phenol to cauterize the mucous membrane is to destroy its secretary function to prevent from cyst formation after the purse string inversion suture.

(5) If the inversion of the stump is unsatisfactory, reinforce it with another purse string suture or one or more figure of "8" sutures. The surrounding fat tissue may also be used to cover it.

4. Closure of the abdomen

Make sure that there is no active bleeding and no gauze or instruments left behind, the abdominal wall is closed layer by layer, including peritoneum (with round needle and medium silk), sheath of internal oblique abdominal muscle (fine silk), aponeurosis of external oblique abdominal muscle (fine silk), subcutaneous tissue (fine silk) and skin (cutting needle and fine silk).

(Zou Baoshan Kong Lingquan)

Chapter 16

Partial Resection and Anastomosis of Small Intestinal

1. Indications of partial resection of small intestine

(1) Strangulated hernia, volvulus, intestinal adhesion, mesenteric thrombosis and other diseases complicated with actual or threatened intestinal necrosis or gangrene.

(2) Intestinal fistula, injury of intestine and other intestinal disorders those are difficult to repair.

(3) Regional or segmental infectious disease of intestine, tuberculoses granuloma and other diseases that may lead to intestinal obstruction.

(4) Intestinal tumor or precancerous disease of intestine.

2. Procedures of partial resection and anastomosis of small intestine

(1) Incision: make an incision as near the lesion as possible. A right rectus muscle splitting incision is usually used for exploratory purpose.

(2) Exploration and determination of the extent of resection: explore the abdomen to confirm the diagnosis first. In case of trauma, much attention should be paid to the possibility of multiple injuries in the abdomen. After thorough exploration, determine the extent of resection.

(3) Expose the intestinal loop to be resected: bring the intestinal loop to be resected out of the abdomen gently, especially the necrotized, to prevent rupture of the intestine and serious contamination of abdominal cavity. Return all normal intestinal loops into the abdominal cavity and place a moist gauze or pad around the extracted intestinal loop. The extent of resection is usually 3–5cm beyond the lesion, i.e. sever the intestine 3–5cm away from the margins of the lesion. However, in resection of an intestinal malignancy, the lines of severance should never be less than 5cm proximal and distal to the tumor mass, in addition, the regional lymph nodes should be removed together. The cut ends of the intestinal loop must be healthy to ensure good healing after anastomosis.

(4) Management of the mesentery: search for the main blood supply in the corresponding mesentery of the intestinal loop to be excised. Two curved clamps are applied on the proximal part of the exposed paired vessels (including artery and vein) and a third one distally. The vessels are cut at the proximal side of the distal clamp. The proximal stump is ligated with a triple knot followed by a transfixion ligation as described formerly. The distal stump of the divided vessels is ligated once only. From the point where the vessels are severed, cut the mesentery in fan fashion (Fig.90). If the vessels in the mesentery are not clearly seen because of thick fat tissues, observe through light.

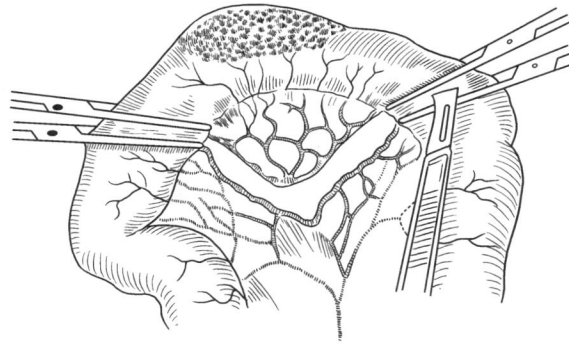

Fig.90   Fan shaped section of the mesentery

(5) Resection of intestinal loop: detach the mesentery about 1cm from the mesenteric border of the intestine beyond the 2 proposed lines of section. This is beneficial to invert the mucosal layer of intestinal wall in anastomosis of cut ends later (Fig.91). After confirming that the reserved loops have good blood circulation, two Kocher clamps are applied on each cut end of the resected segment with the tip of the clamps at the antimesenteric side. The clamps should be placed obliquely (not exceeding 300), with more intestinal wall on the antimesenteric side to be cut away than on the mesenteric side. This will ensure the blood supply of anastomosis and prevent anastomotic stenosis caused by inversion sutures. After the application of Kocher clamps, the intestinal contents are gently squeezed away from the proposed cut lines both proximally and distally, and the fecal flow is blocked by applying an intestinal clamp (with elastic arms to prevent injury of intestinal wall by clamping) on each side (Fig.92). This is to prevent leakage of intestinal contents during and after section and anastomosis of the intestine. The fecal flow may also be blocked by rubber bands winding around the intestine. Protect the operative field carefully again. Now, everything is ready for sectioning the intestine between the paired Kocher clamps and the diseased intestinal segment is removed.

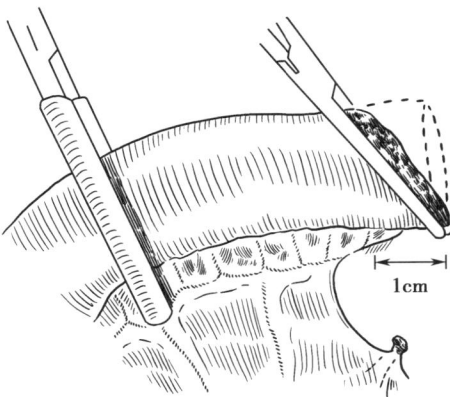

Fig.91   Dissection on the mesentery side of the stump

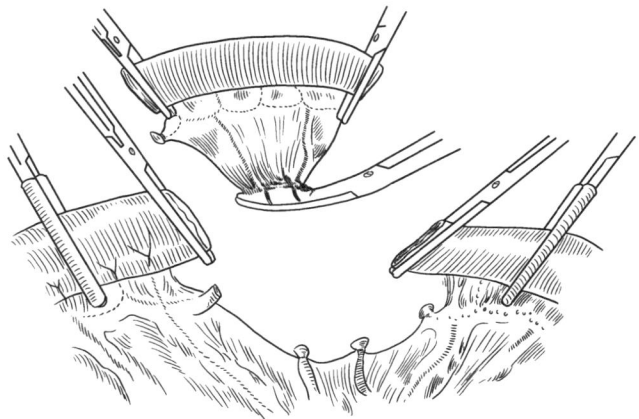

Fig.92   Oblique section of the intestinal loop

(6) Intestinal anastomosis: an intestinal anastomosis may be made closely or openly.

1) Closed end to end intestinal anastomosis: after the resection of the pathologic segment, the Kocher clamps at the healthy cut ends of the intestine are not released. Bring the clamps together with cut ends facing each other. Then make interrupted seromuscular sutures (Cushing or Halsted) close to the clamps circumferentially. All the sutures are not tied temporarily. Pull and straighten the sutures and take away the

Kocher clamps at the same time. After the Kocher clamps are removed, tie the interrupted seromuscular sutures one by one. At last, interrupted Lembert sutures are made around the anastomosis for reinforcement. Closed anastomosis greatly reduces the chance of abdominal contamination by intestinal contents, because the intestinal mucosa is not exposed. One of the disadvantages of this anastomosis is that the blood vessels over the cut intestine are not ligated. If any stitch is made unduly deep, it will penetrate the contralateral intestinal wall leading to blockage of intestinal lumen by an intraluminal diaphragm formed by the deep stitch. Therefore, the stitches should neither be too superficial nor too deep. They should be exactly seromuscular. To prevent intestinal obstruction by an intraluminal diaphragm, check the stoma with fingers from outside before making the Lembert sutures. If a diaphragm is found, the corresponding deep suture should be cut and sutured again.

2) Open anastomosis: bring the Kocher clamps side to side. Two seromuscular stitches are placed about 0.3cm from the clamps, one on the mesenteric side and the other on the antimesenteric side of both cut ends. Tie the two sutures to approximate the cut ends of the intestine. These sutures will serve for traction in later manipulations. Approximate the posterior intestinal wall by a row of interrupted seromuscular sutures. These are the posterior outer sutures of the anastomosis (Fig.93). Now, remove the Kocher clamps and open the intestinal lumen, clean off the residual blood and intestinal contents in it. Check the bleeders over the cut ends. Then, make interrupted full thickness stitches (mucosa of one side in and mucosa of the other side out) as inner sutures of the anastomosis (Fig.94 and Fig.95). After that, make a series of Lembert sutures as the outer sutures of the anastomosis (Fig.96). Though the chance of contamination is high in doing an open anastomosis, it is easy to manipulate and safe if strict aseptic ethnics and preventive antibiotics are used.

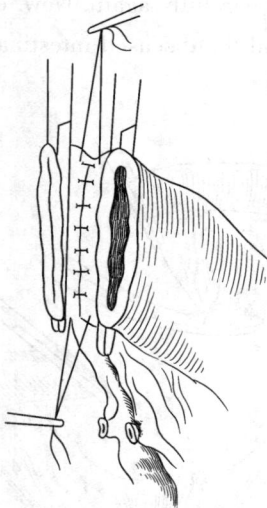

Fig.93   Seromuscular traction sutures and Lembert
sutures on posterior anastomotic intestinal wall

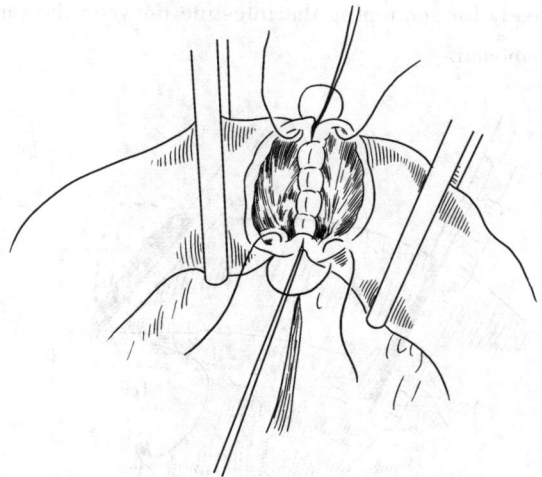

Fig.94   Full thickness interrupted inverting sutures
of the posterior wall of anastomosis

(7) When the anastomosis is finished, whether the inversion of the anastomosis is perfect should be examined, especially at the mesenteric side. If necessary, one or two stitches may be used to strengthen it.

(8) Determine the size and patency of the anastomosis (Fig.97).

(9) After anastomosis, the gap of the mesentery should be closed with several interrupted sutures to prevent from internal hernia (Fig.98).

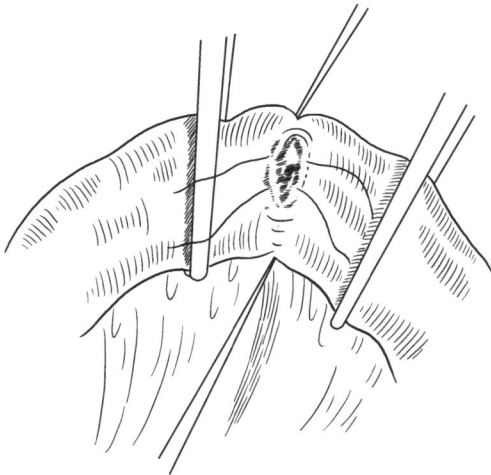

Fig.95 Full thickness interrupted inverting sutures of the anterior wall of anastomosis

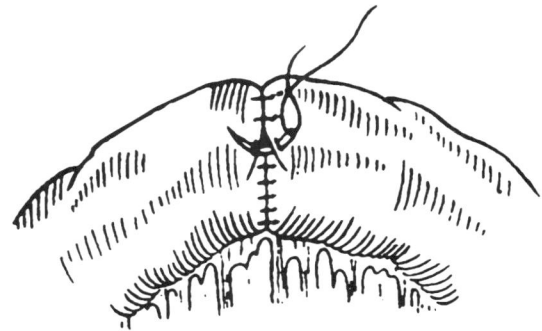

Fig.96 Outer seromuscular sutures of the anastomosis

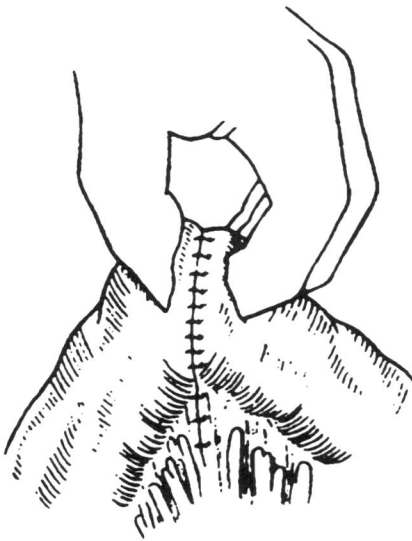

Fig.97 Determine the size and ensure patency of the anastomosis

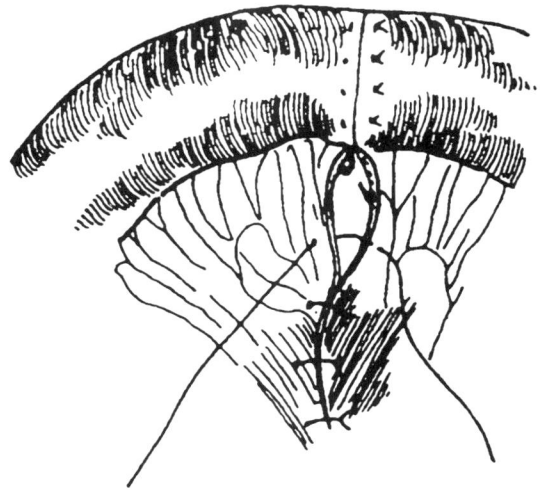

Fig.98 Closure of the mesenteric gap

(10) Clean the operating field, when there is no active bleeding, fluid collection or foreign body left in the abdomen, the incision is closed layer by layer.

There are 3 types of anastomosis to reform the intestinal continuity, end-to-end, side-to-side and end to side. Only end-to-end anastomosis will be described in this chapter. An end-to-end anastomosis conforms to the natural anatomical and physiologic status, but it may cause anastomotic stenosis resulting in intestinal obstruction more easily than the other forms of anastomosis. Furthermore, it is difficult to manipulate if the 2 cut ends are not uniform in their diameters. In a side-to-side anastomosis, close both cut ends first. Then make a longitudinal opening of appropriate length over the antimesenteric border of each of the proximal and distal segments of intestine near their closed cut ends. Sometimes, the pathologic intestinal loops can't be resected (as in case of profuse adhesions), we can leave the pathologic segment alone and bring the segments proximal and distal to the pathologic segment together and anastomose them in a side-to-side manner. There will be no difficulty to anastomose 2 intestinal loops of different diameters, and there is little chance of stenosis of the anastomosis. However, the blind pockets formed between the anastomotic site and the closed cut ends may lead to undesirable complications. In an end to side anastomosis, only one of the 2 cut ends (usually the distal) is closed after the pathologic segment is removed. Make a longitudinal incision on the antimesenteric border of the intestine near the closed cut end and bring the open cut end here to make anastomosis. Sometimes, the pathologic segment may also be left alone without resection of it. An end to side anastomosis is usually used in surgery of ileocecal region and ascending colon. The anastomosis is made between terminal ileum and transverse colon. It mimics the normal anatomy of ileocecal junction.

【Practice】

The class is subdivided into several groups of 2–3 persons to practice the technic of intestinal anastomosis individually. Segments of pork intestine are supplied to practice end to end, end to side and side-to-side anastomosis extracorporeally. Pour some water into the intestinal lumen after each anastomosis is performed to determine the security and patency of it.

Every operative team is required to perform an end-to-end intestinal resection following partial resection in dog through a rectus incision.

(Liu Jiashuo   Kong Lingquan)

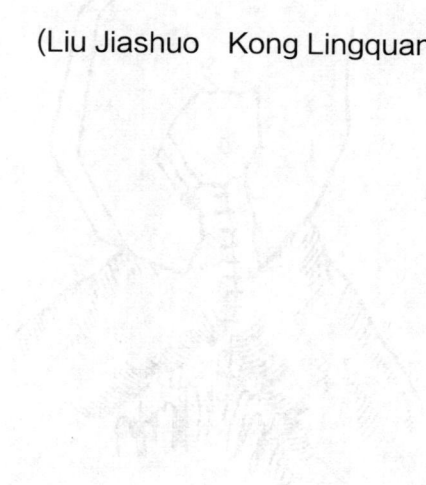

Chapter 17

Gastrojejunal Anastomosis (Gastrojejunostomy)

1. Indications

(1) A gastrojejunostomy may serve to reform the continuity of gastrointestinal tract after gastroduodenal resection, gastrectomy for peptic ulcer or gastric carcinoma, pancreatoduodenectomy for carcinoma of pancreatic head, etc.

(2) It may be used to bypass a pyloric obstruction as in peptic ulcer complicated with cicatrical pyloric obstruction.

(3) It may serve to relieve or prevent a real or expected pyloric obstruction in an irresectable carcinoma of the prepyloric region of stomach.

(4) It is also used to bypass a duodenal lesion, which is difficult to excise like duodenal tuberculosis, duodenal diverticulum, etc.

(5) It may be used to prevent gastric stasis following vagotomy for gastroduodenal ulcer.

2. Surgical mode

A gastrojejunostomy may be antecolic or retrocolic. In the former case, the jejunum is anastomosed with the anterior gastric wall in front of transverse colon, while in the latter it is anastomosed with posterior gastric wall after passing through the mesentery of transverse colon.

3. Surgical procedures

(1) Antecolic gastrojejunostomy

1) Patient's posture and incision: put the patient in supine position and a left upper rectus muscle splitting incision is made.

2) Search for the jejunum and plan the anastomosis: to find the duodenojejunal flexure at the base of the mesentery of the transverse colon, left to the vertebral spine. With the colon been pulled out, the Treitz's ligament, i.e., the beginning of jejunum, can be found at the base of transverse colon mesentery. Pick the first segment of jejunum out, a guide stitch is placed about 15cm from the Treitz's ligament at the antimesenteric border of the intestine with curved needle and fine silk.

Make another guide stitch about 5cm distal to the former one as the stoma of the anastomosis is usually about 5cm.

3) Closure of the mesenteric gap: a gap will be produced between the transverse colon and the jejunal

mesentery when the jejunum is pulled toward the stomach in front of the transverse colon. This gap must be closed to prevent the formation of internal hernia, which may be a fatal complication. Usually three interrupted stitches of fine silk will be enough for this purpose.

4) Plan the site of stoma on the anterior gastric wall: the proposed site of stoma is usually selected at the lowermost part of the anterior gastric wall near the greater curvature crossing a perpendicular line leading from the angular notch. In case of a palliative operation of gastric cancer, the anastomosis should be at least 5cm away from the tumor margin to prevent infiltration and obstruction of the stoma by extension of the tumor later. Bring the segment of jejunum between the two guide stitches upward, in front of the transverse colon to meet the part of the stomach wall chosen for anastomosis, with the proximal end of the segment on the right side. Two traction stitches are made to approximate the stomach and the segment of jejunum (Fig.99). Proceed to make a side-to-side anastomosis.

5) Outer posterior layer sutures of the anastomosis: interrupted seromuscular sutures with small round needle and fine silk are made between the anterior wall of stomach and the posterior wall of jejunum about 0.5cm from its antimesenteric border, within the range of the two traction stitches. The distance between every 2 stitches is about 0.5cm. The sutures are pulled just to make the two walls in approximation, don't tie too tight, nor too loose.

6) Incision of gastric and jejunal wall: protect the operating field with moist gauze. Seromuscular incisions about 0.5cm from the outer posterior sutures are made to cut both the gastric and intestinal walls. All traversed vessels in the submucosal layer are transfixed with small needle and fine silk. A little bit of mucosal tissue is better to be implicated in each transfixion, this makes the later manipulations in inner layer suturing more convenient. Now, the mucous membranes of stomach and intestine are opened (Fig.100). The gastrojejunal contents are removed with suction timely. The incision on both sides should be equal in length and parallel to each other.

7) Inner posterior sutures of anastomosis: started from the middle part of the posterior edge of the stoma and continued in either directions, make continuous full thickness lock-stitch sutures with a long segment of

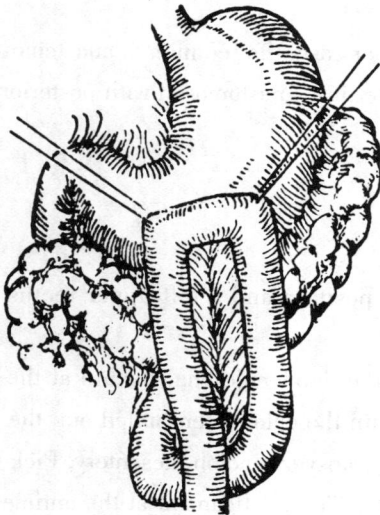

Fig.99   Approximation of stomach and jejunum

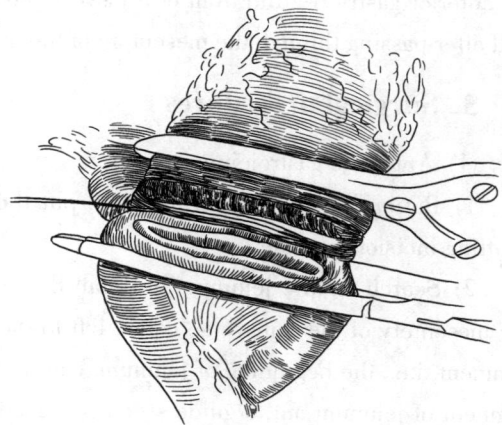

Fig.100   After the outer posterior layer sutures of anastomosis are made, incise seromuscular layer of the jejunum and gastric wall successively, ligate the traversed vessels and then incise the mucosal layer

medium silk. Keep the needle in every stitch mucosa-in-serosa-out on one side and serosa-in-mucosa-out on the other side. Lock the silk before next stitch begins (Fig.101). To hold the silk straightened together with the lock stitches, the stoma is well protected from bleeding.

8) Inner anterior sutures of anastomosis: when the above mentioned lock-stitch sutures run over the entire posterior stomal wall, the sutures at either extremities of the stoma are lead to the serosal surface by passing the needle from mucosal side to serosal side. Now, start to make inner anterior sutures in Connell's fashion. A Connell suture is made by passing the needle serosa-in-mucosa-out on one side and mucosa-in-serosa-out on the same side with a distance about 0.5cm between the 2 needlings. Precede the manipulation in a similar way on the other side. Run the suture on both sides alternatively. The 2 terminal parts of the silk will eventually meet in the middle part of the anterior stomal wall and they are tied together (Fig.102). Take away the gauze protecting the operative field and contaminated instruments used in making anastomosis. Rinse your gloves with saline or change a sterile pair.

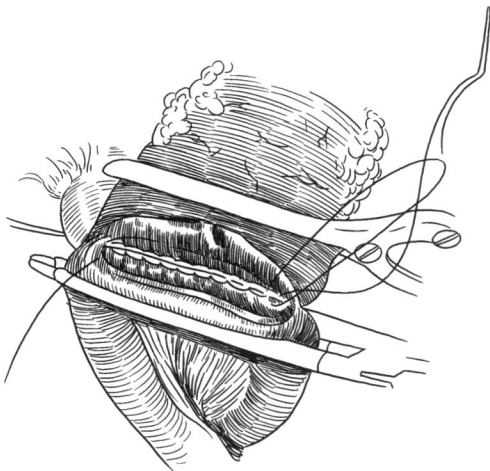

Fig.101 Inner posterior continuous full thickness lock-stitch suture

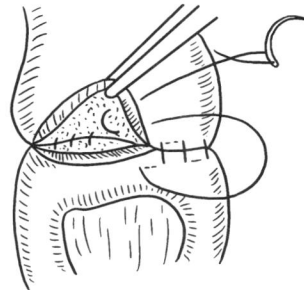

Fig.102 Continuous full thickness inverting sutures of the anterior wall of anastomosis (Connell suture)

9) Outer anterior sutures of the anastomosis: Interrupted seromuscular (Lembert) sutures are made to ensure satisfactory inversion (Fig.103 and Fig.104).

Satisfactory inversion is especially important at the 2 junctions of anterior and posterior walls of the stoma. However, if many tissues are inverted, obstruction of the stoma may be resulted.

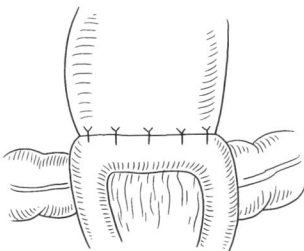

Fig.103 Interrupted seromuscular suture of anterior wall of anastomosis

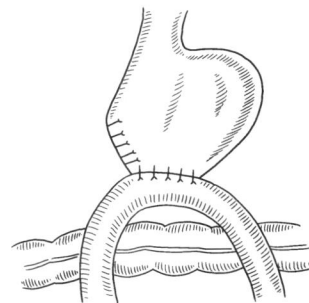

Fig.104 Gastrojejunal anastomosis in front of colon completed

10) Management following anastomosis: be sure there is no intestinal torsion. Check the patency of the stoma including its inlet proximally and outlet distally with fingers. Two to three additional interrupted seromuscular sutures may be made beyond both extremities of the stoma to suspend the afferent and efferent segments of jejunum. This prevents intestinal obstruction at the extremities of the stoma by acute angulation of the intestinal loops at these sites.

Finally, check the number of gauze and instruments. Be sure there is no overlooked bleeding and undesirable fluid collection, and then the abdominal incision is closed layer by layer.

(2) Retrocolic gastrojejunostomy: Patient's posture and incision are same to antecolic anastomosis. After the abdomen is opened, identify the duodenojejunal flexure at the base of the mesentery of the transverse colon, left to the vertebral column. With the colon been pulled out, the Treitz's ligament can be found at the root of the transverse colonic mesentery. Pick up the first segment of jejunum and make two traction stitches at the extremities of the proposed site of stoma about 6cm to 8cm from the Treitz's ligament. Then make a 6 to 7cm opening in an avascular area of mesentery of transverse colon left to the middle colonic artery. Draw the jejunum through the opening approaching the posterior gastric wall near the greater curvature of stomach. Proceed to make anastomosis here by similiar steps in an antecolic gastrojejunostomy (Fig.105). After that, tract the anastomosis down through the opening of colonic mesentery. Interrupted sutures are made between the margin of mesenteric opening and the gastric wall about 1cm above the anastomosis to obliterate the opening. This is an important step in preventing a serious complication (internal hernia) through the opening.

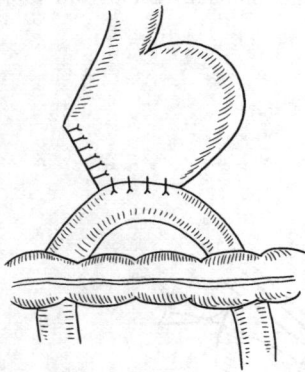

Fig.105   Retrocolic gastrojejunal anastomosis

An antecolic gastrojejunostomy is usually performed in case of short colonic mesentery, too small avascular area in colonic mesentery, thick adhesions between transverse colon and jejunum or stomach, inoperable gastric carcinoma requiring a highly located anastomosis, etc. The manipulations are relatively simple and convenient, however, the afferent intestinal loop (the intestine between the Treitz's ligament and the anastomosis) is relatively long which may cause retention of bile, pancreatic fluid and other intestinal contents. While in retrocolic gastrojejunal anastomosis, the afferent intestinal loop is short, but more complicate in manipulation. A secondary operation, if necessary, may be more difficult.

(3) Points of attention

1) A short afferent jejunal loop, i.e., the preanstomotic loop, will lessen the chance of anastomotic marginal ulcer or jejunal ulcer especially in case of gastrectomy for peptic ulcer. If the afferent intestinal loop is too short, it may cause acute angulation of the intestinal loop at the inlet of the stoma which will result in intestinal obstruction and pressure upon transverse colon by the jejunum (only in case of antecolic type) and lead to intestinal obstruction. In the gastric side, the anastomosis should be made at a lower part near the greater curvature to facilitate satisfactory gastric evacuation.

2) The efferent end of the stoma should be lower than the afferent end. This is also important in ensuring good evacuation.

【Practice】

Fix a dog in supine position on the operating table, make a gastrojejunostomy in front of transverse colon.

(Kong Lingquan)

Chapter 18

Tracheotomy

1. Indications

(1) To relieve respiratory difficulty caused by severe laryngeal edema, spasm or obstruction.

(2) To ensure a free respiratory passage in comatous patients or patients with risk of asphyxia, because a tracheotomy is convenient for sputum extraction, oxygen inhalation or intratracheal drug spraying.

(3) To facilitate the performance of certain maxillofacial operations, pharyngeal, cervical operations or operations in comatous patients to ensure the patency of respiratory tract.

2. Operative procedures

(1) Routine tracheotomy

1) Posture of patient: put the patient in supine position facing exactly upward. A pillow is put under the shoulder to make the neck over extended and the trachea prominent (Fig.106).

2) Anesthesia: local infiltration anesthesia is used.

3) Incision: make a midline incision 2 to 3cm long in the neck from the lower edge of cricoid cartilage to the upper border of the sternum, or a transverse incision is made about two fingers breadth above the upper border of the sternum. Incise both the superficial and deep cervical fascia in the midline. The anterior cervical muscles and anterior tracheal fascia are splitted and retracted bilaterally for the exposure of trachea. Push the isthmus of the thyroid gland away carefully, if it is too broad, cut it with complete hemostasis (Fig.107).

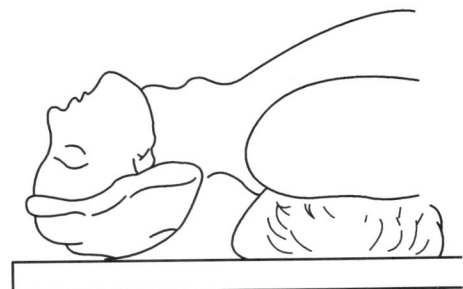

Fig.106   Posture of patient for tracheotomy

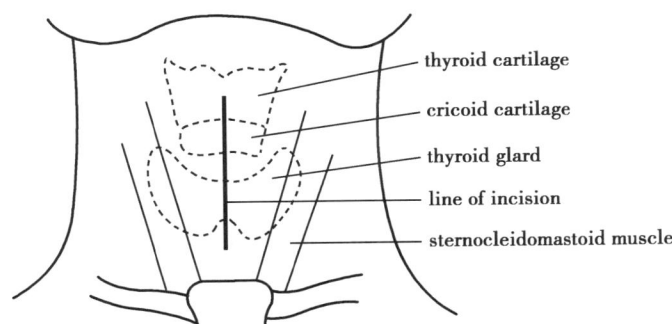

thyroid cartilage

cricoid cartilage

thyroid glard

line of incision

sternocleidomastoid muscle

Fig.107   Incision for tracheotomy

4) Incision of trachea: a vertical incision is made to cut the third and fourth cartilaginous rings of the trachea (Fig.108). This is usually made by piercing and pricking the anterior trachea wall by a scalpel with pointed blade. Sometimes, a part of the cartilages may be excised leaving a small hole on the tracheal wall, which will make the insertion of the tracheotomy tube much easier. Don't prick the anterior tracheal wall too deep lest the posterior tracheal wall may be injured and leading to the formation of tracheoesophageal fistula. Too high a cut on the trachea will cause difficulty in removal of the tracheotomy tube later and too low a cut may cause injury to vessels.

5) Insertion of tracheotomy tube: keep the incision of trachea open with a curved clamp or small retractors (Fig.109), and insert tracheotomy tube of proper size into the trachea. Withdraw the inner cannula right after the insertion of the tube. The intubation is successful when some excretion is coughed out of the tube or the gauze fibers put over the orifice of the tube flutters with respiration. A catheter is inserted through the tube into the trachea to suck out the secretion after assuring the tube is no doubt in the trachea.

6) Suture of incision: The skin incision is sutured loosely with two to three stitches. Too tight sutures may cause subcutaneous collection of air (emphysema).

7) Fixation of the tracheotomy tube: A tracheotomy tube is composed of 2 tubes, a bigger covering a smaller. The outer one is fastened with cotton tapes, which are tied behind the neck to fix the tube (Fig.110).

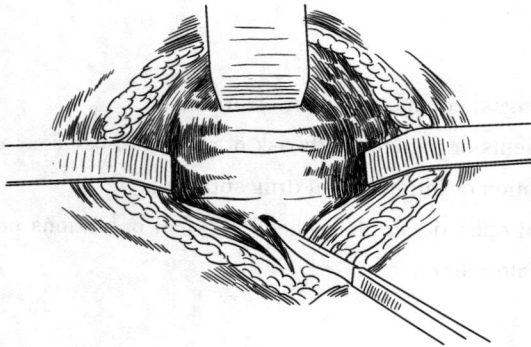

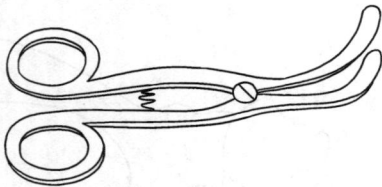

Fig.108   Piercing and pricing the anterior tracheal wall by a scalpel with pointed blade

Fig.109   A clamp to keep tracheal cut open

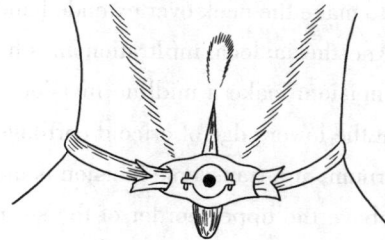

Fig.110   Tracheotomy tube in place

(2) Emergency tracheotomy: In emergency conditions, to race against time, any conveniently acquired knife can be used to do emergency tracheotomy without considering sterilization and anesthesia. The patient is placed in supine position with his head extended, make a transverse incision about 2 to 3cm quickly. After the skin and cricothyroid membrane are cut and the trachea is exposed, stabilize the trachea by fingers at both sides of it and cut it in the midline of its anterior wall. Insert the tracheotomy tube or any similiar tube to release the obstruction as quickly as possible. After, the recovery of ventilation, begin to débride the wound done.

【Practice】

Make routine tracheotomy in a dog. After the operation, the tracheotomy tube is withdrawn. Leave the incision open without suturing. Massage the wound for 1 minute with a piece of gauze in your hand.

(Kong Lingquan)

Chapter 19

Closed Drainage of Pleural Cavity

Pleural cavity is a closed potential cavity. Intrathoracic pressure keeps negative all the time ($-5 - -3$cm H_2O column during inspiration and $-10 - -5$cm H_2O column during expiration). This negative pressure is yielded and maintained by retraction of elastic pulmonary tissues, which makes the respiratory movements and ventilation possible. Any pathological condition that abolishes the negative pressure or changes it into positive will result in collapse of lung of the diseased side. In addition, there will be a shift of mediastinum toward the healthy side during inspiration, because of imbalance of pressure in thoracic cavities of both sides. Mediastinal shift toward the healthy side will further lead to partial collapse of the healthy lung. These changes will certainly impair the respiratory function of both lungs. The purpose of closed drainage of pleural cavity is to re-establish the normal negative pressure in the thoracic cavity surgically. Take a drainage tube of proper size. Insert one of its ends into the pleural cavity of the diseased side and connect the other end to another tube leading to a glass tube in a bottle containing some water. The other end of the glass tube in the bottle is placed deep in the water and the bottle is placed at a level more than 50cm below the patient's chest. During expiration, some intrathoracic air or fluid (usually present in pathologic thorax) will be pushed out through the tubes into the bottle; while during inspiration, nothing is allowed to get into the thoracic cavity as the tube in bottle is water sealed and the bottle is placed at a low level. By this way a state of negative intrathoracic pressure is re-established in a short time. Remember that the key of closed drainage of thoracic cavity is to establish a water sealed system with the bottle in the system placed at a level lower than the patient's chest.

1. Indications

(1) Serious traumatic hemathorax or pneumothorax.

(2) Acute empyema necessitating continuous drainage of pus.

(3) Empyema complicated with bronchopleural fistula.

(4) Open chest operations.

2. Surgical procedures

(1) Anesthesia: use local infiltration anesthesia.

(2) Preparation of drainage tube: prepare a drainage tube with 0.8cm inner diameter and make several side pores near its thoracic end for fluent drainage.

(3) Incision: make an incision about 1.5cm long in line with the intercostal space between 7th and 8th ribs, on the lateral side of the chest (in pneumothorax, the incision is better made in second intercostal space crossing the middle clavicular line). Cut through the skin, split the subcutaneous tissues, deep fascia and intercostal muscles by a hemostat, and then pierce into the pleural cavity.

(4) Insertion of the drainage tube: the distal end of the drainage tube is clamped with a straight hemostatic clamp. Hold the proximal end with a Kelly clamp and insert it into the pleural cavity through the incision. After that, the distal end is connected to the other tube connected to a water sealed bottle. Release the straight clamp and observe whether the drainage is fluent. Adjust the position of the drainage tube may be necessary to keep it patent.

(5) Suture of incision: the skin incision is usually sutured with only one stitch. After ligation, this stitch is further used to fix the drainage tube to prevent slipping off (Fig.111).

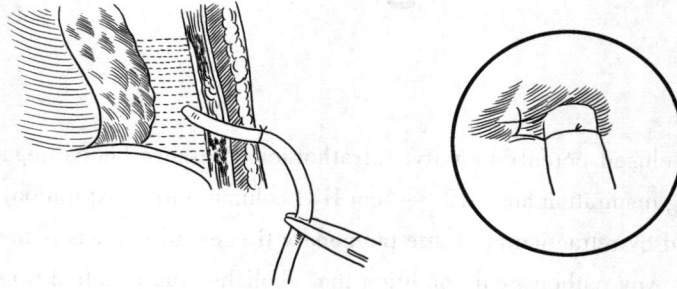

Fig.111   After insertion of the drainage tube, the skin suture is further used to fix the drainage tube

3. Points of attention

(1) Observe frequently to know whether the water column in the glass tube fluctuates with respiration or any fluid or gas is expelled from the end of glass tube in the water. If the water column doesn't fluctuate, it suggests that there may be obstruction somewhere in the tubular system (usually a kink or angulation of certain segment of the tubes) or the tip of the drainage tube has slipped out of the pleura into the interstitial spaces of thoracic wall. If the tip is surely in the thoracic cavity, manipulate the tubes to correct angulation or kink, to change the position of the tubes or to squeeze the drainage tube for several times may relief the obstruction.

(2) The lower end of the glass tube in the bottle must be kept 3 to 4cm below the water level (Fig.112).

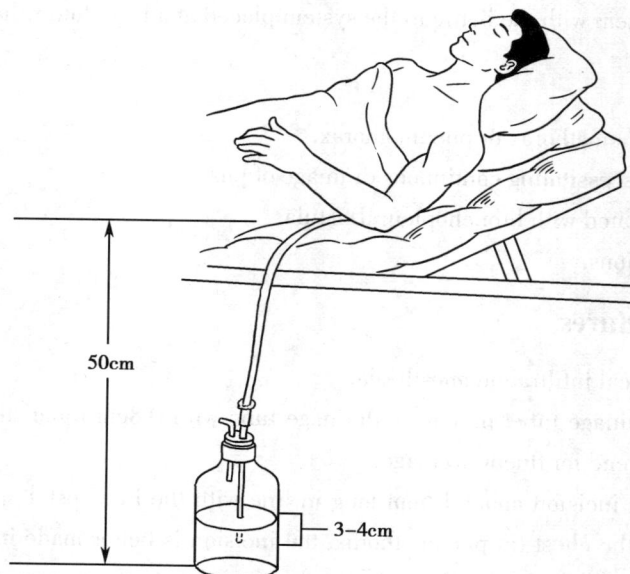

Fig.112   Water sealed system of a closed drainage

(3) All connections of tubes must be tight to prevent leakage or slipping of the tubes.

(4) The water-sealed bottle should be placed at least 50cm below the thoracic cavity.

(5) When no more drainage is required, the drainage tube can be extracted at the end of an expiratory movement. It is important to cover the drainage wound quickly with vaseline gauze right at the movement when the tube is drawn out to prevent suck in of air through the wound at that movement. Massage the wound for half to one minute helps to obliterate the wound. The wound is dressed with gauze finally.

【 Practice 】

Fix a dog in supine position and find the cross point of the seventh intercostal space and mid-axillary line. Then make closed drainage of pleural cavity through this point by the procedures described above. Draw the tube out after the operation is finished.

(Zhu Bing   Kong Lingquan)

Appendix

Writing Requirements of Operative Note and Postoperative Note

Operative note is the special record written by the operator to reflect the general condition, operative procedures, surgical findings and treatment etc, which should be completed within 24 hours after surgery (Critically ill patients should be completed in time).

1. Writing requirements of operative note

(1) Operative note should be written using a separate sheet, and the contents include general item (patients' name, gender, age, department, ward, Bed ID, the hospital medical record number), date of surgery, preoperative diagnosis, postoperative diagnosis, the name of the surgery, the names of operator, assistant and anesthesiologist, anesthesia method, operative procedures, surgical findings and treatment etc. Operative procedures, surgical findings and treatment should be recorded with the following contents:

1) Patients posture during operations, skin disinfection method, operating drape methods, incision direction, incision location, incision length, anatomical level and hemostatic ways.

2) Operative exploration findings, the main lesion site, size, and the relationship with the adjacent organs or tissues; Tumor should be recorded whether with metastasis or lymph node enlargement. If diagnosis during operation is not in accordance with preoperative clinical diagnosis, the records should be more detail.

3) The reason, methods and steps of operation should include the name, scope of lesion tissue or organs which has been dissected or removed, the name of tissue or organs that has been repaired or reconstructed, the size and suture method of the anastomotic stoma, anastomotic suture name and serial number of the thickness, name, number and placement of the drainage material, name, type, quantity and manufacturer of the implants and various special materials. Operation method and steps should be illustrated with drawings when necessary.

4) Before closing the incision at the end of operation, make sure that the number of gauze and instruments must coincide with that counted before operation.

5) The name of submitted samples, cultures, pathologic specimens and the gross appearance of pathological specimens should be recorded.

6) Tolerance, blood loss, intraoperative medication, blood transfusion, special treatment and rescue during the operation should be recorded.

7) Whether the general conditions and anesthesia effects are satisfied or not should be recorded .

8) The reasons of intraoperative changes such as change of the original operation plan, operation method or need to increase the content or expand the scope of operation should be explained.

(2) The operative records should be written and signed by the Chief operator; under special circumstances the operative records can be written by the first assistant, and signed by the Chief operator (Including the outside expert invited).

(3) If an operation must be completed by the various departments and many surgeons, the operative note should be written by the surgeons separately, which can't be written only by one performer.

2. Writing requirements of post-operative note

Postoperative note refers to the postoperative instant operative note written by the doctor who participated in the operation, including operation time, anesthesia, operation method, brief operation procedures, postoperative diagnosis, postoperative treatment, and special postoperative observations etc.

(Li Ming)